On-Site Drug Testing

FORENSIC SCIENCE AND MEDICINE

Steven B. Karch, MD, SERIES EDITOR

ON-SITE DRUG TESTING, edited by ***Amanda J. Jenkins*** and ***Bruce A. Goldberger,*** *2002*

BUPRENORPHINE THERAPY OF OPIATE ADDICTION, edited by ***Pascal Kintz*** and ***Pierre Marquet***, *2002*

BENZODIAZEPINES AND GHB: DETECTION AND PHARMACOLOGY, *edited by* ***Salvatore J. Salamone,*** *2001*

TOXICOLOGY AND CLINICAL PHARMACOLOGY OF HERBAL PRODUCTS, edited by ***Melanie Johns Cupp,*** *2000*

CRIMINAL POISONING: *INVESTIGATIONAL GUIDE FOR LAW ENFORCEMENT, TOXICOLOGISTS, FORENSIC SCIENTISTS, AND ATTORNEYS,* by ***John H. Trestrail, III,*** *2000*

A PHYSICIAN'S GUIDE TO CLINICAL FORENSIC MEDICINE, edited by ***Margaret M. Stark,*** *2000*

BRAIN IMAGING IN SUBSTANCE ABUSE: RESEARCH, CLINICAL, AND FORENSIC APPLICATIONS, edited by ***Marc J. Kaufman,*** *2000*

ON-SITE DRUG TESTING

Edited by

Amanda J. Jenkins, PhD, DABC, DFTCB
The Office of the Cuyahoga County Coroner, Cleveland, OH

and

Bruce A. Goldberger, PhD, DABFT
Department of Pathology, Immunology, and Laboratory Medicine, College of Medicine, University of Florida, Gainesville, FL

Foreword by

Bryan S. Finkle, PhD, DABFT
Chief Consulting Forensic Toxicologist, National Football League; Senior Consultant, New Drug Development, BioTechnology, Cameron, MT

HUMANA PRESS TOTOWA, NEW JERSEY

999 Riverview Drive, Suite 208
Totowa, New Jersey 07512
www.humanapress.com

The content and opinions expressed in this book are the sole work of the authors and editors, who have warranted due diligence in the creation and issuance of their work. The publisher, editors, and authors are not responsible for errors or omissions or for any consequences arising from the information or opinions presented in this book and make no warranty, express or implied, with respect to its contents.

Due diligence has been taken by the publishers, editors, and authors of this book to assure the accuracy of the information published and to describe generally accepted practices. The contributors herein have carefully checked to ensure that the drug selections and dosages set forth in this text are accurate and in accord with the standards accepted at the time of publication. Notwithstanding, since new research, changes in government regulations, and knowledge from clinical experience relating to drug therapy and drug reactions constantly occur, the reader is advised to check the product information provided by the manufacturer of each drug for any change in dosages or for additional warnings and contraindications. This is of utmost importance when the recommended drug herein is a new or infrequently used drug. It is the responsibility of the treating physician to determine dosages and treatment strategies for individual patients. Further, it is the responsibility of the health care provider to ascertain the Food and Drug Administration status of each drug or device used in their clinical practice. The publishers, editors, and authors are not responsible for errors or omissions or for any consequences from the application of the information presented in this book and make no warranty, express or implied, with respect to the contents in this publication.

This publication is printed on acid-free paper. ∞

ANSI Z39.48-1984 (American National Standards Institute) Permanence of Paper for Printed Library Materials.

Cover design by Patricia F. Cleary.

Cover photo courtesy of Robert McCulley, Ismir Oil & Spice Company, Quesnel, B.C., Canada. www.ismirpoppy.com.

For additional copies, pricing for bulk purchases, and/or information about other Humana titles, contact Humana at the above address or at any of the following numbers: Tel: 973-256-1699; Fax: 973-256-8341; E-mail: humana@humanapr.com or visit our website at http://humanapress.com

Printed in the United States of America. 10 9 8 7 6 5 4 3 2 1

Library of Congress Cataloging in Publication Data

On-site drug testing / edited by Amanda J. Jenkins and Bruce A. Goldberger.
p. cm. -- (Forensic science and medicine)
Includes bibliographical references and index.
ISBN 0-89603-870-X (alk. paper)
1. Drug testing--United States. 2. Employees--Drug testing--United States. I. Jenkins, Amanda J. II. Goldberger, Bruce A. III. Series.

HV5823.5.U5 O5 2002
658.3′822--dc21

2001039632

For Sylvester, Jasper, Oliver,
and Penny who brighten my life.
And for TC.

–AMANDA J. JENKINS

For Mom and Dad,
with enduring love.

–BRUCE A. GOLDBERGER

Foreword

It is at least a decade since scientists turned their imaginations to creating new compact, portable test instruments and self-contained test kits that could be used to analyze urine and saliva for alcohol, drugs, and their metabolites. Although the potential applications for such tests at the site of specimen collection, now called "on-site" or "point-of-care" testing, range far beyond hospital emergency rooms and law enforcement needs, it was catalyzed by the requirements of workplace drug testing and other drugs-of-abuse testing programs. These programs are now a minor national industry in the United States and in some western European countries, and cover populations as diverse as the military, incarcerated criminals, people suspected of driving under the influence of alcohol and other drugs, all athletes from college to professional ranks, and of course the general employed population, which is monitored for illegal drug use and numbers in the millions. It is not surprising, then, that the need for rapid and precise tests, conducted economically by trained professionals, has become a major goal. Current government approved and peer reviewed laboratory methods for urine analysis serve present needs very well and have become remarkably robust over the past twenty years, but the logistics of testing some moving populations, such as the military, the Coast Guard, workers on off-shore oil platforms, and athletes—perhaps the most mobile of these groups—are unacceptably cumbersome. So, scientists have turned their attention to the possibility of testing these and other populations on-site at least as a screening test. Happily, the vast majority of all tests for drugs of abuse are negative and making this determination at the site of collection has both efficiency and economic attractions, as well as relieving the specimen donor of the anxiety of awaiting the result of laboratory analysis. There are some important exceptions to this; for example, people suspected of impaired driving have a very high rate of positive tests for alcohol or other drugs and this is also true for persons arrested for a wide variety of crimes.

Devising new test systems that can meet the very strict criteria for unimpeachable science embodying sensitivity, accuracy, and precision, as well as convenience and acceptable economics, is very difficult. Because it is relatively noninvasive, testing a saliva specimen is attractive for on-site testing but in matters of specificity and sensitivity, particularly for marijuana metabolites, it has turned out to be quite a challenge. So, as is often the case with new ideas, development and application is neither quick nor easy. It is these issues—at a time when a pause for critical review and assessment is needed—that *On-Site Drug Testing* addresses.

The eighteen chapters successfully review all aspects of on-site testing from the needs of many various programs, evaluation of devices and test kits, and the legal and medical contexts that form the background against which this science must be applied. The authors are international authorities with a huge aggregate professional experience in analytical toxicology of alcohol and drug detection in biological specimens. They provide for the careful reader a critical review, conclusions, and recommendations concerning the present status and future viability of point-of-care, on-site testing. They include current research such as the European, international ROSITA study, the relationship between on-site analytical test results and the observations of trained drug recognition experts, and even include the effects of deliberate adulteration of specimens on the actual analytical tests. *On-Site Drug Testing* is timely and will serve as a landmark in the progress of this science.

***Bryan S. Finkle,* PhD, DABFT**
Consulting Forensic Toxicologist
Cameron, MT

Preface

Drug testing of individuals is considered the most objective means of determining drug use. Many people are currently tested through workplace programs and within the justice system (probation and parole), hospital emergency rooms, physician offices, and rehabilitation programs. Traditionally, urine, the specimen of choice for testing for illicit and licit drugs, has been analyzed with laboratory-based instruments. With expansion of the drug testing market there is increased interest not only in the use of other biological specimens for testing, but also in noninstrument-based screening tests that may be conducted at the collection site. Advantages of such testing include a rapid turnaround time for initial screening of presumptive results, lower program cost, no requirement for expensive instrumentation, and minimal training needed to conduct the tests. However, since the overall objective of drug testing is to detect drug use, these noninstrument-based or on-site testing devices must be validated.

The objective of *On-Site Drug Testing* is to provide a comprehensive discussion of the on-site devices currently marketed, their validation studies, and the use of the devices in a variety of settings. Each chapter is written by an investigator familiar with the subject and, where possible, authors are independent and have no connection with the company whose product they are discussing. Experts in the field have been utilized to discuss the use of these devices in society.

Amanda J. Jenkins, PhD, DABC, DFTCB
Bruce A. Goldberger, PhD, DABFT

Contents

Chapter 13

Contributors

DAVID ARMBRUSTER • Abbott Laboratories, Abbott Park, IL
JAMES BAER • U.S. Probation and Parole Officer (Retired), Central District of California, Santa Ana, CA
DENE BALDWIN • Cozart Bioscience, Abingdon, Oxfordshire, UK
YALE H. CAPLAN • National Scientific Services, Baltimore, MD
FRANCA CASTAGNA • Forensic Toxicology and Antidoping, University Hospital, Padua, Italy
JOHN T. CODY • Academy of Health Sciences, Interservice Physician Assistant Program, Fort Sam Houston, TX
DENNIS J. CROUCH • Center for Human Toxicology, University of Utah, Salt Lake City, UT
KURT M. DUBOWSKI • Department of Medicine and Forensic Science Laboratories, The University of Oklahoma Health Sciences Center, Oklahoma City, OK
LAUREL J. FARRELL • Colorado Bureau of Investigation, Denver, CO
SANTO DAVIDE FERRARA • Forensic Toxicology and Antidoping, University Hospital, Padua, Italy
CHRISTOPHER HAND • Cozart Bioscience, Abingdon, Oxfordshire, UK
LEO J. KADEHJIAN • Biomedical Consulting, Palo Alto, CA
SCOTT A. KUZDZAL • School of Medicine, Johns Hopkins University, Baltimore, MD
JAMES H. NICHOLS • School of Medicine, Johns Hopkins University, Baltimore, MD
MARINUS G. PELDERS • Hospital Pharmacy Gelre Hospitals, Lukas Hospital, Apeldoorn, The Netherlands
JOHANNES J. W. ROS • Hospital Pharmacy Gelre Hospitals, Lukas Hospital, Apeldoorn, The Netherlands

SALVATORE J. SALAMONE • Advance BioTech Consulting, LLC, Sergeantsville, NJ

SERGE SCHNEIDER • Division de Toxicologie, Laboratoire National de Santé, Centre Universitaire de Luxembourg, Luxembourg

THEODORE F. SHULTS • American Association of Medical Review Officers, Research Triangle Park, NC

VINA SPIEHLER • Newport Beach, CA

LUCIANO TEDESCHI • Department of Forensic Toxicology and Antidoping, University Hospital, Padua, Italy

RAFAEL DE LA TORRE • Pharmacology Research Unit, Institut Municipal d'Investigació Médica, Barcelona, Spain

JANE S-C. TSAI • Roche Diagnostics, Indianapolis, IN

JIMMIE L. VALENTINE • Department of Pediatrics and Pharmacology, Section of Pediatric Clinical Pharmacology and Toxicology, College of Medicine, University of Arkansas for Medical Sciences; Arkansas Children's Hospital, Little Rock, AK

J. MICHAEL WALSH • The Walsh Group, Bethesda, MD

ROBERT WENNIG • Division de Toxicologie, Laboratoire National de Santé, Centre Universitaire de Luxembourg, Luxembourg

ROBERT E. WILLETTE • Duo Research, Denver, CO

ALAN H. B. WU • Department of Pathology and Laboratory Medicine, Hartford Hospital, Hartford, CT

Chapter 1

Clinical Point-of-Care Testing for Drugs of Abuse

Jimmie L. Valentine

1. General Considerations

The decision to utilize point-of-care testing (POCT) devices for detecting drugs of abuse to augment clinical care of a patient must be primarily assessed by the clinician since it is that person who will decide how the test result will be used to care for the patient. Often clinicians will seek the advice or counsel of laboratorians in trying to decide the appropriate POCT device and how it should be used to care for the patient. Answers to the following questions should be addressed:

- In what type of clinical practice will the POCT device be used? That is, does the clinician need only information on one particular drug, for example, alcohol or marijuana metabolite, or have the patients seen in the practice been known to abuse multiple drugs? Such needs would influence whether single or multiple analyte POCT devices are used.
- Will confirmation testing be utilized? As will be discussed below, as well as, in other sections of this book, drugs of abuse POCT are based upon either enzyme- or immuno-assay. Both technologies are known to produce false positive and false negative results. In most clinical situations, confirmatory testing will be required.
- How will the POCT results be used? Most often in a clinical setting POCT results are used in a confrontational manner but have been used otherwise as will be discussed below.

From: *Forensic Science: On-Site Drug Testing*
Edited by: A. J. Jenkins and B. A. Goldberger © Humana Press, Inc., Totowa, NJ

- Will POCT results be utilized to establish sobriety or compliance? Certain physiological considerations need to be addressed if the devices are so used.

POCT is seductive for clinicians to consider. No instrumentation is required, turn-around-times are extremely fast, and little training is required for the person performing the test. As with any new technology, end users have to learn how to best utilize the technology. Manufacturers have provided the clinician with a potentially powerful tool to immediately assess whether an abused drug in the patient should be considered or excluded as part of a differential diagnosis. If the decision to include or exclude drugs of abuse in the differential diagnosis is made, the clinician should be aware of potential pitfalls. This chapter has several aims:

1. Considerations a clinician should make to most effectively utilize POCT drug abuse results in various age groups, and
2. Physiological considerations necessary to interpret POCT results.

2. Pediatric Clinical Considerations

Positive results from urine drugs of abuse POCT of children normally have legal implications since the test results should be negative. With neonates, the implication is that maternal passage of drug has occurred and opens up the social issue of whether the mother should be permitted to keep the child. With toddlers and younger school age children, positive results suggest that the child is residing in an environment where illicit drugs are present and the child had access to the drug(s) by virtue of accidental ingestion or deliberate introduction of the drug(s) to the child. Because of the possibility of a false positive test occurring, POCT results from a neonate or child should never be used as a basis for legal action without a confirmatory analysis, preferably gas chromatography-mass spectrometry (GC-MS) *(1,2)*. If a positive test is observed with a neonate or younger child, most states provide for temporary protective custody of the child until a confirmation test(s) can be completed. With a large number of certified laboratories, such confirmatory results should be available within 24 h.

Because of the legal considerations of a positive test result, the clinician utilizing a POCT device must initiate a chain of custody that proceeds forward with the specimen. This chain of custody must reflect who collected the specimen and at what time, followed by who performed the POCT and at what time, and anyone else who had possession or access to the specimen prior to transportation to a laboratory for confirmation testing. A lack of an appropriately executed chain of custody may invalidate even the confirmatory results in subsequent legal hearings. Chain of custody documentation has become such an integral part of court cases involving drugs that improper execution can invalidate acceptable analytical results. Use of POCT devices as the initial screening test is often the most vulnerable link in the test process since documentation is often lacking to demonstrate that no other person removed specimen or that the specimen was only opened once for testing purposes. Thus, with neonates and children it would be preferable to utilize a POCT device that incorporates the device as an integral part of the collection cup such that once the cup is sealed, there is no need to unseal it outside of a certified testing laboratory. Such devices are discussed in other parts of this book.

3. Adolescent Clinical Considerations

As children enter the adolescent years (13–19 yr of age) experimentation with drugs of abuse usually becomes a concern for adult caregivers (parents, guardians, school officials, etc.) and sometimes the criminal justice system. Clinicians often find themselves juxtaposed between the adolescent and the adult groups interested in their welfare. A valid concern of the clinician is whether the presenting adolescent's symptoms or condition are related to drugs of abuse. Acute care examples would be injuries due to motor vehicle accidents, traumatic injury due to violence, chest pain, or suicide gesture. Most often, positive findings in such situations can be used to confront the adolescent concerning their behavior and as an avenue to recommend further treatment for potential drug abuse as well as, to counsel adult caregivers. Use of POCT devices in such clinical scenarios can be and is usually conducted without confirmatory testing. The clinician is depending upon the adolescent, when confronted with the test results, admitting drug use and a potential problem they may have in dealing with drugs. However, there are some potential situations in which the clinician must be prepared to utilize confirmatory testing. These are as follows:

1. Vehement denial of using the drug producing the positive test(s). A confirmatory test will be required to decide the issue. Many adolescents will admit to drug use only if confronted with unequivocal scientific results, such as that offered by GC-MS. The clinician may confront the adolescent with such results and use phrases such as "this additional test is never wrong" or "this result tells me that you did use the drug." On the other hand, if the confirmatory test result is negative, the adolescent has scored points with his/her physician and perhaps his/her family for being truthful.
2. An accident involving injury or death to another party or significant property damage. Obviously, this situation may have legal implications as a result of the adolescent's negligence. Chain of custody documentation must be utilized as dis-

cussed above and confirmatory testing performed. The effect of drugs on behavioral tasks, such as driving, have profound implications in the legal arena and testing performed as part of the patient's care is often introduced in both criminal and civil actions.

3. Denial of active drug use. The adolescent (or adults as discussed below) will often argue that everyone else at the party was doing drugs and that they inhaled the drugs and hence produced a positive test, the so-termed "passive inhalation defense." The POCT devices currently in use have cutoff levels mandated by United States Department of Defense and Department of Transportation guidelines. These guidelines were designed for the workplace environment where chronic use of a drug of abuse might have profound implications as to how the person performed in assigned tasks, particularly safety sensitivity areas. In an effort to ensure that the occasional or infrequent user of drugs would not produce a positive drug screen, the cutoff values have been set sufficiently high to prevent this type of user and the passively exposed person from producing a positive test. Thus, the clinician can be relatively certain that a positive test on a POCT device is not the result of passive exposure. This of course, does not rule out a false positive test and a confirmatory test will answer not only that question but the quantitative result provided by the confirmation testing will suggest if passive exposure was a remote possibility. A value of the drug 20% of the cutoff value could be used as a guide for active occasional use or passive exposure, whereas, any value above that would suggest only active exposure. Interpretation of the meaning of urine quantitative values is an area currently undergoing intense study, and the guidelines suggested above may not be appropriate in all circumstances, so the clinician should seek expert advice from a clinical toxicologist/pharmacologist for evaluations of borderline urine drug levels.
4. Monitoring for compliance while in a drug treatment program. During drug rehabilitation programs, the monitoring of adolescents for abstinence is a valid use of POCT. While in the resident part of a program, daily or weekly screening of urine specimens will give an indication of whether the adolescent is complying with a no drug policy that is part of most programs. When the adolescent is permitted weekend or holiday passes, compliance with abstinence can be assured. Most treatment programs utilizing POCT devices enable the provider of the specimen to observe the test being performed. A negative result acts a reinforcement for acceptable behavior and a positive test for unacceptable behavior. Again, as discussed previously, vehement denial of a positive test requires confirmatory testing. Physiological considerations that might affect drug clearance and hence POCT results are addressed below.
5. Monitoring at the request of an adult çaregiver. A typical scenario is a parent or guardian who finds some drug paraphernalia in their child's room or has suspicions of the adolescent's behavior and brings them to the physician's office requesting a drug test. Although POCT can be rapidly performed on the adolescent's urine specimen, the results may not produce the desired effects

the parent is expecting. Since the parent has the adolescent at the physician's office, there has already been a breakdown in communication between the parent and adolescent, that is, the adolescent must have denied drug use or there would have been no need for the test. If the result is negative, the adolescent will be angry with the parent for lack of trust. If the test is positive, the parent will be angry with the adolescent for lying. Interposed between both these positions is the possibility that the test result maybe either a false negative or a false positive. Caught in the middle of this parent-adolescent predicament is the person who authorized the test to be performed. In popular vernacular, "it is a no win situation." Many astute clinicians counsel both parent and adolescent prior to agreeing to perform POCT and some even offer a contract to be signed, stating each will not use the test results in a punitive manner.

4. Adult Clinical Considerations

Most of the clinical considerations discussed previously for adolescents also apply to adults, with the obvious exception of point 5. However, there are unique circumstances under which additional adult POCT considerations would be indicated. Some of these additional circumstances include:

1. Custody battles between couples for the right to their children. A divorce or separation will sometimes result in demands by the spouse or courts that drugs of abuse testing be performed. While POCT testing would certainly provide rapid results, the person administering the test may find themselves involved in unwanted legal proceedings, since a positive result will almost certainly result in court appearances for the person performing the test. Therefore, such testing would have to meet all the chain of custody guidelines discussed previously. Even a negative result may lead to claims by the spouse that the person providing the specimen has "beat the test." Therefore, if POCT testing is to be conducted for this type of situation, some determination of urine adulteration should also be performed, e.g., specific gravity, pH, nitrite, etc. Coleman and Baselt have suggested that concentration of drugs at or near the threshold for a particular assay would be most amendable to effects of water or commercial products sold to mask urine test results *(3)*. Confirmatory testing of positive results must be accomplished and signs of adulteration or hydration by the provider should be considered as nullifying the drug screen and should, perhaps result in a request for a specific analyte confirmation test based upon investigative information. Because of all these concerns, clinicians who may be called upon because of their role in providing medical care for family members might better serve their patients by having a certified laboratory perform the required tests. The Canadian experience with such social service agency testing has been reported *(4,5)*.
2. Pre-employment physical examinations. Many physicians, physician's assistants, and nurse practitioners frequently perform pre-employment or pre-insurance

physical examinations. Many companies that contract for such service either expect or require that drugs of abuse testing be part of the physical examination of the prospective employee or applicant. POCT by such medical personnel is attractive since results are available immediately and depending on the needs of the company, the person might be cleared to start a job the same day. Limitations of using POCT in these situations revolve mainly around issues of the accuracy of the test, potential adulteration of the specimen, and initiating an appropriate chain of custody (to accompany any specimen testing positive for mandatory confirmation testing). Schwartz, Clark, and Meek have reviewed many of these issues *(6)*.

3. On the job accidents (postaccident testing). Persons injured on the job are often taken to the health care provider or facility customarily used by the employee's company. A positive postaccident urine drug test will always result in legal proceedings, either in a court because the employee was dismissed as a result of the positive test or before a hearing or tribunal because of denial of workman's compensation. POCT in postaccident situations must be performed in a manner that will permit chain of custody documentation and provisions for the person performing the test to explain the test results in a formal hearing or court proceeding. Therefore, confirmation testing is mandatory.
4. For cause testing. Most companies have policies in place that permit supervisory personnel to request a urine drugs of abuse test based upon behavioral actions of an employee on the job. Because POCT is rapid and can be performed on-site, many companies utilize this test to decide whether an employee is under the influence of a drug. Based upon a positive test an employee is normally disciplined either by dismissal from employment or remanded to a treatment program. Either decision has legal implications, therefore, chain of custody documentation and confirmatory testing is mandatory. Negative results on the POCT may confound the problem. Because of excretion patterns of most drugs of abuse, the person may have been under the influence of the drug, i.e. have discernible blood levels, but yet not excreted the drug in levels greater than the cutoff level of the POCT device. Alternately, the person may have been using a prescription drug not detected by the POCT device that was responsible for the observed behavioral effect. If impairment of the individual is apparent, the specimen should be forwarded along with proper chain of custody documentation to a certified laboratory with a request for comprehensive toxicology testing.
5. Psychiatric outpatient testing. Many adults or older adolescents are followed on a routine basis as outpatients after an in-house treatment program. Shearer, Baciewicz, and Kwong have reviewed the use of various technologies used in such settings *(7)*. Not specifically covered in their review is the practice of using POCT devices by various support groups at weekly meetings in a behavioral modification manner similar to that discussed for adolescents in a treatment program. Again, any positive result that might have employment or legal consequences must be confirmed. An example would be a support group for health care professionals who had previously used illegal drugs or diverted drugs for

their own use. Such groups have regular weekly meetings, and the persons in attendance have previously completed a residence treatment program and are usually attending such meetings under mandate from their respective licensing boards. In such situations, a positive result would have to be reported to the governing professional board and perhaps result in revocation of the licence to practice. Confirmatory testing would be mandatory to protect the rights of the person being tested. While support groups are utilizing POCT devices for such testing, it may be an inappropriate technology for health professionals that have used hydrocodone, meperidine, and fentanyl because the POCT devices will not detect such drugs. Only more robust laboratory-based testing will have the ability to detect these drugs.

5. Physiological Considerations For Clinical Testing

Several mistakes may be made with drugs of abuse POCT because of inappropriate timing of specimen collection. An advantage of POCT is that the test can be performed "on the spot" by individuals with minimal training and knowledge of physiological processes. The first common mistake is to collect a urine specimen as quickly as possible following an event. The second common mistake is to expect a urine specimen to be positive 24 or more hours following an event.

Elimination of the majority of drugs of abuse from the body reaches a maximum 6–9 h following a single dose. Thus, a specimen collected within the initial hours following use of a drug of abuse may have levels below the cutoff for the POCT device resulting in a negative result. Therefore, the time that has transpired following an event will be important in determining whether a test will be successful at detecting prior drug use. As discussed in Subheading 3., item 3, most POCT devices have cutoff levels set high to prevent a positive result for any person except a chronic user. A practical way to prevent a false result is to test the initial two micturitions following a suspected event. If the person providing the specimen is a chronic user, the initial specimen following an incident will most likely be positive because of the residual storage of the drug in deep body compartments and greater, continual excretion patterns. Several drugs have been studied that demonstrate this principle. Valentine et al. demonstrated that levels of methamphetamine and the metabolite amphetamine (used under forensic guidelines to verify the presence of methamphetamine) may be below the designated GC-MS cutoffs in the early time intervals following use of the drug *(8)*. The cutoff, on the other hand, for marijuana was lowered in 1994 by DHHS in the US from 100 ng/mL to 50 ng/mL (of the metabolite) in an effort to increase the ability to detect any use of marijuana *(9)*. Therefore, the regular or occasional marijuana smoker should be detected if tested within 24 h of use. However, if a person is a chronic user of marijuana some difficulty may arise if a POCT device is being used to monitor cessation of use. Huestis and Cone have proposed normalizing the level of marijuana metabolite obtained by GC-MS using creatinine and comparing the ratio of two different urine specimens *(10)*. If the metabolite/creatinine concentration of the later specimen was compared to the earlier specimen, a ratio of 0.5 permitted accurate differentiation of new marijuana episodes from residual excretion. Because of the complexity of such measurements, it is obvious a simple POCT cannot be reliably utilized to differentiate new use from residual excretion.

6. Conclusions

POCT has a supportive role in assisting the assessment of drugs of abuse use by a clinician, in a patient. Because most clinicians are trained in an environment where laboratory test results have been more carefully controlled and reviewed, they have come to expect that a laboratory test can be trusted to provide a reliable result. That is, the result provided by the laboratory can be used to effectively manage the patient's care. POCT devices have now changed the role between the laboratory and clinician since the test is now performed somewhere outside of the laboratory and usually at the site of care. Thus, the clinician is placed in the position of evaluating whether the POCT results meet all criteria for being acceptable and usable in patient care. The possibility for false negative and positive results is a concept that most clinicians do not understand and thus, it is possible that the simple, quick test may provide conflicting information when evaluated in relationship to the clinical presentation of the patient. When such apparently contradictory information occurs, the clinician must either rely on clinical acumen or be willing to seek consultation with a laboratorian skilled in POCT or at least be willing to obtain confirmatory testing. Working in a vacuum without supporting information regarding POCT results is an inappropriate use of the technology for adequate patient care.

Use of POCT in the clinical setting in which results maybe used in a legal manner introduces additional complexity for the clinician. Chain of custody documentation must be included in such testing when a positive result occurs. Since false negative results can occur as a result of inappropriate timing of specimen collection, clinicians should be willing to obtain a later specimen to verify the original result. Only by adopting a rigorous set of guidelines for collection, POCT, and confirmation of positive results can the technology be used in a scientifically defensible manner. Because of the complexities introduced by legal requirements, laboratory-based testing maybe more appropriate than POCT for forensic purposes.

Confrontational use of POCT results to achieve behavioral modification appears to have some clinical utility. Many drug treatment programs and drug dependency support groups have found POCT devices useful for this purpose. However, provisions must be made for confirmatory testing of contested results.

References

1. Valentine, J. L. and Komoroski, E. M. (1995) Use of a visual panel detection method for drugs of abuse: Clinical and laboratory experience with children and adolescents. *J. Pediatr.* **126,** 135–140.
2. Crouch, D. J., Frank, J. F., Farrell, L. J., Karsch, H. M., and Klaunig J. E. (1998). A multiple-site laboratory evaluation of three on-site urinalysis drug-testing devices. *J. Anal Toxicol.* **22,** 493–502.
3. Coleman, D. E. and Baselt, R. C. (1997) Efficacy of two commercial products for altering urine drug test results. *Clin. Toxicol.* **35,** 637–642.
4. Fraser, A. D. (1998a) Urine drug testing for social service agencies. *Toxicol.* **18,** 705–711.
5. Fraser, A. D. (1998b) Urine drug testing for social service agencies in Nova Scotia, Canada. *J. Forensic Sci.* **43,** 194–196.
6. Schwartz, R. H., Clark, H. W., and Meek, P. S. (1993) Laboratory tests for rapid screening of drugs of abuse in the workplace: A review. *J. Addict. Dis.* **12,** 43–56.
7. Shearer, D. S., Baciewicz G. J., and Kwong, T. C. (1998) Drugs of abuse testing in a psychiatric outpatient service. *Toxicol.* **18,** 713–726.
8. Valentine, J. L., Kearns, G. L., Sparks, C., Letzig, L. G., Valentine, C. R., Shappell, S. A., et al. (1995) GC-MS determination of amphetamine and methamphetamine in human urine for 12 hours following oral administration of dextro-methamphetamine: Lack of evidence supporting the established forensic guidelines for methamphetamine confirmation. *J. Anal. Toxicol.* **19,** 581–590.
9. Federal Register (1994) Department of Health and Human Services. Mandatory guidelines for federal workplace drug testing programs. *Fed. Regist.* **59,** 299–312.
10. Huestis, M. A. and Cone, E. J. (1998) Differentiating new marijuana use from residual drug excretion in occasional marijuana users. *J. Anal. Toxicol.* **22,** 445–454.

Chapter 2

On-Site Tests for Therapeutic Drugs

Alan H. B. Wu

1. Rationale for Therapeutic Monitoring and Need for On-Site Drug Testing

There are thousands of therapeutic drugs approved by the United States Food and Drug Administration (FDA) available today for clinical use. These medications are widely used by patients for the acute treatment of illnesses or disease, or for the proper maintenance of health. In addition to approved drugs, there are hundreds of herbal medications that are gaining in popularity, and are not regulated by the FDA. For the vast majority of these drugs regular therapeutic monitoring of blood concentrations is unnecessary because they are safe, and have a low incidence of toxicity and side effects. There are a few drugs for which monitoring is effective for improving the pharmaceutical efficacy of the medication, or for reducing the incidence of unwanted effects.

The criteria utilized to determine whether or not a particular therapeutic drug warrants routine monitoring of blood concentrations are tabulated in Table 1. Therapeutic drug monitoring is the most objective manner to determine if patients are taking their medications. This is particularly true for elderly outpatients on oral prescriptions as they may not remember when or if they took their last dose. Drugs that have a low therapeutic index and therefore will have a narrow target blood concentration range, also warrant therapeutic

From: *Forensic Science: On-Site Drug Testing*
Edited by: A. J. Jenkins and B. A. Goldberger © Humana Press, Inc., Totowa, NJ

Table 1
Rationale for Therapeutic Drug Monitoring

Monitoring patient compliance
Drug has a narrow therapeutic index
Individual variation in drug absorption, distribution, metabolism, and excretion
Alterations in predicted drug concentrations because of disease
Alterations in predicted drug concentrations because of interactions with other medications

monitoring. For example, the therapeutic range for the slow acting barbiturates is only 2–3 fold lower than concentrations that produce coma. Other physiologic, pathologic, and pharmacologic factors have the potential for altering predicted drug concentrations. An individual's genetic makeup may dictate the rate by which drugs are metabolized or cleared (pharmacogenetics) and may also determine if a patient will respond to the medication or not. Coexisting diseases will have variable and unpredictable effects on drug concentrations. Poor cardiac or thyroid function, or the presence of liver or renal failure will reduce the rate of metabolism and clearance of therapeutic drugs, and may therefore, increase the likelihood of toxic reactions. Moreover, because multiple drug regimens are commonly used today, the potential for drug interactions is high. Medications that are potent displacers of plasma protein binding, or those that increase or decrease rates of hepatic metabolism, will alter the blood concentrations of co-administered drugs, thereby warranting therapeutic monitoring. Among the classes of medications that fulfill one or more of these criteria (and therefore are routinely monitored) include the anticonvulsants, antibiotics, antiarrhythmics, and antiasthmatics (e.g. theophylline).

2. On-Site and Point-of-Care (POC) Drug Testing

The clinical need and commercial interest for on-site testing for therapeutic drug monitoring is not in high demand compared with the demand in the workplace drugs-of-abuse testing arena. Quantitative measurement of drug concentrations for routine drug monitoring in serum or plasma is largely conducted by a central hospital or clinic laboratory. Drug concentrations that are outside the desired therapeutic range may affect the quantity and frequency of subsequent dosing. In the majority of cases, a rapid turnaround time (TAT) for results (e.g., <1 h) is not needed for emergencies. The exceptions might be the urgent need to receive rapid results of analgesic (salicylates and acetaminophen), theophylline (especially in children), digoxin, and antidepressant drug concentrations in blood of emergency department patients who have symptoms of toxicity. A quantitative on-site assay for digoxin would be useful for effective patient management, as overdoses can be treated with digoxin antibodies (Digibind) *(1)*. Although there are no FDA-approved POC assays for digoxin at present, one manufacturer has indicated plans to develop this assay (Response Biomedical Corp., Burnaby, Canada) *(2)*. Measurement of digoxin will be difficult due to the low concentration expected, even after overdoses (>2.0 ng/mL).

The development of on-site testing for individual tricyclic antidepressants (TCA) is problematic due to the difficulty of raising antibodies that recognize the target drug, and not metabolites or other structurally-related drugs such as the muscle relaxant, cyclobenzaprine *(3)*. Although there is one point-of-care testing device for the tricyclic antidepressants (Triage, Biosite Diagnostics, San Jose, CA), this assay for TCAs was designed for use in urine for overdose detection (>1,000 ng/mL), and cannot be used for routine quantitative therapeutic drug monitoring in blood. The laboratory-based Syva EMIT tricyclic antidepressant assay (San Diego, CA) has a lower cutoff of 200–400 ng/mL. The clinical utility of the Triage assay was examined in several clinical trials. In separate studies, Poklis et al. and Schwartz et al. found a 95 and 89% agreement of positive results with the Triage Plus compared with thin-layer chromatography *(4,5)*. Baskin et al. found a 85% agreement between Triage and a high-pressure rapid UV-scanning liquid chromatographic assay (Remedi, BioRad Labs., Hercules, CA) *(6)*. In terms of specificity, the Triage assay is superior to EMIT. While both assays produce positive results in the presence of cyclobenzaprine, the Triage assay is not sensitive to phenothiazines such as chlorpromazine and thioridazine (Table 2).

In addition to acute clinical needs, a rapid TAT for drug results may also be useful in routine patient management. On-site testing conducted in physicians' offices may enable a doctor to adjust drug doses while the patient is still in the office *(7)*. Despite this potential for improved medical management, there is very little on-site drug testing currently conducted.

3. Direct On-Site Testing Instruments and Devices for Therapeutic Drugs

There have been a few on-site drug testing instruments and devices developed and studied for therapeutic monitoring that directly measured the

Table 2
Cross-Reactivities of Nontricyclic Antidepressant Drugs for EMIT vs Triage[a]

Drug	EMIT	Triage
Chlorpromazine	200–300	50,000
Cyclobenzaprine	>200	1,500
Thioridazine	>1,500	>100,000
Orphenadrine	>6,000	250,000
Diphenhydramine	>12,000	>1,000,000
Cyprohepatidine	>420	250,000

[a]Concentration of drug resulting in positive results

drug concentrations of interest. The initial use of on-site testing used small chemistry analyzers located in physicians office laboratories (POL) *(8)*. For example, the DT60 analyzer (Ortho-Clinical Diagnostics, Raritan, NJ) was widely used for POL testing. The only therapeutic drug available on the menu, however, was theophylline. Unlike most assays for therapeutic drugs, the DT-60 assay is not antibody-based. Instead, it is based on the ability of theophylline to inhibit beef-liver alkaline phosphatase. The DT-60 requires testing on serum or plasma and cannot use whole blood, therefore a centrifuge is necessary. The Vision analyzer (Abbott Laboratories, Abbott Park, IL) uses serum, plasma, or whole blood, making it more practical for routine POL testing. The instrument uses disposable cartridges and has an on-board centrifuge for separation of serum and plasma from red cells. The only assays for therapeutic drugs available, however, are theophylline and phenytoin. Both of these tests are immunoassay-based. The newest general POL testing analyzer is the Piccolo Portable Blood Analyzer (Abaxis, Inc., Sunnyvale, CA). Multi-analyte reagents are configured in a disposable reagent disk and can test whole blood, serum, or plasma for routine clinical chemistry analytes. Although there are no therapeutic drugs currently available, the manufacturer is considering adding a few to the menu.

The first POC testing device for measuring therapeutic drugs was the AccuLevel (Syntex, Palo Alto CA), a quantitative enzyme immunochromatography assay. AccuLevel assays were available for theophylline *(9)*, carbamazepine, phenobarbital, and phenytoin *(10)*. In an Emergency Department study, use of the AccuLevel theophylline assay at the bedside reduced the length of stay and time required to achieve a therapeutic drug concentration in the acute treatment of asthmatic children as compared with testing from a central laboratory *(11)*. Unfortunately, the AccuLevel assays were discontinued by the manufacturer.

The AccuMeter is an improved POC theophylline test cartridge device that is commercially available (AccuTech, Vista, CA). Figure 1 illustrates the schematic diagram for this device. AccuMeter has been evaluated against a laboratory-based analyzer (TDx, Abbott Labs) using capillary, serum, and heparinized blood samples *(12)*. The analytical correlation of results was good with coefficients of $r = 0.96$, 0.96, and 0.99, respectively. The precision (%CV) for low (8–12 mg/L) and high (19–25 mg/L) controls was 7.4 and 6.6%, acceptable for routine drug monitoring. However, the TAT for this assay is 20 min, which is fairly long for a POC testing assay.

The only other direct POC assay for therapeutic drugs that has received commercial interest is a test for whole blood cyclosporine A. This drug is widely for immunosuppression in patients who have received organ transplants, especially kidney transplants. On-site testing for cyclosporine A may be useful for real time management of transplant patients. A quantitative commercial device is in the development stage.

Further development of POC TDM devices will likely be diminished due to the incorporation of TDM assays onto general chemistry analyzers that have large on-board menu capacities. Most laboratories have the capability to deliver results of TDM assays with the same TAT and convenience as general chemistry analytes. Other than those discussed above, there are unlikely to be additional therapeutic drugs that have a clinical need for a turnaround time of <1 h. On the other hand, there may be a market for POL or at-home testing for therapeutic drugs if compact, rapid, and inexpensive assays can be developed.

4. Indirect On-Site Testing for Therapeutic Drugs

In contrast to direct testing, there is considerable interest in the indirect monitoring of a select few therapeutic drugs. For example, in a patient with insulin-dependent diabetes (Type 1), the direct quantitative measurement of glucose in blood provides an indirect means for determining if the proper insulin doses are being used. Quantitative on-site blood glucose concentrations are routinely used to make dosage adjustments. A discussion of glucometers is beyond the scope of this chapter. However, the next section describes other indirect on-site assays that monitor the efficacy and toxicity of therapeutic drugs.

4.1. Monitoring of Lipid Lowering Medications

Coronary artery disease (CAD) continues to be the major cause of morbidity and mortality in the US and throughout the western world. The risk

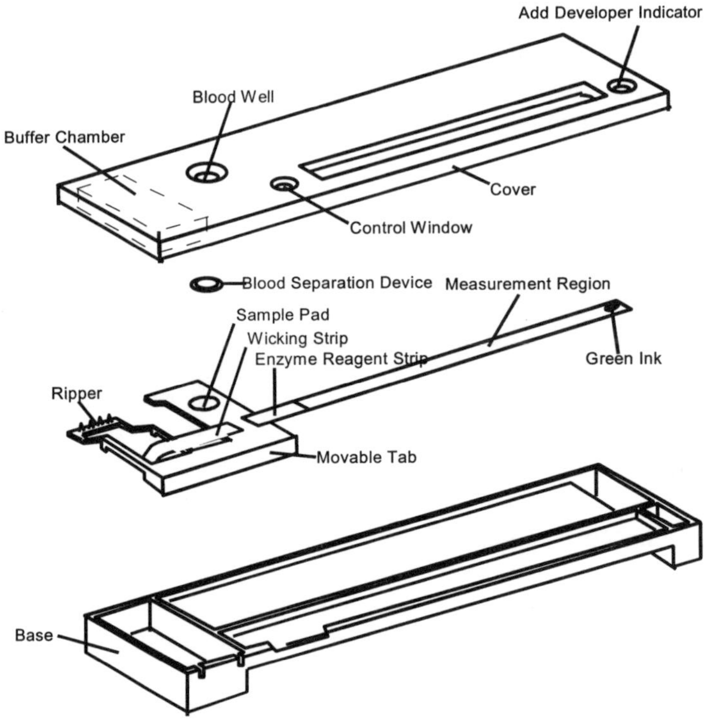

Fig. 1. The AccuMeter for theophylline and cholesterol. The cassette contains a paper strip coated with immobilized antibodies to the target analyte. The sample volume is 3 drops. When whole blood is used, a filter separates the red cells from the plasma. After a 2-min incubation, a cassette "tab" is pulled to initiate the migration onto the paper strip of the sample, and a fixed amount of labeled analyte (with horseradish peroxidase). This sets up a competition for antibody binding sites between the unlabeled (sample) and labeled analytes. The higher the sample analyte concentration, the higher the labeled analyte will migrate on the paper strip. The migration distance of the labeled antigen is determined by the addition of the peroxidase reagent, 4-chloro-1-naphthol, which produces a purple chromophore, which is read off a calibrated scale and converted to the analyte concentration. Used with permission from AccuTech, Carlisbad, CA.

factors for CAD are well established and include a family history of premature heart disease, diabetes, hypertension, cigarette smoking, and high blood concentrations of lipids and lipoproteins. Landmark studies conducted in Framingham, Massachusetts have established a exponential relationship between blood cholesterol concentrations and risk for CAD *(13)*. Guidelines for the interpretation of cholesterol and lipoprotein concentrations in blood have been established by the US National Cholesterol Education Program (NCEP) *(14)*. The NCEP has determined that a desirable total and low density lipoprotein (LDL) cholesterol should be <200 and <130 mg/dL, respectively. Subjects with values between 200 and 240 mg/dL for cholesterol, and 130 and 160 mg/dL for LDL cholesterol are considered at borderline risk. Those with values exceeding 240 and 160 mg/dL, respectively, are designated high risk.

The NCEP guidelines recommend that patients, who are at high risk or borderline risk with two or more CAD risk factors, are treated with a lipid lowering drug. The most effective drugs for lowering cholesterol and LDL are the inhibitors of HMG CoA reductase, collectively known as the "statins." HMG CoA reductase is the rate-limiting enzyme in the hepatic synthesis of cholesterol. In large placebo-controlled clinical trials, statins have been effective in reducing blood concentrations of total and LDL cholesterol, and reducing the incidence of CAD death or nonfatal acute myocardial infarction (AMI) *(15)*. For example, in the West of Scotland Coronary Prevention Study of 6,595 subjects, use of pravastatin led to a reduction of 20% in total cholesterol, 26% in LDL cholesterol, and a 33% reduction in definite and suspected CAD deaths, compared with placebo *(16)*. While the initial studies have focused on high risk groups, more recent trials have shown that the statins such as fluvastatin, are also useful for subjects who have moderate or borderline cholesterol concentrations *(17)*. There are six statins approved by the US FDA for clinical use in the U.S. lovastatin, simvastatin, pravastatin, fluvastatin, atorvastatin and cerivastatin. More drugs will likely be approved in the future.

Blood concentrations of total and high density lipoprotein (HDL) cholesterol, and triglycerides, may be accurately measured using POL instruments and on-site devices. The earliest commercial instruments for lipids and lipoproteins were the DT-60, Vision, and the Reflotron (Roche Diagnostics). These instruments have been used for many years for on-site testing such as POLs, and in unconventional laboratory testing areas such in shopping malls, grocery stores, and health fairs for mass cholesterol screening programs. More recently, other manufacturers have developed improved on-site lipid and lipoprotein analyzers (e.g., L•D•X, Cholestech, Hayward, CA). Accurate results may be obtained on a nonfasting blood specimen for measurement of total cholesterol and HDL. For calculation of LDL cholesterol from the Friedewald equation, a fasting blood specimen is needed because this calculation uses triglyceride concentrations, which increase shortly after eating.

POC testing devices are becoming available for cholesterol determination. The first device was the AccuMeter. The performance of this assay was compared against the L•D•X analyzer, and a US Centers for Disease Control standardized reference laboratory *(18)*, using goals established by the NCEP *(19)*. Both devices met the NCEP accuracy goal of <3%. However, neither device met the 3% precision goal, and both had a significant number of results that exceeded the 8.9% total error allowance. Based on this study, the author concluded that neither device was suitable for therapeutic monitoring for patients being treated for hypercholesterolemia. The results of this study were particularly disturbing considering all comparative assays were performed in duplicate, which is not the current standard of practice. Other investigators have reached the same conclusion for the Cholestech analyzer *(20,21)*, but the opposite conclusion for the AccuMeter *(22)*.

A POC testing device designed for at-home use was recently announced by Lifestream (Sandpoint, ID). The Cholestron measures cholesterol concentration from capillary blood in 3 min, and is projected to sell for $130–$300 (depending on optional features). This device is approved by the FDA.

4.2. Monitoring of Antithrombotic Medications

4.2.1. Heparin

The clotting of blood is a complex system of biochemical reactions. Initiation of the coagulation cascade by either the intrinsic or extrinsic pathways, leads to the conversion of prothrombin to thrombin, which in turn, catalyzes the conversion of fibrinogen to an insoluble fibrin clot. Systemic anticoagulation is widely used to prevent clot formation in patients with AMI and unstable angina, arterial and venous thrombotic diseases, and those undergoing procedures such as coronary artery bypass graft surgery (CABG), angioplasty, and hemodialysis. The most commonly used anticoagulant is unfractionated heparin, an acid mucopolysaccharide of varying molecular weights (10,000 to 30,000 daltons). Unfractionated heparin prevents fibrin formation by accelerating the natural interaction of antithrombin III and thrombin, thereby inhibiting other activated proteases that are involved with hemostasis (e.g., Factor IIa, IXa, and Xa). Because heparin is not well absorbed after oral administration, it is mainly administered intravenously either as a bolus injection or continuous infusion. Relative to use in other patients, very high doses are administered to patients undergoing CABG. The plasma half life of heparin is between 1–2 h. In cases of heparin overdose, protamine sulfate may be administered. This compound binds heparin to inactivate the anticoagulant property *(23)*.

A new anticoagulant widely used in Europe and gaining more acceptance in the US is low molecular weight heparin. This form of heparin is produced from enzymatic degradation of unfractionated heparin to produce polymers that range from 3000–5000 Daltons. Low molecular weight heparin has different pharmacological properties compared with unfractionated heparin. It is a less potent activator of platelets, may lead to a reduced incidence of clinical bleeding, and does not alter prothrombin, thrombin, or activated partial thromboplastin (aPPT) times. However, its effects are not as easily reversed with protamine.

The clinical use of heparin is routinely monitored by measurement of the activated clotting time (ACT), aPPT, and serum heparin concentrations. Because heparin concentrations cannot be directly measured using on-site testing devices, this will not be discussed any further in this chapter. Both ACT and aPTT are measures of the intrinsic coagulation pathway. The tests are performed by measuring the time needed for whole blood or plasma to form a fibrin clot following the addition of a contact reagent such as kaolin, used to accelerate clot formation. ACT is performed on whole blood collected without an anticoagulant. The expected ACT is about 2 min. The ACT requires on-site testing, as the sample begins to clot soon immediately after collection; it therefore cannot be sent to an off-site laboratory. The ACT is most widely used assay in the operating rooms for patients undergoing CABG, where a fast TAT for results is needed. The higher heparin concentration used in these patients makes it more appropriate to use ACT rather than aPTT. The target ACT time for CABG patients is 400–480 s *(24)*. Conditions that limit the accuracy of ACT measurements include hemodilution, platelet lysis, and hypothermia.

The aPPT is performed on citrated whole blood or plasma to which calcium, a thromboplastin reagent, and the clot activator are added. aPPT monitoring is more convenient and universally used than ACT for heparin monitoring, because plasma samples do not have to be tested immediately. Expected values range from 25–35 s. The target therapeutic concentration for heparin monitoring is an aPTT of approx 1.5–2.5 times the upper limit of normal.

4.2.2. Oral Antithrombotic Therapy

Oral anticoagulants such as warfarin, are ideal for outpatient use because these medications have a delayed onset of action, and a prolonged half-life of 2–3 d. Warfarin blocks the reductase enzyme in the vitamin K pathway, thereby producing structurally incomplete clotting factors such as prothrombin, VII, IX, and X. The drug is indicated for treatment of patients with venous and arterial thromboembolic diseases such as deep vein thrombosis, pulmonary embolism, and in survivors of AMI to prevent subsequent thrombosis in these patients

The clinical use of oral antithrombotic therapy is routinely monitored by measurement of the prothrombin time (PT). This test involves measuring the time needed for plasma to clot after adding calcium and tissue factor (thromboplastin), and is a measure of the extrinsic coagulation pathway. There is great variability in reference values for these assays because different thromboplastin reagents have different sensitivities towards clotting factors. Although thromboplastin reagents originating from the human brain are the most sensitive, most reagents used in the US originate from rabbit brain or combination of brain and lung. In order to normalize values between different laboratories, the International Normalized Ratio (INR) was created:

$$(\text{patient PT value} \div \text{mean normal PT})^{\text{ISI}},$$

where the ISI is the International Sensitivity Index *(25)*. The ISI value is dependent on the sensitivity of the thromboplastin reagent used. This calculation enables standardization of PT results from different laboratories. Expected PT values are between 10–14 s, and the INR from 0.9–1.1. The target INR ratios for patients on oral anticoagulant therapy is between 1.3 and 1.6.

4.2.3. On-Site Testing for Anticoagulant Drugs

Therapeutic monitoring of patients on heparin or oral anticoagulants using either ACT or aPTT, and PT, respectively, is well established. There are numerous on-site testing devices for the coagulation markers, including Hemochron (International Technidyne, Edison, NJ), CoaguChek Plus (Roche Diagnostics, Indianapolis, IN), Thrombolytic Assessment System (Dade International, Miami, FL), and proTime (International Technidyne, Edison, NJ).

For the monitoring of heparin, controversy exists as to whether or not ACT testing is superior to aPTT, and studies comparing the two have been conducted. Using quantitative heparin concentrations as a gold standard or reference, some investigators have concluded that measurement of the aPTT is superior to ACT *(26,27)*. Others have suggested that aPTT has the same limitations of hemodilution and hypothermia as ACT *(28)*. While most agree on the need for delivering a rapid TAT, the costs for delivering on-site testing are likely to be higher and therefore need to be justified. There are also issues regarding governmental regulations for on-site testing. Outcome studies have been conducted that compare POC vs central laboratory testing. In the GUSTO-I trial, aPTT monitoring was used to adjust heparin dosing in AMI patients who were treated with thrombolytic agents *(29)*. Figure 2 illustrates the decrease in the incidence of moderate to severe bleeding, blood transfusions, and decreases in hematocrit. Moreover, there were fewer bedside-monitored patients who had subtherapeutic concentrations. Bedside testing did have a slight increase in the incidence of recurrent ischemia. In another study, investiga-

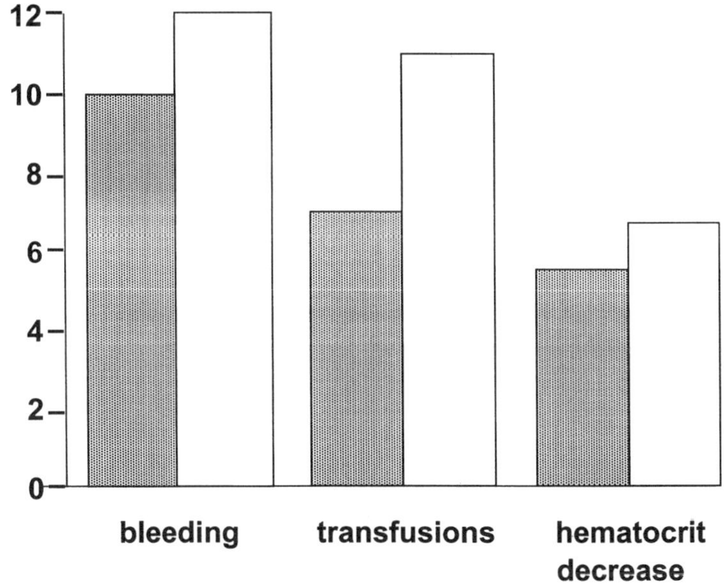

Fig. 2. Comparison of on-site testing for aPTT (shaded bars) vs central laboratory testing (open bars) for monitoring heparin therapy. The rate of complications for bleeding and need for blood transfusions, and % drop in hematocrit are compared. Data from ref. *29*.

tors compared on-site vs central laboratory testing for aPTT in the adjustment of heparin therapy *(30)*. On-site testing significantly reduced the time from when the blood sample was collected to a heparin infusion adjustment (0.4 vs 1.6 h), and the time to reach the therapeutic aPTT range (16.1 vs 19.4 h). These studies illustrate that rapid aPTT testing can be justified when overall hospital costs and improvements in clinical outcomes are taken into consideration.

Equivalent studies demonstrating the clinical advantages of delivering results with a rapid TAT using on-site testing for PT monitoring of oral anticoagulants have not been conducted to date. Published studies have focused on analytical correlation to determine how well POC devices agree with results obtained from the central laboratory. In one study, the CoaguCheck significantly underestimated the INR relative to a central laboratory result, while the TAS was more comparable *(31)*. Use of different thromboplastin reagents may have contributed to the differences in analytical correlations. Despite the lack of evidence-based outcome studies, these devices are being extensively used in physician offices, and are being considered for at-home testing *(32)*.

5. Conclusion

Beyond the markers described in this chapter, the commercial potential for point-of-care therapeutic drug monitoring devices is not extensive. The majority of therapeutic drugs do not need to be measured in an acute manner. Therefore the additional expense to deliver results with a fast turnaround time may not be warrranted. Even though the list of drugs approved by the US FDA increases each year, demands for therapeutic drug monitoring have actually declined over recent years. The development of safer drugs to replace those that are more toxic is one reason for this decline. The overall reduction in reimbursement for laboratory tests is another important factor. Each site must consider a multitude of factors before deciding if on-site testing for therapeutic drugs is warranted.

References

1. Antman, E. M., Wenger, T. L., Butler, V. P., Jr., Haber, E., and Smith, T. W. (1990) Treatment of 150 patients of life-threatening digitalis intoxication with digoxin-specific Fab antibody fragments. Final report of a multicenter study. *Circulation* **81,** 1744–1752.
2. Stephenson, J. (1998) RAMP: a quantitative immunoassay platform takes shape. IVD *Tech.* July/Aug 51–56.
3. Nebinger, P. and Koel, M. (1990) Specificity data of the tricyclic antidepressants assay by fluorescent polarization immunoassay. *J. Anal. Toxicol.* **14,** 219–221.
4. Poklis, A., Edinboro, L. E., Lee, J. S., and Crooks, C. R. (1997) Evaluation of a colloidal metal immunoassay device for the detection of tricyclic antidepressants in urine. *Clin. Toxicol.* **35,** 77–82.
5. Schwartz, J. G., Hurd, I. L., and Carnahan, J. J. (1994) Determination of tricyclic antidepressants for ED analyisis. *Am. J. Emerg. Med.* **12,** 513–516.
6. Baskin, L. B., Morgan, D. L., and Parupia, J. Y. (1996) A rapid immunoassay for drugs of abuse and tricyclic antidepressants. *Lab. Med.* **27,** 193–197.
7. Larkin, J. G., Herrick, A. L., McGuire, G. M., et al. (1991) Antiepileptic drug monitoring at the epilepsy clinic: a prospective evaluation. *Epilepsia* **32,** 89–95.
8. Oles, K. S. (1990) Therapeutic drug monitoring analysis systems for the physician office laboratory: a review of the literature. *Ann. Pharmacother.* 24, 1070–1077.
9. Nguyen, Q. C., Sly, R. M., Boeckx, R. L., and Shier, J. M. (1988) Determination of theophylline concentrations by AccuLevel. *Ann. Allergy* **60,** 521–522.
10. Nielsen, I. M., Gram, L., and Dam, M. (1992) Comparison of AccuLevel and TD: evaluation of onsite monitoring of antiepileptic drugs. *Epilepsia* **33,** 558–563.
11. Shier, J. M., Sly, R. M., Boeckx, R. L., et al. (1988) Impact of AccuLevel on treatment of acute asthma. *Ann. Allergy* **60,** 523–526.
12. Asmus, M. J., Milavetz, G., Teresi, M. E., and Weinberger. M. M. (1998) Evaluation of a noninstrumental disposable method for quantifying serum theophylline concentrations. *Pharmacotherapy* **18,** 30–34.

13. Anderson, K. M., Castelli, W. P., and Levy, D. (1987) Cholesterol and mortality. 30 years of follow-up from the Framingham Study. *JAMA* **257,** 2176–2180.
14. The Expert Panel. Summary of the second report of the National Cholesterol Education Program (NCEP) Expert Panel on detection, evaluation, and treatment of high blood cholesterol in adults (Adult Treatment Panel II) NHLBI. (1993) *JAMA* **269,** 3015–3023.
15. Pearson, T. A. (1998) Primary and secondary prevention of coronary artery disease: trials of lipid lowering with statins. *Am. J. Cardiol.* **82(suppl),** 28S–30S.
16. Shepherd, J., Cobge, S. M., Ford, I., Istes, C. G., Lorimer, A. R., MacFarlane, P. W., McKillop, J. H., and Packard, C. J. (1995) for the West of Scotland Coronary Prevention Study Group. Prevention of coronary heart disease with pravastatin in men with hypercholesterolemia. *N. Engl. J. Med.* **333,** 1301–1307.
17. Herd, J. A., Ballantyne, C. M., Farmer, J. A., Ferguson, J. J., III, Jones, P. H., West, M. S., Gould, K. L., and Gotto, A. M., Jr. (1997) Effects of fluvastatin on coronary atherosclerosis in patients with mild to moderate cholesterol elevations (Lipoprotein and Coronary Atherosclerosis Study). *Am. J. Cardiol.* **80,** 278–286.
18. Volles, D. F., McKenney, J. M., Miller, W. G., et al. (1998) Analytic and clinical performance of two compact cholesterol testing devices. *Pharmacother.* **18,** 184–192.
19. National Cholesterol Education Program. Current status of blood cholesterolmeasurements in clinical laboratories in the United States: a report from the laboratory standardization panel of the National Cholesterol Education Program. (1988) *Clin. Chem.* **34,** 193–201.
20. Bard, R. L., Kaminsky, L. A., Whaley, M. H., and Zajakowski, S. (1997) Evaluation of lipid profile measurements obtained from the Cholestech L.D.X. analyzer. *J. Cardiopulm Rehab.* **17,** 413–418.
21. Kafonek, S. D., Donovan, L., Lovejoy, K. K. L., and Bachorik, P. S. (1996) Biological variation of lipids and lipoproteins in fingerstick blood. *Clin. Chem.* **42,** 2002–2007.
22. McNamara, J. R., Warnick, G. R., Leary, E. T., Wittels, E., Nelson, F. E., Pearl, M. F., and Schaeffer, E. J. (1996) Multicenter evaluation of a patient-administered test for blood cholesterol measurements. *Prevent. Med.* **25,** 583–592.
23. Olson, J. D., Arkin, C. F., Brandt, J. T., Cunningham, M. T., Giles, A., Koepke, J. A., and Witte, D. L. (1998) College of American Pathologists Conference XXXI on laboratory monitoring of anticoagulant therapy. Laboratory monitoring of unfractionated heparin therapy. *Arch. Pathol. Lab. Med.* **122,** 782–798.
24. Esposito, R. A, Culliford, A. T., Colvin, S. B., Thomas, S. J., Lackner, H., and Spencer, F. C. (1983) The role of the activated clotting time in heparin administration and neutralization for cardiopulmonary bypass. *J. Thorac. Cardiovasc. Surg.* **85,** 174–185.
25. Loeliger, E. A. (1985) ICSII/ICTII recommendations for reporting prothromgin time in oral anticoagulatn control. *Thromb. Haemost.* **53,** 155–156.
26. Solomon, H. M., Mullins, R. E., Lyden, P., Thompson, P., and Hudoff, S. (1998) The diagnostic accuracy of bedside and laboratory coagulation. Procedures used to monitor the anticoagulation status of patients treated with heparin. *Am. J. Clin. Pathol.* **109,** 371–378.

27. Reiner, J. S., Coyne, K. S., Lundergan, C. F., and Ross, A. M. (1994) Bedside monitoring of heparin therapy: comparison of activated clotting time to activated partial thromboplastin time. *Cathet. Cardiovasc. Diagn.* **32,** 49–52.
28. Flom-Halvorsen, H. I., Ovrum, E., Abdelnoor, M., Bjornsen, S., and Brosstad, F. (1999) Assessment of heparin anticoagulation: comparison of two commercially available methods. *Ann. Thorac. Surg.* **67,** 1012–1017.
29. Zabel, K. M., Granger, C. B., Becker, R. C., Bovill, E. G., Hirsh, J., Aylward, P. E., et al. (1998) Use of bedside activated partial thromboplastin time monitor to adjust heparin dosing after thrombolysis for acute myocardial infarction: results of GUSTO-I. *Am. Heart J.* **136,** 868–876.
30. Becker, R. C., Ball, S. P., Eisenberg P., Borzak , S., Held, A. C., Spencer, F., et al. (1999) A randomized, multicenter trial of weight-adjusted intravenous heparin dose titration and point-of-care coagulation monitoring in hospitalized patients with active thromboembolic disease. *Am. Heart J.* **137,** 59–71.
31. Hasenkam, J. M., Knudsen, L., Kimose, H. H., Gronnesby, H., Attermann, J., Andersen, N. T., and Pilegaard, H. K. (1997) Practicability of patient self-testing of oral anticoagulant therapy by the international normalized ration (INR) using a portable whole blood monitor. A pilot study. *Thromb. Res.* **85,** 77–82.
32. Gosselin, R. C, Owings, J. T., Larkin, E., White, R. H., Hutchinson, R., and Branch, J. (1997) Monitoring oral anticoagulant therapy with point-of-care devices: correlations and caveats. *Clin. Chem.* **43,** 1785–1786.

Chapter 3

On-Site Workplace Drug Testing

David Armbruster

1. Background

Drug testing is an everyday fact of life for millions of American workers. Truck drivers, retail sales individuals, government workers, and professional athletes are subject to drug testing. Workplace drug testing is now a well-established practice in the U.S. and around the world. Large and small companies and corporations routinely screen job applicants and successfully passing a drug test is often a prerequisite for hiring. After being hired, workers are subject to postemployment testing on a random basis, after an accident, prior to a promotion, or "for cause." Reasons for drug testing include poor productivity, lost profits, defective products, absenteeism, on-the-job accidents, high employee turnover, and employee theft or espionage. Workers engaged in activities related to public safety, such as air traffic controllers, security officers, truck drivers, and nuclear plant workers, are routinely screened for drugs because of the sensitive nature of their jobs.

Traditional workplace drug testing consists of collecting a urine specimen and sending it to a forensic reference laboratory for testing. A new approach, on-site drug screening using commercially available devices, is now becoming commonplace *(1)*. Urine specimens are usually collected at clinics, specimen collection stations, or other central sites and then shipped to reference laboratories for testing. Testing can now be performed immediately at the workplace, without prior notice, and administrative decisions about hiring or continued employment can be made literally on the spot. On-site testing is fueled by the availability of many simple, hand held drug screening kits *(2–15)*.

From: *Forensic Science: On-Site Drug Testing*
Edited by: A. J. Jenkins and B. A. Goldberger © Humana Press, Inc., Totowa, NJ

While the many on-site tests are not equally reliable and accurate and exhibit their individual strengths and weaknesses, the commercially available tests meet minimal technical requirements and are FDA-approved.

On-site tests are not recommended by all forensic toxicologists, for a variety of reasons. Their lack of acceptance by some mirrors the concern over clinical on-site tests, such as the home pregnancy test. Objections were raised about the reliability of home pregnancy tests because the test is conducted by the purchaser and not by trained and certified laboratory workers. Similarly, on-site drug immunoassays require minimal, if any, reagent preparation, and the individual test devices are read visually. As with home pregnancy tests, fertility tests, urine dipsticks, home glucose tests, etc., most nonlaboratorians can perform on-site drug tests competently without professional education or training. While not guaranteed to be foolproof, on-site clinical assays, and now drug tests, are scientifically valid, readily available, and in demand. The challenge is to ensure that these devices are used appropriately for workplace drug testing.

Though very similar in methodology to many clinical assays, on-site drug tests differ in one key way: they are forensic assays. Workplace drug test results are used strictly for administrative and/or legal purposes, not for medical purposes. Forensic test results can have serious consequences for those who test positive, such as denial or loss of employment. This distinction is clearly recognized by the US Clinical Laboratory Improvement Amendments of 1988 (CLIA 88), which specifically exempts forensic laboratories from CLIA regulation. On-site drug testing is not addressed by CLIA, but, by logical extension, it is not exempt from federal regulation.

Traditional reference laboratory testing is well established and considered to be the standard procedure *(17,18)*. Table 1 compares and contrasts reference laboratory testing with on-site testing. There are drawbacks to reference laboratory testing. Employers are turning to on-site drug testing in lieu of the traditional reference laboratory approach for a variety of reasons. One problem with reference laboratory testing is the delay between notification of the candidate to submit a specimen at a collection site and the actual collection. Specimen collection for a reference laboratory can slow down the process and potentially allow some drug users to avoid detection. Typically, job candidates are instructed to report to a collection site to provide a specimen. A drug abuser is thus given considerable warning and may purposely delay going to the collection site to allow illicit drugs to metabolize and clear from the body, attempt to dilute drugs by fluid loading, or acquire an adulterant in order to thwart drug detection. Obviously, employers have an advantage if testing takes place with no delay in specimen collection.

Table 1
Comparison of On-Site and Reference Laboratory Testing for Drugs of Abuse

On-site testing	Reference lab testing
1. Immunoassays based on specific antibodies	1. Immunoassays based on specific antibodies
2. Discrete, single unit, manual test device or kit	2. Bulk reagent kits for automated analysis using instrumentation
3. Test for one drug or several simultaneously using one test device	3. Test for several drugs simultaneously, but requires separate reagents for each analyte
4. Compact, hand-held, portable test device	4. Fixed laboratory facility using automated analyzers
5. Minimal or no test equipment	5. Technologically sophisticated instrumentation
6. Visually read tests; subjective interpretation of test result	6. Analyzer measurement; objective data interpretation.
7. Rapid assay time; 5–10 min to report a result	7. Rapid instrumental analysis but a minimum of several hours to report result
8. Expensive cost per test, but comparable over-all cost	8. Inexpensive screening test cost, but comparable over-all cost

The chain of custody that must accompany a urine specimen to a reference laboratory is also a potential weak link in this approach. An incomplete chain of custody (missing signature, date, identification number, etc.) or a "broken" chain, results in a delay of testing or outright rejection of a specimen for testing. Many chain of custody problems can be successfully resolved by affidavits from the collection site. Nonetheless, time is lost in the process and the employer may wait several days for test results.

Economics is another reason to consider on-site testing. The typical cost of a laboratory based drug test dropped from about $20 at the end of the 1980s to about $15 today *(16)*. On site tests are being sold for approximately the same cost as a reference laboratory test and can thus compete favorably. In addition to the cost of on-site testing, the results are available immediately. On average, it takes about 10 min to obtain results (after specimen collection). Job candidates who test negative can begin work on the same day. While an efficiently run reference laboratory can report results in less than one day, this turn around time (TAT) refers to the in-house TAT once the laboratory receives the specimens. Many specimens are shipped via a commercial air courier service, with overnight delivery expected. For all practical purposes, there is a two day wait between the time a specimen is collected and the time the result is reported. While some laboratories report results to clients electronically (remote printers, facsimile machines, or even by telephone), others send reports through the mail or a courier service, which can add at least another day or more to the TAT. On-site testing is particularly valuable to employers in the instance of job related accidents. The worker may be tested immediately, enhancing the chance of detecting a drug user and allowing the employer to make a timely decision regarding the individual's fitness for duty.

Depending on the location of the specimen collection site, the reference laboratory, and the means of specimen transport, a negative drug test report may be available in 24–48 h. This does not appear to be an unreasonable TAT but employers typically desire results in less time, in order that an otherwise qualified job candidate may start to work immediately. Any delays in reporting results, such as those caused by chain of custody problems, are frustrating for employers. Because of the technology available today, the validity of the test result is taken for granted by employers, who now tend to feel that what they are really paying for is rapid service. The capability of performing the drug screen immediately and making a hiring decision with minimal delay is very attractive. Hence, the obvious appeal of on-site testing.

Naturally, there are also drawbacks to on-site testing. Some individuals argue that on-site tests are not as accurate or precise as standard reference laboratory assays. Indeed, they are not expected to be as results are determined visually and the human eye is not as sophisticated as a spectrophotometer. However, many are US FDA approved and their performance has been shown to be acceptable for routine drug screening. The accuracy of on-site devices is naturally a critical issue. More sensitive assays may yield a positive test even if the drug concentration in a urine specimen is below the stated cutoff for the test. Even the best quality on-site devices have a window of variability around the cutoff concentration. Specimens with drug concentrations slightly below the cutoff may produce positive test results, and, conversely, specimens containing drug levels slightly above the cutoff may yield negative results. However, a certain degree of inaccuracy with a screening immunoassay is an inherent, and understandable, limitation. Similar limitations are also exhibited by standard reference laboratory assays.

On-site tests are generally more likely to yield false positive results compared with reference laboratory screening assays. False positives occur when a specific drug or drug metabolite is not present in a specimen at a predetermined cutoff concentration or when a similar drug molecule crossreacts with the antibody. To eliminate the real possibility of a false positive result being reported owing to a positive screening immunoassay result, confirmation testing by a valid methodology, typically gas chromatography/mass spectrometry (GC/MS), is necessary. The need for confirmatory testing by use of a second, more specific and definitive test methodology applies to both on-site and reference laboratory immunoassay screening procedures. Employers must make provision for confirmatory testing in order to maintain an acceptable on-site testing program. It is critical that users of on-site tests adhere to the well established practice of a two-tiered approach to testing: screening followed by confirmation.

All immunoassays, whether traditional laboratory-based procedures or on-site testing devices, are not created equal and none are always 100% correct. There will be false negatives and false positives. Even a very high quality screening test will not always have a positive result confirmed by GC/MS. Some specimens contain drug concentrations close enough to the screening cutoff to test positive, but they will be negative by GC/MS because it is a more sophisticated and accurate quantitative procedure.

With traditional drug testing, specimen collection is typically conducted at a central site by trained personnel. On-site testing may take place in temporary facilities by less experienced personnel. This problem is not insurmountable and simply requires adequate preparation of the collection site and proper training of the collector/tester. Any standard restroom facility can be modified to support appropriate collection. Collection/testing personnel must undergo training and demonstrate proficiency before performing on-site testing. Certification by the employer or the distributor of the on-site test is highly recommended. Periodic refresher training and continuing proficiency assessment are also advisable. Most test manufacturers or distributors provide both basic training and continuing support to users of their products.

One possible problem with on-site drug testing is the nonlaboratorian who may be reluctant to participate in the collection and testing process. Yet, on-site drug tests are equivalent to CLIA-waived exempt tests because they are designed to require a minimum number of steps and to be simple enough to perform so that anyone who can understand and follow the test directions can obtain valid results. As with their clinical testing counterparts, on-site drug tests can be successfully performed by any layperson, usually with minimal training. Indeed, training personnel to correctly fill out the necessary chain of custody document and conduct a valid collection of the specimen is usually a bigger challenge than actually performing the test.

When a specimen is collected in a forensically acceptable manner, i.e., with a valid chain of custody, adulteration checks, proper specimen seal, etc., it may be sent to a reference laboratory for confirmation. In other words, provided an on-site test program conforms to the standard, well-established protocol used by traditional reference laboratory programs (with the exception that the immunoassay screen is performed on-site), a valid specimen suitable for confirmation testing can be procured. Since the majority of specimens are expected to screen negative, only a few will require the additional effort necessary for confirmation testing. A bonus of on-site testing is that the paperwork and effort required to send a specimen to a reference laboratory is avoided if the specimen screens negative. However, a valid chain of custody is an absolute necessity for valid forensic testing. The chain of custody is vulnerable to a variety of common errors, e.g., missing or erroneous information/annotation, breaks in the chain, etc.

On-site testing sacrifices the anonymity that has traditionally been associated with drug testing. With the traditional approach, the specimen collector has direct contact with the donor, but no role in testing, which is performed in a reference laboratory by personnel who have no contact with the donor. Although it is possible for an on-site program to separate the collection from the testing step, by using two individuals, it is often more practical to use a single person who is both collector and tester, and who, of necessity, knows the identity of the donor.

Another weakness of on-site testing is the potential lack of permanent test result documentation. Laboratory drug screening procedures produce a hard copy of test results — a permanent record — of the testing process. On-site testing devices (with some exceptions) do not produce a permanent record of the test result. The devices are discarded after use, and even if they are stored long term, the test results typically are not stable but fade or dissipate with time. One possible solution to this problem is to photocopy or photograph the results.

2. Conducting On-Site Workplace Drug Testing

A typical on-site workplace drug testing program consists of pre-employment screening of job candidates and post-employment testing of workers for such reasons as: reasonable cause; following on-the-job accidents; prior to promotions /transfers; or before return to work from a layoff or leave of absence. An employer should launch such a program by issuing a company-wide substance abuse policy that clearly states that the use, possession, and distribution of controlled substances is prohibited. Job applicants and current employees should be required to sign a substance abuse policy acknowledgement and consent form.

Drug testing can take place at the facility where a job candidate will be employed. At least two staff members should be trained at each location to collect and test specimens so that the program can continue on a daily basis. Applicants should present photo identification to positively prove identity. Test subjects should be asked to remove jackets and other unnecessary clothing and to wash their hands before testing to minimize the possibility of specimen adulteration. Any standard restroom facility can be used for specimen collection, but toilets should contain bluing agents. Ideally, the restroom should have a water cutoff valve, have only cold water available, or have water faucets that are taped over with seams initialed by staff members. These precautions help preclude adulteration by water dilution and prevent substitution of water for urine.

The on-site devices described in other chapters of this book should be suitable for workplace testing. Those that combine the test device with the urine collection cup have an advantage as the specimen can be tested without aliquoting a sample from the collection device. Combination collection/test devices can be sealed and shipped to a reference laboratory for confirmation testing with forensic integrity. Regardless of what collection system is used, the temperature of the specimen should be tested within a couple of minutes of collection and the specimen should be observed for color and general appearance. Additional adulteration checks may be performed. As with any collection program, suspect specimens should be discarded, the reason documented, and another specimen collected under direct observation, if allowed by the program's protocol. Most manufacturers' of on-site devices design them using the standard cutoffs for the Substance Abuse and Mental Health Services Administration (SAMHSA)-five drugs (THC-COOH, cocaine metabolite, amphetamines, opiates, and PCP), and these are strongly recommended for workplace drug testing programs.

The use of positive and negative controls with any immunoassay is a standard and necessary practice with reference laboratory tests. The better on-site devices include a built-in control that verifies the assay's performance. But these integral controls do not verify conclusively that the test devices will produce the appropriate result with a specimens known to contain a specific drug above or below the cutoff concentration. Only the use of a externally added control will provide that assurance. However, the devices do not permit simultaneous testing of a control and specimen. A typical approach is to test positive and negative controls with on-site devices when a bulk container, perhaps containing 25–100 test devices, is initially opened and placed in service. Daily testing of controls is highly desirable. Of course, test devices used for controls increase the cost of testing as they can not be used for actual donor specimens.

Traditional laboratory based drug testing incorporates the use of blind controls, both internal blinds generated by the laboratory's own quality assurance department and external blinds, submitted to the laboratory by external agencies and indistinguishable from actual donor specimens. It is a problem to challenge on-site testing with blind controls of either type because specimen collection and testing are typically combined, the same individual likely serving as the specimen collector and the test analyst. Proficiency of the collector/analyst and of the on-site testing device may nevertheless be assessed by providing proficiency testing samples for analysis. These samples will not meet the usual criteria for double blind (identity and content unknown), but they would fit the definition of a single blind control (content of sample is unknown, but the sample is recognized as a control or proficiency test sample). It is certainly advisable for on-site programs to participate in some sort of proficiency testing program in addition to the internal quality control/quality assurance program. Another approach to checking the performance of an on-site testing program is to send a certain number of specimens which have screened negative to a reference laboratory for testing (it is assumed that all screen positives will be forwarded for confirmation). Negative results for these specimens at the reference laboratory demonstrate equivalent performance of the on-site assay. On-site negative screened samples that screen and confirm positive at the reference laboratory indicate a performance problem at the on-site testing facility.

If the on-site test device gives a negative result, the job candidate or worker can be immediately approved for hiring or to continue working. If the result is positive, it must be confirmed by a method such as gas chromatography/mass spectrometry (GC/MS). The specimen cup must be sealed with tamper-proof evidence tape and all necessary forensic paperwork properly completed. The specimen and chain of custody are then sent to a reference laboratory for confirmation. A positive immunoassay screening test result is not proof of drug abuse. It is expected that > 90–95% of positive screening tests for marijuana, cocaine, and PCP will confirm positive and indicate the ingestion of a controlled substance. Typically, far fewer screening positive results for amphetamines and opiates are confirmed, and even those that do may be the result of appropriate medical use of amphetamine or opiate drugs.

Positive on-site screening results produce employer dilemmas. For example, a job candidate cannot be hired until the positive test result is confirmed by a medical review officer (MRO). The MRO reviews the record to determine whether the result is because of improper drug use or abuse or a legitimate medical use. The applicant who tested positive by screening may wonder why other individuals were hired and he or she was not. The employer must be prepared to handle these situations. It is appropriate to explain to the donor that the on-site test result was positive and that no employment decision will be made until a confirmatory test result decision is made by an MRO.

While this is a reasonable approach, it is conceivable that some candidates and employees may not accept it, and the on-site testing staff must be prepared to deal with individuals who may want to debate the test results or the entire procedure and, in some cases, perhaps even become belligerent. It is the responsibility of the employer to determine the proper course of action in these situations. It should be emphasized that employers should not wait until such a situation arises. A contingency plan should be designed before the testing program is initiated. Some employers require job candidates who screen positive to have confirmation testing performed at their own expense, the cost of the testing being refunded to the job candidate if a negative confirmation test result is reported. The idea is that job candidates who know that they have not used drugs, or who have a legitimate explanation for a positive test, have nothing to hide. Drug abusers, on the other hand, will have no incentive to pay to have their drug abuse confirmed and will therefore seek employment elsewhere.

3. *The Future of On-Site Workplace Drug Testing*

In April, 1997, the US Department of Health and Human Services' (HHS) Drug Testing Advisory Board (DTAB) met to discuss alternate matrices for drug testing (saliva, sweat, and hair), and the use of handheld, on-site drug testing devices *(19)*. "Field testing" for drugs in the past required reagent preparation and instrumentation. Not so with on-site immunoassays that require minimum or no preparation and whose results are read visually. Specialized training in laboratory testing is simply not required with these devices. Despite the interest shown by the HHS in on-site testing, these devices are not yet approved for use by US government agencies or companies under contract by the government for federally regulated drug testing. In time, the HHS could approve their use, and provide guidelines and controls. Companies not subject to regulation by the federal government, however, are free to choose to use on-site devices.

Screening tests, whether on-site or laboratory based, will not always detect drug use, no matter how accurate they may be. Drugs are metabolized by the human body after administration. Depending on the pharmacokinetics of the specific drug used, and the rate of metabolism of the user (which varies with individuals), a donor's urine specimen may be negative (contains no drug or drug below the cutoff concentration) if it is collected long enough after ingestion of the drug. Thus, a negative test is no guarantee that the donor is not a drug user. In addition, assays cannot be expected to detect the wide range of illicit substances that may be used. If an individual drug is not specifically targeted by a immunoassay, depending on crossreactivity, it may not be detected.

On-site testing will likely be used in the workplace drug testing arena by some companies, but it is probable that traditional reference laboratory drug testing will coexist with on-site testing. Companies that successfully used a reference laboratory based program may have no reason to change to on-site testing, unless it offers a tangible or significant advantage. Companies just beginning a drug testing program, especially smaller businesses with a large number of geographically diverse work sites with no convenient collection sites, may find on-site testing attractive. Some companies may decide up front, or learn from experience, that on-site testing requires too much commitment in terms of personnel and effort. On the other hand, any company that is willing to invest the necessary time, money, and effort, and, perhaps most importantly, train its personnel well, can perform on-site testing in a forensically acceptable manner.

How on-site drug testing will be regulated is an unanswered question, as different approaches are still evolving in the United States. Regulating such a potentially widespread, flexible, and adaptable option in drug testing presents a challenge to government officials, both federal and state. Guidelines and directives are currently lacking because when government mandated workplace drug testing was initiated, on-site testing did not exist as a viable alternative and all testing was conducted at reference laboratories.

References

1. Armbruster, D. A. (1997) On-site drug testing: On the rise and growing strong. *Medical Laboratory Observer* **129,** 40–44.
2. Wu, A. H. B., Wong, S. S., Johnson, K. G., et al. (1993) Evaluation of the Triage system for emergency drugs-of-abuse testing in urine. *J. Anal. Tox.* **17,** 241–245.
2. Buechler, K. F., Moi, S., Noar, B., et al. (1992) Simultaneous detection of several drugs of abuse. *Clin. Chem.* **38,** 1678–1684.
3. Anderson, G., Vekich, A. J., and Scott, M. (1990) Evaluation of a rapid qualitative EIA test for drugs of abuse. *Clin. Chem.* **36,** 1021–1022.
4. Towt, J., Tsai, S.-C, Hernandez, M. R., et al. (1995) OnTrak TesTcup: A novel, on-site, multi-analyte screen for the detection of abused drugs. *J. Anal. Tox.* **19,** 504–510.
5. Schwartz, R. H., Bogema, S., and Thorne, M. M. (1990) of a rapid latex-inhibition screening assay for cocaine in urine. *J. Pediatr.* **117,** 670–672.
6. Cone, E. J., Darwin, W. D., and Dickerson, S. L. (1991) Evaluation of the AbuScreen OnTrak assay for cocaine (metabolite). *Clin. Chem. News* **17,** 40.
7. Armbruster, D. A. and Krolak, J. M. (1992) Screening for drugs of abuse with the Roche OnTrak assays. *J. Anal. Tox.* **16,** 172–175.
8. Koch, T. R., Raglin, R. L., Kirk, S., and Bruni, J. F. (1994) Improved screening for benzodiazepine metabolites in urine using the Triage panel for drugs of abuse. *J. Anal. Tox.* **18,** 168–172.

9. Jenkins, A. J., Darwin, W. D., Huestis, M. A., Cone, E. J., and Mitchell, J. M. (1995) Validity testing of the acuPINCH THC test. *J. Anal. Tox.* **19,** 5–12.
10. Jenkins, A. J., Mills, L. C., Darwin, W. D., Huestis, M. A., Cone, E. J., and Mitchell, J. M. 1993 Validity testing of the EZ-Screen cannabinoid test. *J. Anal. Tox.* **17,** 292–298.
11. Klimov, A. D., Tsai, S.-C, Towt, J., and Salamone, S. J. (1995) Improved immunochromatographic format for competitive-type assays. *Clin. Chem.* **41,** 1360.
12. Baskin, L. B., Morgan, D. L., and Parupia, J. Y. (1996) A rapid immunoassay for drugs of abuse and tricyclic antidepressants. *Lab. Med.* **27,** 193–197.
13. Parsons, R. G., Kowal, R., LeBlond, D., et al. (1993) Multianalyte assay system developed for drugs of abuse. *Clin. Chem.* **39,** 1899–1903.
14. Schwartz, R. H., Bogema, S., and Thorne, M. M. (1990) Evaluation of EZ-Screen enzyme immunoassay test for detection of cocaine and marijuana in urine specimens. *Ped. Emerg. Care* **6,** 147–149.
15. Uehling, M. (1995) Score one for drug screening. *CAP Today June* **9,** 1,5–9.
16. Armbruster, D. A. (1992) A guide to NIDA certification for workplace drug testing. *Medical Laboratory Observer* **24,** 32–36.
17. Pelehach, L. (1996) What happened when employers just said "No." *Laboratory Medicine* **27,** 162–169.
18. Department of Health and Human Services Substance Abuse and Mental Health Services Administration Drug Testing Advisory Board. Scientific Meeting on Drug Testing of Alternative Specimens and Technologies, April 28–30, 1997, Rockville, Maryland.

Chapter 4

Program Requirements, Standards, and Legal Considerations for On-Site Drug Testing Devices in Workplace Testing Programs

Theodore F. Shults and Yale H. Caplan

1. Introduction

On-site testing technology offers the exciting prospect of providing contemporaneous toxicological assessment of biological specimens for drugs of abuse. On-site technology is diverse, rapidly expanding and evolving. New on-site products are being rapidly introduced into the drug testing market. These products are designed to expand the scope of testing and/or to displace existing testing technology. On-site testing of urine, oral fluids, and presumably other biological matrices raises new and old questions as to its appropriate application in regards to the written and unwritten expectations of the law, clients, and society.

Drug testing is modern society's application of technology toward mitigating the very ancient human problem of substance abuse. For any drug testing technology to be successful, it must be effectively integrated with applicable social policy, legal principles, and the pragmatic economic considerations of business. These three factors simultaneously shape, enable, and constrain the application of technology. Neither technical considerations nor market puffery predict success for any technology.

From: *Forensic Science: On-Site Drug Testing*
Edited by: A. J. Jenkins and B. A. Goldberger © Humana Press, Inc., Totowa, NJ

We tend to think of technical validity as separate and independent from legal and social policy issues. One major reason for this construction is that technical validity is objectively measured and reported in the language of science and statistics; crossreactivity, precision around a cutoff value, reproducibility and stability are all measured in statistical terms. Yet even these objective technical criteria are to a large degree a function of legal, economic and cultural standards.

As aptly illustrated in the "debate" that surrounded the World Trade Organization meeting in Seattle in 1999, we live in a world of converging interests, yet wide differences exist in this global economy between economic statuses, employer rights, individual rights and the power of the state. When these fundamental differences are applied to workplace drug testing, the programs implemented in the United States, Mexico, Europe, and Asia look very different *(1)*. As the balance between economic factors, individual rights and employer rights equilibrate so will drug testing standards. Technical requirements, procedural safeguards, and quality assurance are in the final analysis a function of who is being tested, why the individual is being tested, the toxicological nature of the test, what is at stake, who is doing the testing, and even where the test is being performed.

The focus of this chapter is on the U.S. application of on-site drug testing technology in governmental and private sector workplace drug testing programs. Large-scale drug testing is unique to the U.S. social experiment, and while U.S. culture is often criticized, it is at the same time the most emulated. The leadership role the United States has taken in using drug testing technology has been necessitated by the country's economic success and its unfortunate status as the largest consumer of euphoric compounds.

As economic development expands worldwide and barriers to trade are eroded, the problem of illicit drug consumption will grow. Increasing per-capita disposable income and the inefficiency of existing controls on the availability of euphoric compounds are the essential conditions that exacerbate the universal individual and societal problem of substance abuse. As the problem grows, so will the need for cost-effective drug testing programs. The successful experiences in the United States will be models for the rest of the world as economic conditions improve.

2. What Is "On-Site" Testing from a Standards Perspective?

On-site technology is rapidly evolving and diversifying to the point where it appears a broader definition of the term "on-site" is needed. This term initially referred to bench-top automated immunoassay devices used outside of a formal laboratory setting. Over time, as immunoassay methods progressed, instrumental measurement of the immunoassay reaction could be replaced by visual inspection. Immunoassay impregnated on plastic cards became the new "on-site" technology, and the term "noninstrumented on-site testing" was used. This urine-based immunoassay technology has recently been modified to work with oral fluids, and a consensus has quickly formed that oral fluids should be included in a discussion of on-site testing. Sweat is another biological matrix that is being investigated as a viable candidate for rapid immunoassay analysis. Although there are no current products on the market that will give an immediate immunoassay screening result on sweat, such a product is foreseeable, as are the same validity and application questions.

Further, the distinction between instrumented and noninstrumented immunoassay on-site testing is also dissolving. Handheld instrumental devices are in development that will provide an "on-site" analysis of oral fluids and urine. Visual interpretation of a line or no line will be replaced by an automatic report or simply reading a display. Another promising innovation is the integration of an on-site instrument that objectively reads the immunoassay results and transmits the results over the Internet to a centralized facility. The computer at the central facility analyzes the results according to a software program and essentially determines whether the specimen should be sent to a laboratory for further testing (nonnegative, or random quality control). The final results are then reported to a medical review officer. This type of approach is a hybrid of centralized laboratory management and local collection and screening. The first such product, called *eScreen*, is already being marketed. Finally, on the horizon are nonimmunoassay and "noninvasive" handheld or portable instruments that use technology other than immunoassay to distinguish between presence and absence of specific substances in biological specimens. An example of such a nonimmunoassay device is the recently approved wristwatch that monitors glucose levels.

Another term that many providers use is point-of-collection (POC) testing. POC testing is used in clinical laboratory medicine to refer to diagnostic screening tests performed with or near the patient. The terms POC as well as "on-site" communicate another common element of the new technology: in addition to providing contemporaneous results, the testing is performed outside a comprehensive laboratory. Therefore, the challenge when establishing drug testing standards (in particular, technical validity) is to determine the degree to which the intrinsic safeguards of training, quality control, and technical management used in forensic drug testing laboratories are necessary and applicable to on-site testing.

In summary, what these devices and methods have in common is the promise of a fast and generally mobile method of toxicological analysis for a wide number of applications. What is also common is the inability of most consumers to evaluate the validity, effectiveness and risks of these technologies.

3. Establishing Federal Standards for On-Site Drug Testing

From the federal government's perspective, the legal and policy framework within which drug testing must operate is quite clear. Robert Ashby, a government lawyer who has considerable experience with the Department of Transportation's (DOT) mandatory drug testing program, concisely described the legal framework of the program at a meeting with representatives of the drug testing industry in December 1999. Mr. Ashby stated that on the one hand, DOT has the statutory and administrative mandate to implement drug and alcohol testing on public safety grounds, and on the other hand, DOT's program must conform with the constitutional requirements as articulated by the Supreme Court to assure fairness to the individual, accuracy, due process, and reasonableness.

There are other governmental interests in drug testing besides public safety. However, regardless of the government's interest, drug testing is legally a "search" when required by a governmental entity and thus must meet the constitutional requirements. Constitutional standards for drug testing generally exceed the legal requirements as found in employment law. Nevertheless, federal drug testing standards strongly shape and influence private employer practices. Many employer programs meet these high standards.

Technical standards for federally mandated testing were initially developed under the auspices of the U.S. Department of Health and Human Services *(2)*. These standards were formulated in 1988 and published under the title *Mandatory Guidelines for Federal Workplace Drug Testing Programs (3)*. These standards have withstood a number of constitutional challenges and have served as a template for many state Drug-Free Workplace statutes and voluntary employer drug testing programs.

3.1. Drug Testing Advisory Board (DTAB)

A number of years ago, Substance Abuse and Mental Health Services Administration (SAMHSA)'s Office of Workplace Drug Testing Programs created the Drug Testing Advisory Board (DTAB). DTAB is comprised of a diverse group of technical experts who serve as a technical advisory committee for the federal drug testing program. Since 1998, DTAB has been examining alternative specimens and technologies. A separate subgroup has concentrated on the technical validity and standards issues presented by on-site testing.

Opening remarks at a special DTAB industry conference on on-site testing in October 1999 summarized the basic requirements for governmentally mandated on-site testing by reaffirming the recommendations from a 1989 NIDA Consensus Conference *(4)*.

On-site urine screening can reliably identify negative specimens, provided appropriate safeguards are built in to the procedure. These precautions include meeting the basic forensic standards for specimen collection, chain of custody, documentation and security, splitting the collected urine specimen into two portions, participation in open and blind proficiency testing, a rigorous quality assurance program, being subject to on-site inspections, using an FDA-approved screening test that provides objective and documentable results, use of the same cutoff concentrations as used in NIDA (now DHHS, SAMHSA) certified laboratories, and submitting all presumptive positive specimens to a [DHHS] certified laboratory for confirmation.

This is more than an abstract statement about quality or a collection of wishes. It reflects the fact that for any drug testing method to be incorporated into the federally mandated drug testing programs, it must at a minimum meet the constitutionally mandated requirements. This simple legal conclusion does not seem to be appreciated outside of the regulatory and technical community. It is, however, well appreciated by federal agencies and seen as a significant challenge to all new methods.

Unfortunately, merely noting that federally mandated testing must meet constitutional requirements is an oversimplification of the task at hand and sidesteps the more difficult questions of refining abstract essential constitutional elements into specific technical parameters. To its credit, DTAB has taken a disciplined and useful approach to resolving this problem.

With the knowledge that the existing laboratory-based urine drug testing program passes constitutional muster, DTAB has developed a framework for evaluating alternative methods by deconstructing the existing laboratory-based federal drug testing program into a grid of essential elements. Each prospective drug testing method (on-site testing, sweat testing, hair testing and oral fluid testing) has been assessed in terms of how it could fulfill these requirements, currently, or theoretically. The grid has served as a useful tool for all parties in standardizing definitions, focusing discussion, achieving many points of consensus, and particularly facilitating comparisons across the different classes of specimen technology. On-site testing has been redefined to include both urine and oral fluid.

The operating premise is that a federally required laboratory technical standard must be consistently met, regardless of whether the specimen is tested in a laboratory or on-site. This standard must also be consistent across various specimen types. For example, the screening test performs the same function whether conducted in the laboratory or on-site; therefore it must be subject to the same cutoff performance criteria, quality control, and test certification. The current debate revolves around whether on-site testing must include 10% QC and the same level of accuracy and precision discrimination around the cutoff required of the laboratory screening, or whether alternative protocols can assure the same level of performance.

Another example of the attempt to achieve technical parity between existing laboratory-based screening and on-site screening is the current laboratory requirement of "certification" for negative screening test results. How can this procedure be applied to on-site testing? Can a combination of certified analyses using approved devices and procedures suffice *(5)*?

There are ten major categories in the DTAB grid. The following summarizes the key factors and current thinking in each category with regard to urine and oral fluid on-site testing.

3.1.1. Collection Site

The collection site must provide security and privacy, as well as the ability to do an observed collection. These may be more relevant as the collection site becomes the testing site. The routine collection of oral fluid, by its very nature, will take on the appearance of an observed process.

3.1.2. Collector/Tester

In on-site testing the collector now has the additional responsibility of being the "tester"; hence a defined training and certification process will most likely be required. Such on-site tester certification would require a minimum level of education (e.g., a high school diploma), completion of a structured course, and practical, hands-on experience with the device. A proficiency test and a written test would also be part of the process.

3.1.3. Collection Device/Test Device

These may be separate or combined. If separate, protocols used today will continue, but if combined, the device must meet the criteria discussed in Subheading 3.1.6.

3.1.4. Specimen

The specimen itself, in the case of urine, is no different from the basic laboratory specimen. In the case of oral fluid, important issues include the site and nature of the specimen's collection, whether accurate volume can be collected to permit multiple and repeat testing, whether a specimen can be effectively split, and what kind of device would be needed for a split specimen. This is an area that is probably a more global concern. Exactly how is the specimen going to be split and made available for future testing? In addition, there are questions of stability and storage, both prior to and during the testing process.

The collection procedure itself includes the traditional elements of ensuring donor identification and preparation of the donor for the specimen collection. Paramount here will be the issue of the donor's identity and the donor's knowledge of how the actual testing process works. Another element of the procedure is the chain of custody—the appropriate development of documentation, the custody form, and the major issue of specimen integrity evaluation.

3.1.5. Collection Procedure

The collection procedure for urine will follow the standard procedure currently used if a standard collection device is used or an approved procedure if a combined device is used.

3.1.6. On-Site Testing

The introduction of on-site testing in the federal programs encompasses two types of issues: technical-scientific issues and administrative-policy issues.

FDA clearance is recommended. FDA clearance provides preliminary evaluation that a product is at least comparable to other products in limited studies. The limitation of clearance is that, once cleared, products are not evaluated further unless new claims are made.

Chain of custody must be maintained throughout the collection, testing, transfer and storage of specimens. The drug test report must be such that details of the analytical result are documented in a manner that is recoverable.

Specific analytes must be identified and each analyte that is reported must be defined by a predetermined cutoff. The specificity of the analyte for urine must be the same as for laboratory-based testing. For other specimen types, target analytes must be defined and specific cutoffs must be reported.

Calibration and quality control must follow a defined process; i.e., controls must be in the substances tested and must effectively test analytes at the cutoff (± 25% of cutoff discriminator) *(6)*. Additionally, routine testing for adulteration must be included.

Administratively, it will be necessary to decide if confrontation of the donor with the test result is acceptable *(7)*.

3.1.7. Laboratory Testing

On-site testing encompasses the laboratory moving the screening to an on-site location, but confirmation testing must be accomplished utilizing more sophisticated technology in a laboratory. GC/MS or other equivalent technology must be used.

3.1.8. Quality Control/Quality Assurance (QC/QA)

Quality processes are essential to all testing. External proficiency specimen evaluation must be integrated with all batches of specimens.

3.1.9. Reporting

On-site testing will result in final reports for most negative specimens; hence, a procedure to provide certified results and maintain clear, recoverable records at the testing site will be required *(8)*.

3.1.10. Medical Review Officer (MRO)

On-site urine testing may require additional duties for the medical review officer (MRO), such as oversight of collector/tester performance, but it will not alter the MRO's tasks in regard to verification. Verification of on-site oral fluids will strongly resemble the verification of urine in that there is a reasonable correlation of positive tests obtained between current oral fluid and urine methods.

3.2. The DTAB End Game

Although it may not reflect it, the current state of the grid incorporates a great deal of discussion, involving nuances over terminology such as "what is a specimen?" But the more difficult debate is yet to be heard, and that is whether all of the existing safeguards and elements are indeed essential. A strong argument can be made that there was a degree of over-engineering built in to the initial standards and that, over a ten-year lapse of time, technical advances have made some of the stated safeguards obsolete.

There is little doubt that requiring a negative reviewing scientist at an on-site testing site will be problematic. Is there a true need for such an element, and consequently if there is not, is there a need for one in a certified laboratory? The final arbiter of these issues in the United States will be DHHS and ultimately the courts.

4. The Legal Requirements for Confirmatory Testing in Private Sector On-Site Testing

It should go without saying that existing confirmatory testing requirements will continue to be required in the event that on-site technology becomes incorporated into federally mandated drug testing programs. Confirmatory testing is one of the essential constitutional requirements of federally mandated testing. In workplace drug testing, confirmatory testing has become synonymous with GC/MS technology. But in a broader sense, confirmatory tests can be conducted with LC/MS or MS/MS or comparable instrumentation. The essential element of confirmatory testing is the independent definitive nature of the analysis. It is the true technical foundation upon which sound decisions affecting employment can be made.

Although all manufacturers and distributors of on-site products are in the chorus singing the praises and necessity of GC/MS confirmation and MRO review, it is not a foregone conclusion that either of these safeguards will be automatically included in private sector workplace drug testing programs. Most employers do not have a legal duty or mandate to require confirmation testing, and the economics and apparent simplicity of screen-only results are seductive.

The employment-at-will doctrine is a pillar of labor and employment law in the United States. The doctrine essentially states that either party to an employment relationship, the employer or the employee, can terminate the relationship for any reason, or for no reason *(9)*. Thus, it is argued that an employer may terminate an employee based on a screen-only result, but it is an ill-advised practice. First, it is highly unlikely that a screen-only result will be persuasive in any employment proceeding, whether it is an unemployment security hearing, labor arbitration, or a workers' compensation hearing. Further, the employer's publication of a screen-only result to another employer may raise the issue of defamation. This is because for all practical purposes, 99% accuracy is simply not good enough. All the screen-positives claim to be that 1%, and the law allows them to make that claim.

Although the law of evidence establishes evidentiary requirements of the establishment of legal facts, such as beyond a reasonable doubt, clear and convincing evidence, and preponderance of the evidence, it is conceivable that an employer will not prevail in adversarial proceedings when the only evidence produced is a single screening result. The *de facto* and in many cases the *de jure* standard of drug testing is not beyond a reasonable doubt, but beyond all doubt—and this is why confirmatory testing is essential.

Fortunately, most employers seem to exhibit enough instinct for fairness and/or self-preservation to require a confirmatory test as a condition of taking adverse employment action against incumbent employees. The more amorphous issue is what standards are appropriate for testing applicants, where the legal considerations may be insufficient to establish a self-imposed standard of confirmatory testing.

A collateral rule to the employment-at-will doctrine is that an employer is free to hire or not to hire applicants based on the employer's assessments as long as the hiring criteria and decisions are not discriminatory in nature. Thus for many employers the use of a screening device for applicants that produces false positives does not appear to present any significant legal repercussions *(10)*. There is, essentially, no "right" to any job.

Applicant screening is the target market for many on-site testing devices. It is a very large market, and many employers do not perceive a need for confirmatory testing or for medical review officers. In the absence of any state prohibition against screen-only testing of applicants, the argument can be made that the employer who does screen-only testing will run afoul of the Americans with Disabilities Act of 1990 (ADA) (*11*). An applicant who has been denied a job without confirmation testing may bring an action claiming to have been discriminated against because the employer thought the applicant was an illegal drug user and had a disability, yet the applicant does not use illegal drugs and does not have a disability. Although this argument may technically be true, it is not a strong discouragement of screen-only practices.

The broader danger of widespread screen-only practices will be the undermining of the public's acceptance of drug testing. The unwritten social pact is that drug testing is accurate and reliable, and that there will be no adverse impact on an individual who is not currently engaging in illegal drug use.

From time to time a call is received at the office of the American Association of Medical Review Officers (AAMRO) from a family member of an applicant who was denied employment because of a "false positive screening test." Their stories of hardship, broken families, and anger are statistically unlikely to have been caused by a false positive. More likely it was caused by a true positive.

The need to premise adverse action on confirmatory results is ultimately an ethical issue as opposed to a legal or business issue. If the manufacturers, promoters and users of on-site testing have a difficult time understanding the ethical aspects of the manner by which they champion the elimination of illegal drugs from the workplace, then they undermine the very foundation of drug testing.

5. The Legal Requirements for a Medical Review Officer in Private Sector On-Site Testing

The MRO performs a number of critical functions in a comprehensive drug testing program. There is the interpretation of results, the determination of alternative medical explanations, the assessment of shy bladder, the management of split specimens, and the management of specimen integrity (adulteration testing). These functions are often referred to as the MRO verification of results.

The MRO fulfills the legal and policy requirements that cannot be fulfilled by technology. The MRO provides a degree of technical oversight of the process and is the appropriate interface between the employer and the donor. In addition, many MROs provide collection services, make recommendations to clients, and provide expert testimony.

The MRO role is an essential element of federal programs, but it is not universal in workplace drug testing programs—even though sound legal arguments, risk management, and technical management plus court cases support the need for MRO verification of results. The legal argument is based on the employer's compliance with the Americans with Disabilities Act and in some cases, with state medical confidentiality and privacy laws.

The ADA has been characterized as the most significant federal employment legislation of the decade. Although the ADA does not afford disability protection for a current illegal drug user, and excludes a drug test from the restrictions imposed on employment-related medical examinations, the ADA does impose one fundamental standard on all workplace drug testing practices for covered employers *(12)*. That standard is the use of a competent MRO. The term "medical review officer" is not used in the act, but it is not possible to perform a drug test in compliance with the ADA without using an MRO.

One of the predictions made following the passage of the ADA was that the widespread practice of employers requiring applicants and employees to disclose all of the prescription drugs that they were taking would be eliminated. This practice was a way for employers to deal with what they thought was prescription drug abuse and opiates in the days before MRO practice was developed. The practice without the ADA is ineffective and invasive, and although much less widespread, is still prevalent. All too often employers are simply unaware of the legal issues or are ill advised. The first court decision that illustrates the legal issue for employers and their counsel was the case of *Roe vs Cheyenne Mountain Resort (13)*. In this case, an employer's mandatory requirement that applicants disclose all drugs that they were currently taking, or had recently taken, was found to be a violation of the ADA.

6. New Liability Risks of Drug Testing Providers and On-Site Drug Testing—Another Factor in Establishing Standards

Much attention is given to the legal aspects of workplace drug testing in respect to the employer's interests and how the employer's risk/benefit assessment will determine what technical and programmatic quality assurance procedures will be required for on-site drug testing. As noted above, when it comes to liability, an employer who is protected by the employment-at-will doctrine has little civil liability exposure. The applicant/employee simply does not have a cause of action against the employer for a defective, inaccurate or negligently performed drug test.

In the past there has not been much attention given to the liability of drug testing providers who market, sell, provide, and perform on-site testing. Historically, the legal doctrines of contractual privity and limited duty to third parties had been used to insulate the laboratories, and to a great degree MROs, collectors, and third-party administrators, from liability. It is a common misconception that if a laboratory makes a mistake, such as reporting a false positive, the employee or donor can sue the laboratory for negligence. Strictly speaking, donors have not been able to sustain negligence actions against laboratories or drug testing providers.

Although a service provider such as a laboratory has a contractual obligation to the employer (written, verbal or implied), the law had not recognized a "legal duty of care" to the third-party donor of the specimen (the applicant or employee). As a result, the employee or applicant could bring a lawsuit against the employer, but had no direct avenue to the provider (laboratory).

Thus, with employment-at-will protecting the employer, and no legal duty attaching to the provider in the event of a negligently performed drug test that results in termination or other economic damage, the donor might not have any legal recourse. Naturally, with drug testing an almost universal employment practice, this insulation was not going to last forever. The law adapts, and it is in that process.

Over the past five years there has been a case-by-case, jurisdiction-by-jurisdiction expansion of what is essentially the scope of legal liability to cover various drug test providers. In the first significant case, *Stinson vs Physicians Immediate Care, Limited*, Stinson alleged that the laboratory had been negligent in performing a drug test on him and had reported a false positive result for cocaine *(14)*.

Stinson alleged that the test result was false or, in the alternative, the report of the test result was false. As is characteristic in this type of case, he alleged that the defendant (Physicians Immediate Care) was negligent by committing one or more of the following acts:

1. Failed to instruct its employees of the danger of specimen contamination
2. Failed to use specimen containers with sealable and tamper evident lids
3. Failed to seal the specimen containers
4. Failed to obtain the plaintiff's initials or otherwise identify the specimen as belonging to the plaintiff
5. Conducted the drug screening test so that the results were not accurate and were in error
6. Erroneously tested and reported that the plaintiff had cocaine in his body

7. Failed to use routinely followed precautionary procedures, including the use of sterile specimen containers, the use of tamper evident seals, the use of identifying marks on specimen containers, and otherwise conducted the drug screening test so that the results erroneously diagnosed cocaine in the plaintiff's body.

The trial court dismissed Stinson's case on the grounds that a laboratory does not have any legal duty to the donor of the specimen. The Appellate court in Illinois, however, reversed this decision and held that a drug testing laboratory owes a duty of reasonable care to persons whose specimens it tests for employers or prospective employers. The court noted that it is reasonably foreseeable that the tested person will be harmed if the laboratory negligently reports the test results to the employer, that the laboratory is in the best position to guard against injury, and that the laboratory is better able to bear the burden financially than an individual who is wrongly maligned by a false positive report.

Thus a terminated employee, and presumably a frustrated applicant, has a basis to state a claim against a drug testing laboratory by alleging that it performed a drug screening test on the employee's urine specimen, that the laboratory had duty to the employee to act with reasonable care in collecting, handling, and testing the specimen, that the laboratory falsely reported to the employee's employer that the result was positive, that the false report was the result of any of several allegedly negligent acts, and that the employee lost his job and suffered other damages as a result of the laboratory's negligence.

This expansion of legal duty is not limited to the laboratory. In November 1999, the Wyoming Supreme Court cited the Stinson case when it held not only that a collector (and a collection company) owes a duty of care to the donor but that it also has a duty of care as a consultant, where the collection company recommended a urine alcohol test (*Duncan vs Afton, Inc.*) *(15)*.

Duncan vs Afton, Inc. is a recent example of a court finding that a drug test provider (in this case, a collection company) owes a duty of care when collecting, handling, and processing urine specimens for the purpose of performing substance abuse testing. This duty is not only to the employer, but to employees and applicants as well.

Duncan was an employee of Solvay Minerals. Solvay contracted with Afton to collect urine specimens of Solvay's employees from time to time for drug and alcohol testing. Solvay separately contracted with a laboratory to analyze the specimens and report the results to Solvay. On December 15, 1997, Solvay ordered Duncan to submit a urine specimen for drug and alcohol testing. Duncan was randomly selected for the test in accordance with Solvay's substance abuse policy. Leigh Ann Shears, an employee of Afton, supervised the collection of a urine specimen from Duncan at Solvay's place of business. Duncan's specimen was subsequently reported as positive for alcohol.

Based on the report, Solvay terminated Duncan's employment on December 23, 1997. He filed suit in June 1998, naming Afton and Shears as defendants, claiming that Afton negligently instructed and trained Shears, failed to employ proper collection and handling procedures for urinalysis of alcohol content, failed to inform Solvay that urinalysis is unreliable if specific procedures are not followed, and misrepresented to Solvay the accuracy and reliability of urine alcohol testing.

Afton and Shears answered the complaint and filed a motion to dismiss, contending that they did not owe a duty of reasonable care in the collection of the urine specimen, and filed for a protective order to stay discovery, pending the ruling on dismissal, which order was granted on October 1, 1998. That order prevented investigation of all other stages of the testing process to determine if other defendants should be named. The suit was dismissed before discovery, thus precluding Duncan from amending the complaint to name the employer and the laboratory performing the test as defendants.

The district court ruled that the relationship did not extend to create a duty of care to be imposed on Afton and its employee. Holding that a duty of care was not created by contract, statute, or common law, the district court entered an order dismissing the action, and this appeal to Wyoming's Supreme Court followed.

The Wyoming Supreme Court concluded that a legal duty of care must be imposed. The court stated:

In assessing the moral blame factor, several considerations make it appropriate to impose a duty of reasonable care upon a collection company: its direct financial benefit in providing alcohol testing services to Duncan's employer; its direct control over establishing and ensuring proper collection and handling procedures; its ability to hire and train competent personnel to perform services; and its ability to contract with the employer to ensure test results are properly interpreted and utilized.

Perhaps the most important factor in this analysis is whether the policy of preventing future harm is at issue. Afton does not present an argument on this particular factor. Companies like Afton provide services that present a risk of harm great enough to hold them accountable. The particular services provided demand adequate protection of employees' interests to prevent future harm, and the imposition of a duty to act reasonably will reduce the likelihood of injury. There is little question that our ruling that Afton owes a duty places a burden upon Afton to act in a "scientifically reasonable manner" and guard against human error; however, Afton is in the best position to guard against employee injury arising from its collection and handling procedures. (Elliot, 588 So.2d at 176.) Because Afton is paid for its services, it is better able to bear the burden financially than the individual wrongly maligned by a false positive report. (Stinson, 207 Ill.Dec. 96, 646 N.E.2d at 934.)

The types of allegations made in both the Stinson and Afton cases are the same as might arise with on-site testing. Thus, a provider of these services carries additional litigation risk, and the risk is not merely limited to the few states that have litigated this issue. These two cases and a line of other cases provide strong precedence for future courts, which will have to deal with the same issue.

The objective of the Mandatory Guidelines and the National Laboratory Certification Program was to assure technical validity and legal supportability of results. This objective has been achieved so well that successful actions against laboratories that adhere to the Mandatory Guidelines are almost nonexistent.

The change in the risk exposure for providers of on-site drug testing, which is implicit in these cases, should strongly encourage providers to confirm results in a laboratory that follows the Mandatory Guidelines in terms of quality control and quality assurance, and to incorporate MRO review in these processes.

7. Conclusion

Drug testing is essentially a professional service that requires expertise in a number of areas. Most consumers of drug testing services cannot adequately evaluate the legal, technical and interpretative aspects of the product. It is said in business that when you purchase a service you often do not know what you have purchased until it is not delivered. In drug testing, it is during a compliance inspection, arbitration, hearing, or civil litigation where the product is or is not found to be sufficient.

The overall goal of the federal technical requirements is to achieve a level of zero-defect management in regards to the reporting of a positive result, while minimizing the inherent incidence rate of false negatives. The concept of zero-defect testing is not, however, synonymous with the concept of "legally defensible." Additional technical, administrative, and ministerial elements are often needed to fulfill the judicial needs. Meeting the federal requirements has been the soundest assurance that the legal requirements have been met. This is why the majority of workplace drug testing programs mimic the federal program, despite its apparent limitations.

It is worth noting that there was much resistance to GC/MS as a requirement in the initial Mandatory Guidelines. The concern was that GC/MS confirmation testing would be prohibitively expensive as compared with existing clinical methods. Today, workplace drug testing conducted in accordance with the guidelines is performed with extraordinary safeguards and quality and is less expensive than anyone would have anticipated. Quality is not an expense; it is a disciplined efficiency strategy.

Most important is the fact that drug testing has been built on a foundation of public trust and confidence. The public trust is not that every drug user will be deterred or identified, but that the drug testing process is effective and will not falsely accuse a worker or applicant of illicit drug use or substance abuse.

The only open question is whether appropriate on-site standards will be adopted voluntarily or legislatively. For, despite the public's support for eliminating drugs from the workplace, there is little public appetite for "collateral" damage caused by false-positive screening results by this or any other drug testing methodology.

Notes

1. To a lesser degree, regional differences within the United States (as reflected in state laws and judicial decisions) create a mosaic of policy and technical standards as well.
2. At the time, the division that led this project was NIDA (National Institute on Drug Abuse), and "NIDA Guidelines" and "NIDA 5" became common usage. After a governmental reorganization, a new entity was created called the Substance Abuse and Mental Health Services Administration (SAMHSA).
3. *Mandatory Guidelines for Federal Workplace Drug Testing Programs* June 9, 1994 [59 FR 29908]. The Mandatory Guidelines were first published on April 11, 1988 [53 FR 11970].
4. *Technical, Scientific and Procedural Issues of Employee Drug Testing*, Consensus Report, National Institute on Drug Abuse, Department of Health and Human Services, Public Health Service, Alcohol, Drug Abuse and Mental Health Administration, 1990, Editors Bryan S. Finkle, Robert V. Blanke and J. Michael Walsh.
5. Laboratory screening is performed on a batch basis, and essentially, the negative certification is the review of the batch QC. On-site testing is not done on a batch basis, thus it is a fundamentally different process, with no "batch" QC to review. In addition, laboratory quality control software can review, assess, and approve screening batches as efficiently or more efficiently than a certifying scientist. This raises the question of whether the certifying scientist is superfluous even in the laboratory.
6. A general consensus of manufacturers and technical experts is that the current technology may not achieve this level of performance. (It appears that most devices achieve a performance of ± 50%.) This does not disqualify the methods, but it necessitates the creation of a different technical model for on-site performance that meets the goal or the justification of this standard.
7. The language of DTAB's working document does not recommend confrontation between the donor and the collector/tester in the on-site screening process.

8. Data management is not a formal element of the grid, but it is a critical practical consideration of on-site testing.
9. The exception to this general rule is that employers are prohibited from terminating employees for reasons such as race, age, sex and disability discrimination, whistle-blowing and refusing to participate in illegal activity.
10. Some state laws may prohibit this practice.
11. The ADA was signed into law on July 26, 1990.
12. The provisions went into effect for employers with more than 25 employees in July 1992.
13. Roe v. Cheyenne Mountain Conference Resort, Inc., 124 F.3d 1221 (10th Cir. 1997).
14. Stinson v. Physicians Immediate Care, Ltd., 269 Ill. App.3d 659, 207 Ill. Dec. 96, 646 N.E.2d 930, 932–934 (1995).
15. Harvey J. Duncan, a/k/a Jim Duncan, Appellant (Plaintiff) v. Afton, Inc., a Tennessee corporation, d/b/a Healthcomp Evaluation Services Corporation, d/b/a National Ameritest, a/k/a Ameritest; and Leigh Ann Shears, an individual, Appellees (Defendants). No. 99–24. Supreme Court of Wyoming. Nov. 30, 1999. (Cite as: 1999 WL 1073434 (Wyo.))

Chapter 5

On-Site Testing Devices in the Criminal Justice System

Leo J. Kadehjian and James Baer

1. Drug Testing in the Criminal Justice Arena

1.1. Introduction

The prevalence of drug use by those under supervision in the criminal justice system is alarmingly high. Current (1998) data from the U. S. Alcohol and Drug Abuse Monitoring program (ADAM, replacing the Drug Use Forecasting (DUF) program) in surveying arrestees in 35 cities across the U.S. indicated that more than half of all individuals brought into criminal justice systems have substance abuse problems. In 15 of the cities, 2/3 of adult arrestees tested positive for at least one drug, while 1/2 of male juveniles tested positive *(1)*. Urine drug testing has been recognized as an objective and effective tool to identify substance abusers within the criminal justice system *(2–40)*. Accordingly there has been a great demand for effective urine drug testing programs within the criminal justice arena. These urine drug testing programs include pre-initial appearance drug testing of arrestees, testing as a condition of pretrial release *(11–31)*, pre-sentence testing, testing while on probation (supervised release) or parole *(32–35)*, testing within jails and prisons *(36–40)*, as well as on-site testing in a variety of specialized drug courts, community corrections programs, and court-mandated treatment programs.

From: *Forensic Science: On-Site Drug Testing*
Edited by: A. J. Jenkins and B. A. Goldberger © Humana Press, Inc., Totowa, NJ

1.2. On-Site Testing

These programs historically utilized commercial laboratories, often with frustrating delays between specimen collection, testing, reporting of the result, and ultimate response to the substance user. With the availability of simple, robust and accurate automated benchtop immunoassay analyzers, many testing programs began to implement their own on-site testing facilities. The first court-based testing laboratory was established in 1971 in the Superior Court of the District of Columbia. In 1982, the Federal Probation office in Seattle, Washington, established a pilot program of on-site testing using instrument-based immunoassay. In 1984, the National Institute of Justice funded an on-site drug testing program for Washington D.C. Pretrial adult arrestees. Since that time a wide variety of on-site testing programs have been implemented. These programs have recognized the value of rapid drug test results with the benefit of immediate responses to and graduated sanctions for ongoing drug use and rewards for drug abstinence. For many of these criminal justice applications, on-site benchtop automated immunoassay analyzers have been successfully used for several years. For example, within the U.S. federal courts, pretrial drug testing using benchtop analyzers is now in place in over 30 federal locations, and instrument-based on-site drug testing of federal probationers is conducted in at least 9 locations, some using sophisticated high-volume analyzers as used in commercial laboratories. These federal on-site testing programs were initiated as a pilot program in 8 federal districts between 1989–1991 as authorized under the 1988 Anti-Drug Abuse Act, Pub. L. 100–692 § 7304, and have expanded dramatically. These on-site testing programs with automated immunoassay analyzers generally employ manufacturer-trained officers as operators, are subjected to rigorous on-site inspections, and participate in quarterly blind proficiency testing, demonstrating excellent performance. Test results from these on-site testing programs have been repeatedly upheld in numerous challenges. A 1991 National Institute of Justice study of drug testing technologies recognized that on-site automated immunoassay analyzers demonstrated performance equal to commercial laboratory-based testing *(2)*.

Although on-site benchtop automated analyzers offer the benefits of rapid turnaround time, objective hard copy results, reduced per test costs based on volume, and a proven track record of performance and admissibility in a variety of legal and administrative proceedings, not all criminal justice testing programs have a sufficient volume of specimens to justify an on-site automated analyzer. Although such instrumented on-site testing offers more rapid turnaround times than specimen shipment to commercial laboratories, they still may not be able to offer the benefits of immediate results obtained in the presence of the donor.

Table 1
Comparison Between Instrument and Noninstrument Drug Test Devices

Automated benchtop analyzer	Noninstrument devices
Objective read	Subjective read
Suitable for high volume	Suitable for low volume
Rapid turnaround time	Immediate turnaround time
Lower cost/test ($1/drug)	Higher cost/test ($1–3/drug)
Daily calibration/controls	No calibration/use internal control(s)
Established QC practices	Undefined QC requirements
Established proficiency testing programs	Proficiency testing programs available
Hard copy print-out	No hard copy print-out
Established case law	Little case law
Repeat testing often meets due process	Due process requirements uncertain

Furthermore there may be remote field testing situations for which a simple hand-held noninstrumented device would be more appropriate.

1.3. Use of Noninstrument Drug Testing Devices

With the increased availability and technological improvements in noninstrument urine drug testing devices, with promise of simple, immediate, and accurate drug test results, there has been widespread interest in their use from a variety of criminal justice drug testing programs. These noninstrument devices are available in a variety of test formats, from simple dipsticks which are briefly inserted into a specimen and then allowed to develop over a few minutes, to cassettes where a few drops of the specimen are added with a plastic pipet or calibrated syringe. Even specimen collection cups with the test strips incorporated directly into their walls, which obviate any handling or pipetting of the specimen, have been developed. Furthermore many of the noninstrument test devices are available in single- or multi-drug assay formats. For all of these devices the test results are available after 3 to 15 min. These devices utilize antibodies against the drug and/or metabolites in question, and so are solid-phase immunoassays, similar to the automated instrument homogeneous immunoassay technologies.

Some of the key comparative issues between on-site automated analyzers and noninstrument drug testing devices within a criminal justice setting are shown in Table 1. Although there have been published scientific studies addressing the performance parameters of these devices, unfortunately there has been little published on the use and performance of these noninstrument devices in the context of the criminal justice system.

In 1995, President Clinton issued an executive directive that all federal arrestees be subjected to drug testing, directing Attorney General Reno to develop a policy by March the next year. As part of this policy initiative the Administrative Office of the U.S. Courts in conjunction with the Department of Justice instituted a two-year program called Operation Drug TEST (Testing, Effective Sanctions, and Treatment). In this program, the utility of both noninstrument and instrument immunoassay-based urine drug testing technologies is being evaluated in 53 federal sites across 24 urban, suburban, and rural districts over 2 years. The program includes both pre-initial appearance testing as well as testing of all defendants released pending trial. In 1998 the program involved the testing of over 10,000 defendants. This program has recently been extended for another year.

After the issuance of President Clinton's Executive Order in 1995, the Administrative Office of the U.S. Courts commissioned a study of the noninstrument drug testing devices currently marketed. This comprehensive and challenging study was carried out in 1996 by Duo Research, whose results are presented elsewhere in this volume. That study of 15 noninstrument devices found that many of these devices performed well, especially considering a challenging specimen set weighted around the immunoassay cut-off concentrations. The accuracy of these devices was (against the gold standard of GC/MS confirmation) comparable to a commonly used benchtop automated analyzer. The noninstrument devices demonstrated an overall accuracy of 71% (52–79%) vs the automated analyzer's average of 80% (78–82%). A second similar study was commissioned in 1998 by the Substance Abuse and Mental Health Services Administration (SAMHSA) with similar results, with the 15 devices demonstrating an overall accuracy of 70% (61–78%) vs automated analyzer 76% (the data from the SAMHSA-sponsored study can also be found elsewhere in this text and also on the Internet at: www.health.org/workplace/summary.htm). These devices are expected to demonstrate even higher accuracies with specimen populations actually encountered in routine criminal justice settings.

Although most of these noninstrument devices offer convenience and ease of use, they do have the limitations of a subjective read (requiring a visual determination of the presence or absence of a colored line). However, rigorous and challenging scientific studies, although relatively limited in number, have demonstrated that the limitations of subjective reading is not a significant issue. Furthermore, there are newer on-site testing devices being developed that utilize a small electronic reader to provide an objective reading of the result. Such readers are being developed not only for urine test devices, but for saliva testing as well. In fact a study has been initiated by U. S. Probation in the Central District of California to examine on-site saliva collection and saliva drug testing devices. Note that saliva has been recognized as a suitable specimen for alcohol testing and is allowed under the Department of Transportation's nonevidential on-site alcohol testing procedures.

Although the noninstrument devices generally have greater unit costs per test than instrument based assays, these unit test costs are highly test volume dependent. In addition, there are several other factors to consider with an instrument-based test system such as costs associated with the purchase or rental of the instrument (with these costs often included in the cost of the tests), costs associated with hiring of technical staff (although current on-site urine drug testing instrumentation is robust such that nontechnical staff can perform accurate and reliable testing, as has been demonstrated within the Federal Courts' on-site testing programs), costs of appropriate laboratory space and facilities, and instrument calibration costs.

Another issue faced in drug testing programs is adulteration/dilution of specimens. Automated analyzers can offer objective indications of inappropriate, altered, or diluted specimens. Noninstrument devices may also offer indications of inappropriate specimens or failure of the test to perform properly through the use of built-in control checks. Most of these devices have a single control line or window to indicate proper test performance. In addition there are noninstrument adulteration check dipstick devices available which can measure pH, creatinine, specific gravity, nitrites, and even an adulterant called UrinAid (glutaraldehyde). Hand-held refractometers have also found utility in the on-site determination of specific gravity as a marker of dilution.

There are some additional issues to consider when an officer is asked to perform drug testing in the presence of a defendant or offender. Officers may be resistant to taking on testing responsibilities as they may feel it is not part of their job function. The officers may also fear increased risk of exposure to infectious disease in handling urine specimens (although the 1991 OSHA Bloodborne Pathogen Regulations, 56 FR 64004, have recognized the extremely low risk from casual exposure to urine specimens). There is also the potential for harm when confronting a violent offender with a positive drug test result. It may be easier for the officer to deal with a confirmed positive report from a formal laboratory than with a presumptive positive test result from a noninstrument device. Despite these concerns, there are clear benefits in the use of these noninstrument drug test devices in front of the offender. Many offenders when told of the accuracy of the device will admit to drug use even as the test is administered. Furthermore when faced with a positive test result many will admit to drug use. In contrast, it is rare for an offender to admit to drug use when the specimen is collected for shipment to an off-site laboratory. Also, when on-site test results are negative, the officer can provide immediate positive reinforcement for maintaining abstinence. When on-site test results are positive, the officer can confront the issue directly and immediately, rather than later dealing with "prior" drug use.

One final issue is the availability of these devices to the defendants/offenders. Those subjected to a court-ordered drug testing condition could use these devices themselves to determine when they are safely negative for reporting for a drug test. A few of these devices are now available over-the-counter, and are approved for home use by the FDA. Some of these drug testing devices are being marketed through the Internet.

Thus, several of these noninstrument urine drug testing devices have shown themselves to be easy to use, giving virtually immediate results, with demonstrated accuracy in challenging scientific studies, and offering real benefits to criminal justice testing programs. What remains to be established is how the courts will view the use of these devices in fulfilling legal requirements for admissibility of scientific evidence and due process in various administrative, disciplinary and criminal contexts. Such judicial scrutiny and decisions will dictate policy in the practical use of these noninstrument drug testing devices.

2. Legal Admissibility, Evidentiary Weight, and Due Process

One of the issues involved in the use of noninstrument drug testing devices is their legal admissibility in various administrative and criminal contexts and, if determined to be admissible, what weight such evidence is given by the trier of fact. There is ample case law precedent for the admissibility in many criminal justice contexts of instrument immunoassay urine drug testing, both when performed in a laboratory as well as when performed on-site. Most of these cases uphold the use of repeat immunoassay testing as meeting the due process requirements for use in prison disciplinary hearings and even in probation revocations, without additional confirmation testing.

The Federal Bureau of Prisons has a statutory requirement that for those serving their sentence in a contract community treatment center, all positive-test results be validated to substantiate the positive result (28 CFR §550.42[c]). The current federal probation regulations also require that if a probationer is to be returned to prison based on a drug test, it must be confirmed by GC/MS at a SAMHSA certified laboratory. Otherwise corrections-based urine drug testing programs are generally not otherwise regulated. However in order to withstand legal scrutiny, such on-site testing programs should comport with standards of good laboratory practice, including quality control practices and participation in proficiency testing. The on-site testing programs of the U.S. Federal Courts utilizing automated analyzers have been following such practices for many years, including on-site inspections and participation in external proficiency testing. Quality control practices, external proficiency testing, and appropriate inspection criteria are now being developed for such programs utilizing noninstrument drug testing devices.

Whether these noninstrument devices can enjoy the same level of judicial acceptance as their instrument counterparts is uncertain at this time. There has been little significant case law review of the accuracy and reliability of these devices and whether they can meet due process requirements in the various criminal justice contexts. But with their growing use we can expect to see this case law develop, thereby establishing some policy guidelines for their use.

2.1. Standards for Admissibility of Scientific Evidence

There are currently two broad standards applied to the admissibility of such scientific evidence. The older standard, known as the Frye test or rule, was established in a 1923 Washington, D.C. Federal Court of Appeals case (Frye vs U.S., 293 F. 1013 (D.C.Cir. 1923)) where the court held that novel scientific testimony (in this case a blood pressure test to determine truthfulness) must have the "consensus" of the relevant scientific community in order to be admissible. This case law standard was gradually adopted by most state and federal courts. The early challenges to instrument based immunoassay drug testing in the 1980's were decided (almost always favorably) using this standard. These early cases recognized the high levels of accuracy of instrument based immunoassay testing, with several cases citing research studies demonstrating accuracies on the order of 97–99%, even noting that these levels of accuracy surpass the "beyond a reasonable doubt" standard. However the Frye test was eliminated from all federal courts in 1993 as a result of the U.S. Supreme Court's decision in Daubert vs Merrell Dow Pharmaceuticals, Inc. (509 U.S. 579 (1993)).

In this landmark case, the Supreme Court's first addressing admissibility of scientific testimony, the court ruled that the Federal Rules of Evidence, established in 1975, superseded the case law Frye test established in 1923. The Federal Rules of Evidence say nothing about requiring a consensus within the relevant scientific community, but do require that the scientific testimony be relevant and reliable. In Daubert, the Supreme Court ruled that consensus within the relevant scientific community is certainly one of the criteria which could be examined to determine reliability, as well as false positive and false negative rates, peer review publications, and a few other factors. However consensus is no longer absolutely required in federal court. It is felt by many that the new Daubert standard represents a more lenient approach to the admissibility of scientific testimony. Note that state courts are not absolutely required to follow the Supreme Court's Daubert ruling. Although many state courts have taken the Supreme Court's lead, still about 1/3 of the states have decided to continue to use the supposedly more stringent Frye test.

2.2. Cases Addressing the Use of Noninstrument Drug Testing Devices

Whether these noninstrument drug tests fulfill the Daubert standards and/or the Frye standards has apparently not been decided by higher level state or federal courts. In fact there is little significant case law addressing the use of these devices and the admissibility of their results.

A 1993 federal case did address in part the use of a first generation noninstrument drug test device (OnTrak) in prison discipline (Ransom vs Davies, 816 F.Supp. 681 (D.Kan 1993)). However this case did not specifically address the scientific accuracy or admissibility of the noninstrument drug test per se, but rather focused on whether prison officers should be granted qualified immunity for using these devices alone, without any further testing. In this case, a single noninstrument OnTrak test was positive, and, without any further repeat or confirmation testing, the prison inmate was sanctioned for disciplinary violations. The court held that whether a single noninstrument OnTrak test constituted "some evidence" was not clearly established in 1990 and so granted the officers qualified immunity, since they could not be held responsible for knowing about the scientific acceptability of such tests. It should be noted that the prison thereafter changed its policy to require repeat testing.

In a 1994 unpublished federal appellate case, (Easton vs U.S. Corrections Corp., 45 F.3d 430 (6th Cir. 1994)) a first generation noninstrument device (OnTrak) gave a positive result which was confirmed by an established on-site instrument immunoassay (Emit-st). Prison discipline based on the confirmed result was upheld, but there was no discussion in the opinion as to the accuracy or reliability of the noninstrument test device.

2.3. Requirements for Repeat and/or Confirmation Testing

There are other earlier cases where even single (not repeated nor otherwise confirmed) on-site instrument immunoassay tests (Emit® method) have been held to be sufficiently reliable to comport with due process. *(41–45)*. There are certainly numerous corrections cases where repeated on-site instrument immunoassay tests (almost all using the Emit method) have been found to be sufficiently accurate to meet due process requirements. *(46–68)*

A question which requires resolution is whether noninstrument devices are accurate enough to be used alone or with repeat testing, but without further confirmation testing by an alternative technique, such as GC/MS. Alternatively, will an admission of use after confrontation with the positive results of a noninstrument device suffice to fulfill due process requirements? It has been argued that an admission of use is the best form of confirmation.

In order for noninstrument drug test results be used in these various corrections contexts, not only must the inherent performance of the devices be demonstrated, but also whether the devices are properly used. Issues such as operator training, proper chain of custody, specimen handling, device and ancillary storage conditions, and recordkeeping procedures must be documented. On-site inspection of these noninstrument testing programs as well as participation in external proficiency testing programs will also be important components in assessing the admissibility and weight such noninstrument drug testing evidence should receive. Within the federal courts pretrial and probation on-site testing programs, appropriate inspection checklists and proficiency testing programs are being developed and implemented for use of these noninstrument drug test devices.

It must be recognized that the due process requirements vary depending upon the corrections context, from a fairly low "some evidence" standard in prison disciplinary hearings, to a "beyond a reasonable doubt" standard in criminal cases. With these noninstrument drug test devices demonstrating accuracies on the order of 70%, even in studies with especially challenging around the cut-off specimens, it seems clear that these device results should meet even the preponderance of the evidence standard (>50%) and possibly even the clear and convincing evidence standard. However, it is unlikely that these devices alone would be held to meet the beyond a reasonable doubt standard (95% or higher). It is important to note that these devices would be expected to demonstrate accuracies well beyond the 70% observed with near-cut-off specimens, when testing specimens within the criminal justice context with a less-challenging concentration distribution. Furthermore when examining the performance of these devices against the criteria of drug presence or absence (rather than GC/MS confirmation cut-off criteria) these devices have positive predictive values of virtually 1. That is, a positive on-site noninstrument drug test result, at least for cocaine or cannabinoids, can be relied on to indicate the presence of drug in the specimen, even though there may be insufficient amounts to be confirmed positive when using standard confirmation cut-offs.

3. Conclusions

There is no question that several of the noninstrument drug testing devices are not only rapid and easy to use, but also are sufficiently accurate and reliable for use within a variety of criminal justice programs. Until case law recognizes these devices' levels of accuracy and reliability and how they comport with various due process requirements, these devices will likely need to be used with some form of confirmation testing.

The discussion of legal issues involving on-site drugs of abuse testing in criminal justice is intended for informational use only. Any legal information or opinions presented herein are not intended to be considered legal advice from the authors, nor to substitute for professional legal advice. Consult your own legal counsel for professional guidance.

References

1. Alcohol and Drug Abuse Monitoring (ADAM) Program Internet address: http://www.adam-nij.net/index.htm.
2. Visher, C. and Mc Fadden, K., (1991) A Comparison of Urinalysis Technologies for Drug Testing in Criminal Justice, National Institute of Justice.
3. Torres, S. (1996) The Use of a Credible Drug Testing Program for Accountability and Intervention. *Fed. Prob.* **60,** 18.
4. The Impact of Systemwide Drug Testing in Multnomah County, Oregon, National Institute of Justice, 1995.
5. Carver, J. (1986) Drugs and Crime: Controlling Use and Reducing Risk Through Testing, National Institute of Justice.
6. Wish, E. and Gropper, B. (1990) Drug Testing by the Criminal Justice System: Method, Research, and Application, in *Crime and Justice, Vol. 13: Drugs and Crime*. University of Chicago Press.
7. BJA Monograph, Urinalysis as a Part of a Treatment Alternatives to Street Crime Program, Bureau of Justice Assistance, 1988, NCJ 115416.
8. Wish, E. Drug Testing, National Institute of Justice, NCJ 104556.
9. Wish, E. et al., Identifying Drug Users and Monitoring Them During Conditional Release, National Institute of Justice, 1988. NCJ 108560.
10. Stephens, R. and Feucht, T. (1993) Reliability of Self-Reported Drug Use and Urinalysis in the Drug Use Forecasting System. *Prison J.* **73** (3&4), 279.
11. Drug Testing. Guidelines for Pretrial Release and Diversion, National Association of Pretrial Services Agencies, 1995.
12. Rhodes, W. et al., Predicting Pretrial Misconduct with Drug Tests of Arrestees. Evidence from Six Sites, National Institute of Justice, Research in Brief, January, 1996. NCJ 157108.

13. Rhodes, W. et al. (1996) Predicting Pretrial Misconduct with Drug Tests of Arrestees: Evidence from Eight Settings. *J. Quant. Criminol.* **12,** 315.
14. Goldkamp, J. et al. (1990) Pretrial Drug Testing and Defendant Risk. *J. Crim. L. Criminol.* **81,** 585.
15. Smith, D. and Polsenberg, C. (1992) Specifying the Relationship Between Arrestee Drug Test Results and Recidivism. *J. Crim. L. Criminol.* **83,** 364.
16. Toborg, M. et al., Assessment of Pretrial Urine Testing in the District of Columbia, National Institute of Justice, 1989.
17. Visher, C. (1990) Using Drug Testing to Identify High-R isk Defendants on Release: A Study in the District of Columbia. *J. Crim. Justice* **18,** 321.
18. Visher, C. Pretrial Drug Testing, National Institute of Justice, 1992.
19. Visher, C. (1992) Pretrial Drug Testing: Panacea or Pandora's Box? *Ann. Am. Acad.* **521,** 112.
20. BJA Monograph, Estimating the Cost of Drug Testing for a Pretrial Services Program, Bureau of Justice Assistance, 1989.
21. Rosen, C. and Goldkamp, J. (1989) The Constitutionality of Drug Testing at the Bail Stage. *J. Crim. L. Criminol.* **80,** 114.
22. Abell, R. (1989) Pretrial Drug Testing: Expanding Rights and Protecting Public Safety. *Geo. Wash. L. Rev.* **57,** 943.
23. Meyers, P. (1991) Pretrial Drug Testing: Is It Vulnerable to Due Process Challenges? *BYU J. Pub. Law* **5,** 285.
24. Walton, R. et al. (1991) Pretrial Drug Testing – An Essential Component of the National Drug Control Strategy. *BYU J. Pub. Law* **5,** 341.
25. Carver, J. (1991) Pretrial Drug Testing: An Essential Step in Bail Reform, *BYU J. Pub. Law* **5,** 371.
26. Skousen, R. A (1991) Special Needs Exception to the Warrant and Probable Cause Requirements for Mandatory and Uniform Pre-Arraignment Drug Testing in the Wake of Skinner vs Railway Labor Executives' Association and National Treasury Employees' Union vs Von Raab. *BYU J. Pub. Law* **5,** 409.
27. Nielson, D. (1991) Consenting to Searches After Being Arrested: Pretrial Drug Testing. *BYU J. Pub. Law* **5,** 439.
28. Jensen, C. (1991) Survey of Current and Prior Pretrial Drug Testing Sites, *BYU J. Pub. Law* **5,** 451.
29. BJA Monograph, Integrating Drug Testing Into a Pretrial Services System, Bureau of Justice Assistance, 1993, NCJ 142414.
30. Carver, J. (1993) Using Drug Testing to Reduce Detention. *Fed. Prob.* **57,** 42.
31. Smith, D. and Polsenberg, C. (1992) Specifying the Relationship Between Arrestee Drug Use Test Results and Recidivism. *J. Crim. L. Criminol.* **83,** 364.
32. BJA Monograph, Drug Testing Guidelines and Practices for Adult Probation and Parole Agencies, Bureau of Justice Assistance, 1991. NCJ 129199.
33. Rosen, C. (1990) The Fourth Amendment Implications of Urine Testing for Evidence of Drug Use in Probation. *Brooklyn L. Rev.* **55,** 1159.
34. delCarmen, R. and Sorensen, J. Legal Issues in Drug Testing Probation and Parole Clients and Employees, Department of Justice, National Institute of Corrections, 1989.
35. delCarmen, R., and Sorensen, J. Legal Issues in Drug Testing Probationers and Parolees. *Fed. Prob.* **19** (Dec. 1988).

36. Bird, A. et al. (1997) Harm Reduction Measures and Injecting Inside Prison Versus Mandatory Drug Testing: Results of a Cross Sectional Anonymous Questionnaire Survey. *BMJ* **315,** 21.
37. Gore, S. and Bird, A. (1996) Cost Implications of Random Mandatory Drug Tests in Prisons. *Lancet* **348,** 1124.
38. Gore, S. et al., (1966) Prison Rights: Mandatory Drug Tests and Performance Indicators for Prisons. *BMJ* **312,** 1411.
39. Gore, S., and Bird, A. Mandatory Drug Tests in Prisons, *BMJ* **310,** 595 (1995).
40. Epstein, R. (1987) Urinalysis Testing in Correctional Facilities. *Boston Univ. L. R.* **67,** 475.
41. In re Johnston, 745 P.2d 864 (Wash. 1987).
42. Soto vs Lord, 693 F.Supp. 8 (S.D.N.Y. 1988).
43. Thompson vs Hall, 883 F.2d 70 (4th Cir 1989), 88-6525, (unpublished opinion)
44. Harrison vs Dahm, 911 F.2d 37 (8th Cir. 1990).
45. Burdette vs Legursky, Civil Action 91-C-341 (W.V.Cir., Marshall Cty.).
46. Jensen vs Lick, 589 F.Supp. 35 (D.N.D. 1984).
47. Storms vs Coughlin, 600 F.Supp. 1214 (D.N.Y. 1984).
48. Peranzo vs Coughlin, 608 F.Supp. 1504 (D.C.N.Y. 1985).
49. Vasquez vs Coughlin, 499 N.Y.S.2d 461 (A.D. 3 Dept. 1986).
50. Spence vs Farrier, 807 F.2d 753 (8th Cir. 1986).
51. State vs Johnson, 527 A.2d 250 (Conn.App. 1987).
52. Peranzo vs Coughlin, 675 F.Supp. 102 (S.D.N.Y. 1987).
53. People vs Walker, 517 N.E.2d 679 (Ill.App. 5 Dist. 1987).
54. Lahey vs Kelly, 518 N.E.2d 924 (N.Y. 1987).
55. Brown vs Scully, 524 N.Y.S.2d 486 (A.D. 2 Dept. 1988).
56. Amaro vs Ternullo, 529 N.Y.S.2d 153 (A.D. 2 Dept. 1988).
57. Peranzo vs Coughlin, 850 F.2d 125 (2nd Cir. 1988).
58. Jones vs U.S., 548 A.2d 35 (D.C.App. 1988).
59. Berrios vs Kuhlmann, 532 N.Y.S.2d 593 (A.D. 3 Dept. 1988).
60. Pella vs Adams, 702 F.Supp. 244 (D.Nev. 1988).
61. Pella vs Adams, 723 F.Supp. 1394 (D.Nev. 1989).
62. Rucker vs Johnson, 724 F.Supp. 568 (N.D.Ill. 1989).
63. Higgs vs Bland, 888 F.2d 443 (6th Cir. 1989).
64. Driver vs State, 576 So.2d 675 (Ala.Ct.App. 1991).
65. Works vs State, 575 So.2d 622 (Ala.Cr.App. 1991).
66. Moley vs Coughlin, 591 N.Y.S.2d 845 (A.D. 2 Dept. 1992).
67. Koenig vs Vanelli, 971 F.2d 422 (9th Cir. 1992).
68. Penrod vs State, 611 N.E.2d 653 (Ind.App. 2 Dist. 1993).

Chapter 6

On-Site Testing Devices and Driving-Under-the-Influence Cases

J. Michael Walsh

1. Introduction

Evidence gathered over the last 50 years has established a direct relationship between increasing blood alcohol concentrations (BAC) in drivers and increasing risk of motor vehicle accidents *(1)*. As a result, over the last ten years major prevention initiatives in the United States focusing on driving-under-the-influence of alcohol (DUI) have resulted in a significant reduction in accidents/deaths because of alcohol intoxication *(2,3)*. To some extent this success is because of the fact that biochemical devices used to rapidly assess breath-alcohol-concentration on-site are widely available, relatively inexpensive, and are used universally by law enforcement agencies to determine DUI and enforce the associated laws. Unfortunately, until recently there have been no similar devices available to test for illegal drugs.

In comparison with the alcohol literature, relatively little information is available regarding the true incidence and prevalence of illegal drug use in reckless driving and driving accidents. Breath-alcohol testing is the most frequently performed and the most widely used forensic science procedure. This technology has established a scientifically sound basis for the estimation of the prevalence of alcohol use among reckless drivers *(4)*. The principal problem with estimating "drugged" drivers has been the relative unavailabil-

From: *Forensic Science*: *On-Site Drug Testing*
Edited by: A. J. Jenkins and B. A. Goldberger © Humana Press, Inc., Totowa, NJ

ity of drug detection devices to test for illegal drugs. In general, such testing devices have been limited to highly specialized forensic laboratories *(5,6)*. Some data have emerged over the last 20 years, however, which gives insight as to the extent of the problem. Lundberg et al. reported that the presence of psychoactive drugs other than, or in addition to, alcohol was common in a pooled sample of 765 persons with driving behavior problems in Nevada and California *(7)*. Williams et al. reported on a "high risk" sample of 440 young male auto drivers killed in California traffic accidents where blood specimens collected from these drivers indicated 70% contained alcohol and over 40% contained other drugs *(8)*. Soderstrom et al. found that of 1023 patients admitted to The Maryland (Baltimore) Shock-Trauma Unit, 34.7% had recently used cannabis (i.e., greater than 2 ng/mL delta-9-tetrahydrocannabinol in serum) and 33% had BAC's greater than 100 mg/dL *(9)*. Marzuk et al. examined postmortem blood and urine of motor vehicle fatalities in New York City [1984–87] and found that at least one in four dead drivers [ages 16–45] had used cocaine within 48 h of death. Marzuk et al. detected either cocaine metabolites, alcohol or both in 56% of those killed in fatal traffic accidents in New York City *(10)*.

In a collaborative effort between the US National Institute on Drug Abuse [NIDA] and the National Transportation Safety Board (NTSB) an investigation of fatal-to-the-driver trucking accidents was conducted in eight states over a one-year period *(11)*. Comprehensive drug screens on blood specimens collected from 168 fatally injured truck drivers indicated that one-or-more drugs were detected in 67% of the drivers and 33% of the drivers had detectable blood concentrations of psychoactive drugs or alcohol. The most prevalent drugs were cannabinoids and ethanol (each found in 13% of the dead drivers), cocaine was found in 8% of the cases, and amphetamine-like substances in 7%.

2. On-Site Testing in DUI Cases

As a result of the overall prevalence of drug abuse in the nation and the growing body of evidence of illegal drug use by drivers, a number of states (AZ, GA, IL, MN, RI, UT, IA, and IN) have enacted *per se* laws for driving under the influence of drugs *(12)*. These laws generally state that the presence of detectable levels of illegal drugs/metabolites in body fluids can be used as evidence of being "under-the-influence" of a drug (DUID) *(13)*. Under such statutes individuals can be found guilty of "driving under the influence" if he/she were operating a motor vehicle while any illicit drugs were present in his/her system. This legal *per se* strategy to deal with DUI is the same philosophy underlying alcohol-DUI statutes. This tactic creates an important legal distinction between having to prove that observed driver impairment is the result of taking a drug (causal relationship) and demonstrating that observed impaired driving behavior was associated with specified concentrations of drug/metabolite in the individual's body fluids.

Within the last five years new technologically advanced rapid immunoassay drug-testing devices have been developed that can provide qualitative information about the presence of drug/drug metabolites in body fluids within minutes of testing. These devices have been designed primarily for use with urine specimens and marketed for workplace testing. A variety of these devices are being marketed worldwide and an outline of the parameters of currently available devices is listed in Table 1. In addition, recently new products are entering the market designed for use with saliva and sweat as alternative test matrices. Among the available devices there are significant differences in the performance of these products. However, most of the FDA approved products are capable of providing immediate accurate and reliable results "on-site" and provide a unique opportunity to effectively apply this technology in traffic safety, the enforcement of drugs and driving laws, and the conduct of epidemiological research into the prevalence of drugged driving.

In an early drugged-driving evaluation of on-site immunoassay technology conducted in Memphis, Tennessee individuals arrested for reckless driving who were not apparently impaired by alcohol [no odor of alcohol or tested negative by breath analysis or both] were tested using a Drug Screening Systems Inc. (DSSI) rapid immunoassay urinalysis test for marijuana [100ng/mL] and cocaine [300 ng/mL] *(14)*. Each specimen was analyzed twice on-site with two separate DSSI kits. Only specimens that were positive on two consecutive tests were considered to be positive. Result of the on-site assay indicated a 59% test positive rate (18% for both drugs, 33% for marijuana alone, and 20% for cocaine alone). When specimens were re-analyzed in a forensic laboratory (Emit-Dau screening with GC/MS confirmation) results indicated that the DSSI device performed well for cocaine (all on-site cocaine positives confirmed) however the device produced unacceptably high false positive and false negative results for marijuana. Of the 60 on-site positive marijuana results 30% failed to confirm. In addition, control specimens from 50 drivers who tested negative on site were sent to the laboratory and 20% tested positive for marijuana.

In a more recent field evaluation of on-site kits, specimens were collected by police officers from DUI suspects in Tampa, Florida (15,16). Four kits were evaluated (Triage [Biosite Diagnostics], TesTcup [Roche Diagnostics], Accusign [Princeton Biomeditech], OnTrak [Roche Diagnostics]) analyzing the same specimens on site. All positives and 10% of negatives were sent to a Substance Abuse and Mental Health Services Administration

Table 1

Road Immunoassay Drug-Testing Devices

PRODUCT	AccuSign	EZ-Screen Profile	First Check	Frontline
Test Panel	Multi-Test	Multi-Test	Multi-Test	Multi-Test
Drugs Tested				
Marijuana	X	X	X	X
Cocaine	X	X	X	X
Amphetamines	X	X	X	
Opiates	X	X	X	X
PCP	X	X		
Barbiturates	X			
Benzodiazepines	X			
Other	Methamphetamine			
Urine Handling	Yes	Yes	No	Yes
Reagents	No	Yes	No	No
Mixing	No	No	No	No
Reaction Timed	Not Required	Not Required	Not Required	Not Required
Reading Timed	Yes	Not Required	Yes	Not Required
Storage	Room Temp	Refrigeration Req	Room Temp	Room Temp
Manufacturer Name	Princeton BioMeditech	Editek Inc	Worldwide Medical Corp	Boehringer Mannheim
Address	P O Box 7139 4242 US Rt 1 Monmouth Junction, NJ 0852	P O Box 908 1238 Anthony Rd Burlington, NC 27216	199 Technology Dr -Ste 150 Irvinge, CA 92718	Sandhofer StraBe 116 D-68298 Mannheim, Germany
Phone#	(908) 274-1000	(910) 266-6311	(714) 727-0711	
FDA Approved (12/05/97)	Yes	Yes	Yes	Some Drugs/Pending
Cost/Test[a]	$2.10	$2.50	$2.19	Unknown
Comments	PCP is an Additional test	Many unconfirmed positives	FDA approved as AccuSign Same Test as AccuSign	Dip Stick Amphets Not Available

[a]Price will vary significantly depending on the volume of purchase. Prices stated estimate a medium to high volume purchase.

Table 1 (Continued)
Road Immunoassay Drug-Testing Devices

PRODUCT	Mach IV Microline	OnTrak	Pharmscreen	Pharmscreen Card
Test Panel	Multi-Test	Single-Test	Single-Test	Multi-Test
Drugs Tested				
Marijuana	X	X		X
Cocaine	X	X		X
Amphetamines	X	X		X
Opiates	X	X		X
PCP	X	X		X
Barbiturates				
Benzodiazepines				
Other			Methamphetamine	
Urine Handling	Yes	Yes	Yes	No
Reagents	No	Yes	No	No
Mixing	No	Yes	No	No
Reaction Timed	Yes	Not Required	Yes	Yes
Reading Timed	Yes	Not Required	Yes	Not Required
Storage	Refrigeration Req	Refrigeration Req	Refrigeration Req	Room Temp
Manufacturer Name	Drug Screening Systems, Inc	Roche Diagnostic Corp.	PharmChem Laboratories	PharmChem Laboratories
Address	PO Box 579 1001 Lower Lndg Rd-Ste 304 Blackwood, NJ 08012	9115 Hague Rd Indianapolis, IN 46256	1505 O'Brien Dr-Bldg A Menlo Park, CA 94025	1505 O'Brien Dr-Bldg A Menlo Park, CA 94025
Phone#	(609) 228-8500	(800) 737-9667	(800)-446-5177	(800) 446-5177
DA Approved (12/05/97)	Some Drugs/Pending	Yes	No	No
Cost/Test[a]	$3.00	$1.85	Unknown	Unknown
Comments	Not FDA Approved	Product being	2 Tests only	New Product
for BZEdiscontinued	Card placed in urine			

***Table 1* (Continued)**

Road Immunoassay Drug-Testing Devices

PRODUCT	Rapid Drug Screen	Rapid Test (Syva)	Status DS	SunLine Five
Test Panel	Multi-Test	Multi-Test	Multi-Test	Multi-Test
Drugs Tested				
Marijuana	X	X	X	X
Cocaine	X	X	X	X
Amphetamines	X	X	X	X
Opiates	X	X	X	X
PCP	X	X	X	X
Barbiturates		single test		X
Benzodiazepines		single test		X
Other		Methadone, Methamp-single tests		Methamphetamine, Methadone
Urine Handling	No	No	Yes	Yes
Reagents	No	No	No	No
Mixing	No	No	No	No
Reaction Timed	Yes	Not Required	Not Required	Not Required
Reading Timed	Yes	Not Required	Not Required	Not Required
Storage	Room Temp	Room Temp	Room Temp	Room Temp
Manufacturer Name	American Bio Medica Corp	Behring Diagnostics Inc	Orion Diagnostica	Sun Biomedical Laboratories, Inc.
U.S. Address	102 Simons Rd Ancramdale, NY 12503 Blackwood, NJ 08012	PO Box 49013 San Jose, CA 95161	71 Veronica Avenue Somerset, NJ 08873	604 VPR Center 1001 Lower Lndg Rd
Phone#	(800) 227-1243	(800) 227-9948	(800) 526-2125, ext. 911	(609) 401-1080
FDA Approved (12/05/97)	Yes	No	No	Some Drugs/Pending
Cost/Test[a]	$2.75	Unknown	$4.50	$2.25
Comments	Non-Nida Cutoffs Video-Poor laboratory Practices	Not Available Yet		FDA Approved as Visualine (not for PCP)

[a]Price will vary significantly depending on the volume of purchase. Prices stated estimate a medium to high volume purchase.

Table 1 (Continued)
Road Immunoassay Drug-Testing Devices

PRODUCT	SureStep	TesTcup	TestStick	Triage	Verdict
Test Panel	Multi-Test	Multi-Test	Single-Test	Multi-Test	Single-Test
Drugs Tested					
Marijuana	X	X	X	X	X
Cocaine	X	X		X	X
Amphetamines	X	X		X	
Opiates	X	X		X	X
PCP		X		X	X
Barbiturates				X	
Benzodiazepines				X	
Other	Methamphetamine			Tricyclics, Methamp	
Urine Handling	No	No	Yes	Yes	Yes
Reagents	No	No	No	Yes	No
Mixing	No	No	No	No	No
Reaction Timed	Not Required	Not Required	Not Required	Yes	Not Required
Reading Timed	Yes	Not Required	Not Required	Yes	Not Required
Storage Temp	Room Temp	Room Temp	Room Temp	Room Temp	Room
Manufacturer Name	BioChem Immunosystems	Roche Diagnostic Corp.	Roche Diagnostic Corp.	Biosite Diagnostics Inc.	Editek Inc.
Address	100 Cascade Dr Allentown, PA 18103-9562	9115 Hague Rd. Indianapolis, IN 46256	9115 Hague Rd. Indianapolis, IN 46256	11030 Roselle St San Diego, CA 92121	PO Box 908 1238 Anthony Rd Burlington, NC 27216
Phone#	(800) 345-3127	(800) 737-9667	(800) 737-9667	(619) 455-4808	(910)266-6311
FDA App (12/05/97)	Yes	Yes	No	Yes	Some Drugs/Pending
Cost/Test[a]	Unknown	$2.15	$1.85	$4.00	$2.80
Comments	Immerse a card Oversensitive High False Positive		New product not on market		Amps and PCP not available

(SAMHSA) certified laboratory for rescreening and confirmation using the SAMHSA cutoff concentrations. Over the course of the study the data indicated that 26% of the total specimens (78/303) were confirmed positive by GC/MS in the certified laboratory for one or more illegal drugs. Forty-one percent of those individuals who were able to pass the breathalyzer test (i.e. BrAc <0.08) tested positive for one or more illegal drugs. Comparisons of the kit results indicated differences in the ease of handling, the time to conduct the test, specimen handling, reagent mixing, and readability of results. The kit evaluations clearly indicated the superiority of the Accusign and TesTcup devices. A major consideration was the elimination of the need for reagent mixing, and in the case of the TesTcup there is no specimen handling. Comparisons of specificity, sensitivity, positive, and negative predictive values were made and overall the results indicated that all four immunoassay products worked at an acceptable level. All four kits were in close agreement on prevalence: 15.5–15.8% for THC, all at 13.2% for cocaine, and all at 0.7% for opiates. The evaluation indicated that non-medical personnel are quite capable of learning to use the devices and demonstrated the feasibility of integrating on-site urine testing into routine police operations. In a follow up project all Tampa DUI squad officers have been trained to perform on-site immunoassay tests and the evaluation is continuing.

The National Highway Traffic Safety Administration (NHTSA) recently completed a project in which police officers in Houston, TX, and Long Island, NY, evaluated five on-site drug kits (Triage®, TesTcup5®AccuSign®, Rapid Drug Screen®, and TesTstik®) with DUI suspects. The officers participating in this project were certified "Drug Recognition Experts," having been trained in the NHTSA-approved "Drug Recognition and Classification Program." Overall results indicated that the on-site devices performed well, and the DRE officers participating in the study "favored the use of on-site devices in the enforcement of impaired driving laws." *(17)*.

Another major on-site drug testing evaluation has been completed recently in Europe. The ROSITA project is a multinational drugged-driver study funded by the European Commission and carried out in eight countries (Belgium, Spain, Italy, France, Germany, Norway, Finland, and Scotland). The objective of the Roadside Testing Assessment [ROSITA] project is to identify the requirements for roadside testing equipment, and to conduct an international comparative assessment of existing devices and prototypes. Equipment designed to test various matrices, including blood, urine, saliva, and sweat, were used in the project. The assessment addressed roadside drug testing, result validity, equipment reliability, practical usability, and cost. Ultimately the

European Commission would like to develop drugged-driver legislation around the findings and recommendations of the ROSITA project that would be adopted in all EU countries. Progress reports on the ROSITA project are available on the internet at http://www.rosita.org.

3. Summary

There is ample evidence that DUID is a growing problem worldwide. In the United States eight states have enacted *per se* DUID laws, however, none of these states are currently using on-site rapid immunoassay technology to enforce these laws. In fact, a recent informal survey of the state prosecutors in these states (conducted by the author) indicated that there is very little enforcement of driving under the influence of drugs at all. It seems clear that the US Department of Transportation regulations for commercial drivers could easily be adapted at the state level to cover all motor vehicle operators and that the use of on-site technology for screening could make enforcement of such laws quite feasible. While further research is needed and many of the issues (i.e. legal, and technical) have yet to be clarified, the European Union is moving forward to integrate the latest technology into a political strategy and legislation to deal directly with the problem of drugs and driving.

In order to prevent drug-related traffic accidents, law enforcement officials must be able to detect drivers under-the-influence of drugs as they routinely do now with alcohol detection devices. The availability of technologically advanced on-site drug-testing devices that are capable of providing immediate accurate and reliable results provides a unique opportunity to effectively apply this technology in traffic safety and the enforcement of drugs and driving laws. The routine availability of drug testing for DUI and DRE officers could be used as a powerful prevention tool to detect and deter drugged driving behavior.

References

1. Council on Scientific Affairs. (1986) Alcohol and the Driver. *J. Amer. Med. Assoc.* **255,** 522–527
2. (1997) *Morb. and Mortal. Wkl. Report.* **46,** Dec. 5.
3. National Highway Traffic Safety Administration. (1997) *Traffic Safety Facts,* 1996: Washington, DC: US Department of Transportation, National Highway Traffic Safety Administration, National Center for Statistics and Analysis, Research, and Development.
4. Dubowski, K. M. (1992) The Technology of Breath-Alcohol Analysis, US Dept. of Health and Human Services, DHHS Pub. No. ADM-92-1728.

5. Turk, R. F., McBay, A. J., and Hudson, P. (1974) Drug involvement in automobile driver and pedestrian fatalities. *J. Forensic Sciences.* **19,** 90–97.
6. Willette, R. E. and Walsh, J. M. (1983) Drugs, Driving and Traffic Safety, *World Health Organization, Pub.* #78, World Health Organization, Geneva, Switzerland.
7. Lundberg, G. D., White, J. M., and Hoffman, K. I. (1979) Drugs (other than or in addition to Ethyl Alcohol) and Driving Behavior: A collaborative study of the California Association of Toxicologists. *J. Forensic Sciences* **24,** 207–215.
8. Williams, A. F., Peat, M. A., Crouch, D. J., Wells, J. K. and Finkle, B. S. (1979) *Public Health Reports* **100,** 19–25,1979.
9. Soderstrom, C., Trifillis, A., Shankar, B, Clark, W., and Cowley, R. (1988) Marijuana and Alcohol use among 1023 patients, *Arch. Surg.* **123,** 733–737.
10. Marzuk, P. M., Tardiff, K., Leon, A. C., Stajic, M., Morgan, E. B., and Mann, J. J. (1990) Prevalence of recent cocaine use among motor vehicle fatalities in New York City. *JAMA* **263,** 250–256.
11. Crouch, D., Birkey, M., Gust, S., Rollins, D., Walsh, J. M., Moulden, J., Quinlan, K. and Beckel, R. (1993) The Prevalence of Drugs and Alcohol in Fatally Injured Drivers. *J. Forensic Sciences* **38,** 1342–1353.
12. Preliminary Estimates from the 1995 National Household Survey on Drug Abuse. U.S. Department of Health and Human Services, Public Health Service, August, 1996, DHHS Pub. No. (SMA) 96-3107.
13. Lewis, M. F. and Buchan, B. J. (1998) The drugged driver and the need for a per se law. *Fl. Bar J.* July/Aug.
14. Brookoff, D., Cook, C. Williams, C. and Mann, C. (1994) Testing Reckless Drivers for Cocaine and Marijuana. *New England J. Med.* **331,** 518–522
15. Buchan, B. J., Walsh, J. M., and Leaverton, P. E. (1998) Evaluation of the accuracy of on-site multi-analyte drug testing devices in the determination of the prevalence of illicit drugs in drivers. *J. Forensic Science* **43,** 395–399.
16. Walsh, J. M., Buchan, B. J., and Leaverton, P. E. (1997) Detection of Illicit Drugs in Drivers, in Proceedings of the 14th International Conference on Alcohol, Drugs and Traffic Safety, C. Mercier-Guyon (ed.) Vol. 2, pp. 485–491, CERMT, Centre d'Etudes et de Recherches en Medecine du Trafic, Annecy, France.17.
17. Hersch, R. K., Crouch, D. J., and Cook, R. F., Field Test of On-Site Detection Devices, Report #DOT-HS-809-192, Oct. 2000, National Highway Traffic Safety Administration.

Chapter 7

Analysis of Ethanol in Saliva

Kurt M. Dubowski

1. Introduction

Since the inception of regulated testing for drugs-of-abuse in the civilian workplace setting, there have been continuing calls for on-site testing and for use of specimens alternative to the primary specimen for nonethanol drugs, urine, and the primary specimen for alcohol[1], breath. Testing of saliva (now often referred to as "oral fluid") for alcohol can serve both of those goals. The effect of oral exposure to alcoholic fluids and alcohol ingestion on saliva was first studied about 100 years ago *(1)*, and during the 1930s and 1940s there were many of studies and publications on the detection and measurement of alcohol in saliva after consumption of alcoholic beverages *(2)*. The methods of that era had 3 characteristics:

- They required collection of saliva specimens with or without stimulation,
- They measured the alcohol content of saliva in the laboratory by the procedures of the day such as distillation plus wet chemical oxidation and titration, and
- The saliva alcohol results were usually correlated with the alcohol concentration of blood, serum, or plasma collected at the same time.

Because early methods for alcohol measurement had sensitivities typically limited to the milligram or microgram range, a major emphasis in the early saliva-alcohol studies was the collection of adequate saliva volumes and the means for stimulating saliva flow. Instrumental measurements for alcohol

[1]The unmodified term *alcohol* in this chapter refers to ethanol.

From: *Forensic Science: On-Site Drug Testing*
Edited by: A. J. Jenkins and B. A. Goldberger © Humana Press, Inc., Totowa, NJ

did not become commonplace until the post-World War II era. By that time, interest in saliva collection and analysis for alcohol and other analytes had greatly waned.

The need for immediate results and simple alcohol testing methods for clinical and law enforcement and corrections applications had greatly accelerated development of methods for analysis of alcohol in breath—an even less invasive sample than saliva. Saliva alcohol measurement was relegated to obscurity for the next 45 years or so. The advent of more sensitive physical (e.g., gas chromatography) and chemical methods for alcohol measurement (e.g., enzymatic oxidation) brought about a resurgence of work on biological, physiological, and analytical aspects of saliva alcohol *(3–15)*. New single-use disposable commercial devices for saliva alcohol made their debut about this time (1984–1985) using mixed saliva ("oral fluid") and, initially, modifications of the solid-state enzymatic test strip technology then widely used for urine analyses.

The last phase of this cycle is the initially slow development of commercial devices that combine collection of mixed saliva with on-site single-use disposable tests for alcohol. This trend accelerated with the U.S. Department of Transportation's (DOT) decision to study, and later to authorize, use of on-site saliva-alcohol screening tests as an alternative to breath-alcohol screening tests for workers in the transportation industries *(16–17)*. Most of the single-use saliva-alcohol tests developed by industry never reached the market or did not remain commercially available for a long period of time. The definitions and other aspects of the DOT rulemaking process about 1994 stimulated commercial device development in the right directions. A new category of alcohol test devices was recognized by DOT – "Disposable Alcohol Screening Devices: Alcohol screening devices designed for a single use" *(16)*. Alcohol Screening Device was defined as: *"A device that is used to detect the presence of 0.020 or more BAC. The device may measure any bodily fluid for this purpose, but shall provide output in BAC units. Test results may be indicated by numerical read-out or by other means, such as by the use of lights or color changes" (16)*. The rulemaking discussion also described saliva-alcohol screening tests as a combination of the collection of saliva (with a swab) with immediate testing for alcohol in saliva transferred from the swab to the analytical device. Thus, recent and current commercial developments for such tests were influenced in a direction which would yield devices able to achieve Conforming Products List status under the DOT regulations.

2. Saliva as a Specimen; Saliva Collection; Relationship of Saliva and Blood-Alcohol

It is accepted scientific doctrine that alcohol taken into the body through the mouth or other entry sites is thereafter distributed throughout the body and, at equilibrium, partitions into the various organs, tissues, and biological fluids (other than breath) in approximate proportion to their respective water content. Saliva with its high water content (~994 g/L) is a good candidate body fluid as a specimen for alcohol measurement, especially since the alcohol concentration vs time profiles are very similar for blood, breath, and saliva *(18)*. Saliva is produced mainly by bilateral pairs of salivary glands - parotid, submandibular, submaxillary, and sublingual. In the context of clinical or workplace on-site saliva-alcohol testing, only in vivo pooled mixed saliva collected from the oral cavity is widely used. In humans, 0.5–1.5 L of saliva is produced per day, but not at a uniform rate of secretion. There are age-related, health-related, and psychologically-induced differences in volume and rate of saliva secretion. Because saliva flow is largely controlled by the parasympathetic nervous system, saliva flow may be impaired and adequate collections may be difficult in persons on anticholinergic medications ("dry mouth") and in some elderly persons with chronic suppressed salivation (Xerostomia or hyposalivation). More than 400 drugs suppress salivation; atropine is a textbook example. Stimulation of saliva flow by tactile, olfactory, or gustatory means is mainly used in research applications of saliva analysis. Recent comprehensive reviews of saliva as a specimen for drug analysis have been published *(19–20)*. Human mixed saliva, when devoid of such artifacts as bubbles, foam, food particles, cell debris, etc., is a clear, colorless liquid with pH ~6.7 and low concentrations of proteins, electrolytes, carbohydrates, hormones, and some enzyme activity. There is no endogenous alcohol in saliva in any relevant concentration in alcohol-abstaining subjects.

Saliva, in regulated workplace testing for alcohol, shares with breath traceability to the specimen donor by direct observation, without invasion of privacy.

Alcohol reaches the saliva mainly by passive diffusion from blood plasma as the main transport mechanism, in accordance with Fick's Law of Diffusion. There is no known active transport mechanism for alcohol secretion into saliva. Other contributions of alcohol to saliva during and after secretion may occur through ultrafiltration, from mucous, and from interchange with mucous membranes. Because the mixed saliva commonly used as a specimen for alcohol and other drug analysis may differ significantly from the initial secreted state of the several mixed saliva components, the term "oral fluid" is becoming fashionable to describe the collected sample. Saliva, of course, shares with breath the possibility of contamination with alcohol remaining in the mouth (mouth alcohol) after recent ingestion of alcoholic beverages or use of alcohol-containing medications, mouthwash, breath fresheners, candy, etc., or from vomit or other contact with alcohol-containing stomach contents. Saliva in the mouth can be diluted by ingested water or other liquids. A 15-min deprivation/observation period prior to breath sample collection has been shown to eliminate mouth alcohol or water dilution as factors in breath-alcohol analysis *(21)* and is equally applicable to saliva sampling. Routine rinsing the mouth with water prior to saliva collection, or drinking of any liquid, is not recommended practice because alcohol re-equilibration and elimination of residual water require time to overcome dilution effects. None of the known physiological components of mixed saliva *(22)* have been demonstrated to have any positive or negative effect on saliva-alcohol measurements by gas chromatography or enzymatic oxidation.

2.1. Saliva Collection

The procedural details for saliva collection differ for the various disposable test devices; but all fall into 2 categories:

1. Direct application of mixed saliva in the mouth to an indicator device such as an alcohol-sensitive test strip, and
2. Collection of mixed saliva with a small sponge or absorptive material mounted on a plastic handle, by swabbing, or by aspiration of mixed saliva from the sublingual area of the mouth with a disposable plastic pipet.

The volume of saliva needed for the current commercial tests is small and can be collected in one or two minutes or less. There are several commercially available collection devices that can be used to absorb pooled mixed saliva from the mouth. They are then placed into a closed container for transport and laboratory testing for human immunodeficiency virus (HIV) screening and other clinical purposes. Use of such collection-only devices without immediate saliva retrieval and alcohol analysis is clearly not an on-site screening test procedure.

2.2. Relation of Saliva-Alcohol to Alcohol in Other Body Fluids

After the initial flurry of methodological developments and evaluations conducted in the 1930s and 1940s, relatively few studies were performed on the correlation between alcohol concentrations in saliva and in other body fluids. Still fewer of these studies met established and rigorous requirements for scientifically acceptable approach and procedures for comparative experimental studies. Alcohol in blood was first measured long ago and blood became the testing specimen for most early studies concerning the effects of alcohol. Therefore, the unfortunate decision was made decades ago to attempt to correlate the alcohol concentrations in breath, saliva, urine, and tissues with that in whole blood at the same time and to use the resultant experimental ratios to derive conversion factors for transforming alcohol measurement results in other biological specimens to the supposedly coincident blood-alcohol concentration. That conversion was unnecessary, scientifically unsound, and predictably strewn with major and minor scientific and legal obstacles. It caused 50+ years of turmoil in the application of breath-alcohol measurement to traffic law enforcement and other purposes, and is still an occasional subject of controversy in litigation involving breath-alcohol testing. The same treacherous path has been followed with respect to saliva-alcohol measurements - instead of directly correlating measured alcohol concentrations in saliva with the effects of alcohol on individuals, their performance in specific tasks, and measurable impairment of fitness-for-duty, if any.

In 1932, Linde (who with Liljestrand had also studied and published on alcohol in breath) suggested the use of saliva for alcohol measurement *(23)*. He concluded that the parotid saliva alcohol concentration was about 10% greater than that of mixed saliva, and that the mean saliva/blood alcohol ratio was 1.21 to 1. In an extensive Canadian study, Coldwell and Smith found a mean saliva/blood ratio of alcohol of 1.12 to 1 and concluded that it did not vary significantly with time, after mouth-alcohol clearance and alcohol equilibration had occurred *(24)*. Jones subsequently confirmed the stable relationship of postabsorptive saliva-alcohol to blood-alcohol, and concluded that the mean saliva/blood ratio of alcohol was 1.07 to 1 *(25)*. Elbel reported that the mean ratio of alcohol in saliva and blood, in the postabsorptive alcohol distribution phase is 1.25 to 1 *(26)*. Jones also reported another study in which the mean saliva/blood alcohol ratio was about 1.09 to 1 one to six hours after alcohol intake, with overall 95% confidence limits of 1.02–1.12 to 1 *(27)*. Based on relative water content, at 85.0% w/v for whole blood and 99.4% w/v for saliva, the expected equilibrium saliva/blood alcohol ratio should be 0.994/0.850 = 1.17 to 1. Extensive differences between experimental studies make comparisons of findings and conclusions problematic. It is to be noted that none of the studies cited above employed any commercial screening test devices, which would add another major variability factor, but rather relied on direct laboratory measurements of alcohol in separately collected parotid or mixed saliva and blood.

Because of the obvious, significant differences between the results of published studies, other scientific considerations, and for other pragmatic reasons, the DOT has chosen to avoid the issue of alcohol concentration differences between blood and saliva for workplace alcohol screening test purposes in which the previously promulgated decision points were breath or blood-alcohol concentrations. The agency did so essentially by fiat, requiring that screening test devices "may measure any bodily fluid (including blood, breath, or saliva), but that the output must be in blood alcohol concentration (BAC) units," and thus defining "Alcohol Screening Device: A device that is used to detect the presence of 0.020 or more BAC. The device may measure any bodily fluid for this purpose, but shall provide output in BAC units," and further declaring that "NHTSA considers use of a one-to-one conversion factor between blood and saliva to be appropriate" for alcohol *(17)*. This approach, of course, leaves unresolved the issue of identity or equivalence of blood-alcohol and saliva-alcohol concentrations in the context of other applications than those regulated by U. S. DOT. It is clear that the attempted conversion of the results of mixed saliva-alcohol measurements, even if accurately quantitative, to supposedly coincident whole blood or serum-alcohol concentrations cannot be validly performed in the forensic science context. Obviously, the same is also true for alcohol screening tests on mixed saliva. The scientifically most defensible position is to measure saliva-alcohol as accurately as possible, report the actual analytical findings, and to base any decision making on acceptability/ unacceptability thresholds established by policy reflective of accepted scientific principles and information, and on sound patient care considerations in clinical practice.

The remainder of this chapter concerns only single-use, disposable saliva-alcohol tests yielding immediate results by means of an integral indication, e.g., colored negative (–) and positive (+) symbols or thermometer-like numerical scales, etc.

3. Saliva-Alcohol Testing Principles and Procedures

The saliva-alcohol screening test devices listed hereafter in this chapter all use the predominant analytical principle of enzymatic oxidation of alcohol with alcohol dehydrogenase (ADH) which, after various stepwise coupled intermediary reactions, produces a colored endpoint product. In schematic form, the generalized coupled reactions are:

$$\text{Basic Reaction: } C_2H_5OH + NAD^+ \xrightleftharpoons{\text{ADH}} CH_3CHO + NADH + H^+$$

$$\text{Diaphorase Reaction: } INT + NADH + H^+ \xrightleftharpoons{\text{Diaphorase}} \text{Colored Formazan} + NAD^+$$

In the basic reaction, ethanol is oxidized to acetaldehyde in the presence of the enzyme alcohol dehydrogenase (catalyst), with simultaneous reduction of the coenzyme nicotinamide adenine dinucleotide (NAD) on a mole-for-mole basis. In the diaphorase reaction, the reduced nicotinamide adenine dinucleotide (NADH) reacts with the tetrazolium salt INT as a chromogen and a suitable hydrogen acceptor to yield a highly colored formazan compound, whose color intensity obeys Beer's Law, in the presence of the enzyme diaphorase as a catalyst, with simultaneous oxidation of the reduced nicotine adenine dinucleotide. These coupled reactions are quite selective for ethanol and under usual screening test conditions are not significantly affected by methanol or isopropanol. The several current commercial devices use different variants of the above generic reactions. Other commercial saliva alcohol tests not currently on the market used a variant of the above coupled reactions in which alcohol oxidase instead of alcohol dehydrogenase was the enzymatic catalyst for the basic reaction.

The saliva-alcohol screening test procedure typically consists of five sequential steps:

1. Preparations for testing and preparation of the test subject
2. Collection of a mixed saliva sample and its delivery to the test device, or direct saliva contact in the mouth with the test indicator device
3. The chemical reactions process within the device
4. Observation, after a specified time interval, of the result indication and any associated quality control signal
5. Preparation of the record and report of the result and other incidental information

Some procedural details vary among the different commercial saliva-alcohol screening test devices, e.g., in the length of development time for the endpoint or the method of associating saliva with the test device.

Given the testing situation discussed above, it is of great importance that there be complete and strict, not merely substantial, compliance with all of the details of the test procedure set forth in the particular manufacturer's instructions or directions. This is also a regulatory requirement. Further, performance of alcohol screening tests in both clinical and nonclinical settings is not an occasion for experimentation or individual initiative by the tester.

In step (1) above, the preparations involve at least procuring and making ready the necessary supplies and materials, accomplishing required documentation (such as the confirmed identity of the tested person, place, date and time of the test, designation of the test performed, name of the screening test technician, etc.). They also include adequately informing the test subject about the relevant test details; and performing any other required subject preparation. The screening test device manufacturers uniformly recommend a deprivation interval

Table 1
Saliva-Alcohol Screening Test Devices on the DOT/NHTSA Conforming Products List

Device	Manufacturer
ALCO-SCREEN 02	Chematics, Inc.; North Webster, IN
On-Site Alcohol®	Roche Diagnostic Systems, Somerville, NJ
Q.E.D. A150 Saliva Alcohol Test	STC Diagnostics, Inc., Bethlehem, PA

before testing. The statement appearing in the Fact Sheet for the Q.E.D. Saliva Alcohol Test is typical: "Wait ten minutes after eating or drinking to allow the mouth to clear residual food or beverage" *(28)*. The remaining test steps (2), (3), (4), and (5) in DOT-regulated testing must conform to the details of the DOT-prescribed screening test procedure, which consists of 13 steps *(29)*.

Because the test is associated with body fluid(s) and may result in contact by the screening test technician with such fluid(s), certain minimum universal safety precautions must be used by the technician. These include use of eyeglasses (or safety goggles or face shield), hand washing, and use of surgical gloves which should be changed for every test subject. All materials which did contain or had contact with saliva, such as the saliva sampler, should be disposed of safely.

4. Commercial Saliva-Alcohol Screening Test Devices

The three saliva-alcohol devices listed in the U. S. DOT NHTSA Conforming Products List of Alcohol Screening Devices *(30)* appear in Table 1.

The three devices exemplify three different means of indicating the test result, although all employ enzymatic oxidation of alcohol and the color formation principle outlined above.

ALCO-SCREEN 02 is a plastic test strip with an indicator bar which becomes visible in the presence of alcohol in a saliva sample at and above 0.02 g/dL. The reactive pad on the test strip is placed under the test subject's tongue until saturated with saliva, or is immersed into collected saliva. Once the pad is saturated, the test strip is removed and the strip is examined two minutes later for presence or absence of a greenish bar on the reactive pad. Absence of the bar constitutes a negative result; its presence is a positive result. ALCO-SCREEN is another version of this device (not on the NHTSA Conforming Products List) that yields semi-quantitative results for saliva-alcohol between 0.02 and 0.30 g/dL, by visual comparison of the strip pad color with a green - blue green - blue color chart printed on the package. A clinical evaluation of this latter device has been reported *(31)*. When the blood-alcohol concentration was 0.10 g/dL or greater, the ALCO-SCREEN test was reported as 90.9% sensitive, 71.4% specific, and 92% efficient.

The On-Site Saliva-Alcohol Test is a self-contained assay which consists of a 65 × 40 × 10 mm compartmented plastic tray ("Test Card") with reagent, reaction, and sample wells. A reagent transfer pipet and a sample pipet and saliva swab are also included. The reaction well is charged with one drop of reagent by means of the small plastic transfer pipet. The saliva swab is then saturated with saliva by the test subject's pressing its foam head against the inner mouth area and tongue for 15 or 20 s. The saturated swab is press-fitted into the circular sample well. After two minutes, the reaction well of the test card is examined for presence or absence of a reddish-purple plus sign (+) in the center of the initially pale yellow detection pad. Its appearance constitutes a presumptive positive test for saliva-alcohol of 0.02 g/dL or greater. Absence of the + sign constitutes a negative test result. The manufacturer has reported some performance characteristics of the device, including its accuracy in aqueous alcohol control tests. At an alcohol control concentration of 0.008 g/dL, there were 0 positives and 52 negatives (0% reported as positive); at a control concentration of 0.020 g/dL, there were 36 positives and 16 negatives (69% reported as positive); and at a control concentration of 0.032 g/dL, there were 50 positives and 2 negatives (96% reported as positive) *(32)*. In 20 replicate control tests at 0.015 g/dL, there were 45% false positive test results and 0.020 g/dL there were 5% false negative test results *(32)*. Isopropanol and methanol did not react in this system at 0.10 and 1.00 g/dL, respectively.

The Q.E.D. A150 Saliva Alcohol Test consists of a plastic saliva collection stick with end-mounted cotton swab, and a 73 × 20 × 4 mm plastic indicator that incorporates a reaction capillary and a saliva port (Fig. 1). The indicator has scales calibrated from 0 to 150 mg/dL and 0 to 0.15% w/v like a miniature old fashioned wooden bath thermometer. Saliva is collected by having the subject (or tester) actively swab around the subject's cheek, gums, and under the tongue for 30–60 s or until the cotton swab is saturated. It is then friction-fitted into the saliva port and kept there with gentle pressure until the capillary fills, as indicated by a color change in the "QA Spot" at the top of the capillary. Readings are taken after 2 min, at which point the "QA Spot" should be purple and filled. A positive test result consists of a purple bar ascending the capillary to the scale reading calibrated in 10 mg/dL and 0.01 g/dL increments. In a negative test result, there is no visible purple segment of the capillary, or one below 0.02% w/v. If the "QA Spot" does not fill correctly, the test is invalid. Ten tests per hour can be performed using this device.

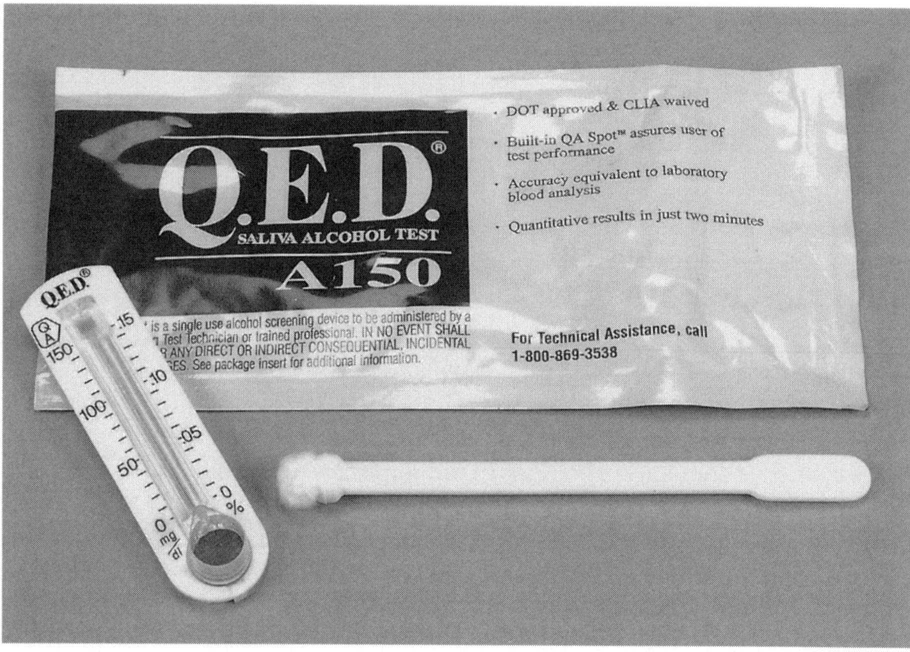

Fig. 1. Q.E.D. saliva-alcohol test device.

There is also a Q.E.D. A350 version of this device (not on the NHTSA Conforming Products List) that has a saliva-alcohol range of 0–345 mg/dL. The Q.E.D. A150 device has been the subject of several evaluations. In one clinical study, 42 subjects provided 168 blood specimens containing from 0 to 145 mg/dL of alcohol, and paired saliva specimens. At all BACs less than 10 mg/dL saliva testing was reported as negative, and in no instance did the saliva blood difference exceed 15 mg/dL *(33)*. Jones performed an in vitro and in vivo evaluation of the device. He found that the Q.E.D. device had a cutoff of approx 10–15 mg/dL; alcohol concentrations below this threshold yielded zero readings *(34)*. It was concluded that the Q.E.D. device is capable of distinguishing between saliva-alcohol concentrations of 20–40 mg/dL (0.02–0.04 g/dL) but that there was much greater uncertainty when Q.E.D. is used to estimate various blood-or-breath alcohol concentrations. It should be noted that despite its ability to display quantitative results, the Q.E.D. A150 device is only approved for use in alcohol screening tests under U. S. DOT rules.

All of the manufacturers listed in Table 1 have posted information about their saliva-alcohol test devices on the Internet, including a variety of technical details and some performance data.

5. Quality Assurance

As in other forms of alcohol analysis in biological specimens, quality assurance of saliva alcohol testing encompasses preanalytical, analytical, and postanalytical aspects. Therefore, a comprehensive program includes:

1. Test subject preparation and other test preparations
2. Specimen collection
3. The analysis process
4. Test result records and reports
5. Performance and proficiency testing, inspections and evaluations
6. Facilities and personnel

In recognition of the fact that workplace on-site saliva-alcohol testing is limited to screening test status under applicable federal regulations and in view of the characteristics and limitations of the single-use saliva alcohol test devices, the quality assurance program is necessarily simplified and modified, compared to those for clinical or evidential analysis for alcohol in other human biological specimens in a laboratory setting. This limited quality assurance/quality control feature is one major reason why all positive saliva-alcohol screening tests results should be confirmed by appropriate quantitative evidential analyses for alcohol in blood or breath. Confirmation of positive saliva-alcohol screening tests results by quantitative evidential breath-alcohol analysis is mandated by DOT rules.

Commercial products available for saliva-alcohol screening tests are single-use disposable devices which are essentially self-contained. Any individual single test device is not susceptible to multiple specimen testing, or to calibration in the field or to such normal quality control measures as analysis of replicates and accompanying control specimens used in within-run manual or automated analyses of alcohol in biological liquids. For these reasons, and in accordance with federal regulations *(16)*, many enumerated quality assurance activities and aspects have become the responsibility of the manufacturer of each disposable device rather than the user.

Good manufacturing practices and good quality assurance in the production of saliva-alcohol devices are fundamental on the part of the manufacturer. The maker of each device must determine such quality assurance factors as shelf-life of the device under various environmental storage conditions; acceptable environmental operating temperature range; and stability of result indication; and the usual analytical characteristics, e.g., accuracy, precision, results, sensitivity (limit of quantitation), specificity for ethanol, allowable variability in results for given saliva-alcohol target concentrations, etc. Pertinent information must also be provided to users of the device by means of package inserts or other printed information, together with directions for use of the device, precautions, sources for technical assistance, and any disclaimers or restrictions. For devices intended for clinical applications, the manufacturing, labeling, and other market clearance requirements of the U. S. Food and Drug Administration (FDA) applicable to such "medical devices" must be met.

The Centers for Medicare and Medicaid Services (CMS, formerly HCFA) have granted "waived" test status under the Clinical Laboratory Improvement Amendments of 1998 (CLIA) to some saliva-alcohol test devices *(35)*. This eliminates requirements for a daily quality control check and for test performance by a qualified laboratorian. Manufacturers of saliva-alcohol devices intended for DOT regulated workplace alcohol testing or traffic law enforcement uses must comply with pertinent FDA regulations. To be eligible for listing in the NHTSA Conforming Products List, such manufacturers must prepare, and submit for DOT approval, comprehensive labeling instructions for the devices and provide self-certification of compliance with FDA's Good Manufacturing Practices regulations for medical devices (21 CFR Part 820) and with FDA's labeling regulations for medical devices (21 CFR Part 809.10) *(16)*.

There are limitations on quality assurance and quality control practices which can be carried out in association with single-use disposable saliva-alcohol test devices. The focus of these practices, therefore, shifts from the customary fact-finding and interpretation of analytical system performance by the user to becoming fully and currently informed about the manufacturer's directions for use and other labeling information, and fully conforming to the directions and limitations specific to the particular device used. The user must establish under the relevant circumstances (location, ambient conditions of temperature, humidity, light, air quality, etc., and testing personnel) that the device when used in conformity with the manufacturer's directions, instructions, limitations, and other labeling information yields results within the manufacturer's designated limits. Such testing of functionality and performance can be done with acceptable control specimens containing alcohol at the critical concentration(s)—most commonly 0.02 or 0.04 g/dL. Alcohol in an artificial saliva matrix or aqueous alcohol solutions are appropriate as positive controls. Their validated target alcohol concentration(s) should be traceable to National Institute of Standards and Technology Aqueous Ethanol Standard Reference Material SRM 1828a. Other user checks at the time of a screening test include examination of the integrity of the factory-packaged device, expiration date for use of the device, and any obvious defects such as missing or damaged testing components. Some devices include an integral indication (e.g., a colored spot) that adequate sample introduction has occurred; that quality control feature must show the proper response before the test is completed and reported. Unknown positive control tests, or replicate control tests with a single disposable device are not possible. The best alternative is periodic performance of consecutive replicate tests of an alcohol-positive control specimen with individual devices randomly selected from each numbered lot. All should yield results within the model specifications. Negative results should be similarly checked by the user with alcohol-free water or with artificial saliva or with saliva from alcohol-free persons. Stability of the positive and negative result indications for at least 20 min should be established. Although single-use devices typically lack serial numbers, the applicable lot number should be recorded for each device used; and the procedures outlined above carried out for every lot.

The result indication given by single-use disposable devices is typically a visual signal or indication, such as a colored + symbol or a thermometer-like numbered scale reading, signifying a saliva-alcohol concentration of 0.02 g/dL or greater. Recording and reporting of these results must be accomplished manually by the tester, for one test and one device at a time. In unusual circumstances, a black-and-white or color photo or xerographic reproduction of the device, e.g., by copying machine or Polaroid camera, can be made within the result reading time limit if the necessary equipment is at hand. Any unusual or unexpected occurrences that prevent test completion or confound the result indication should be recorded in the test log. These include refusal to undergo testing, loss of a collected specimen by dropping it or failure of built-in quality control indicators in devices which have them. The latter should not be over interpreted. For example, a dark spot at the top of the sample capillary of the Q.E.D. A150 device merely indicates that the sample liquid has reached that location, presumably reflecting an adequately filled capillary tube; it does not indicate validity of either negative or positive test results. Details of any incomplete or otherwise faulty test should be recorded, and the test then repeated from start to finish, using a new device for saliva collection and testing. The time when a saliva-alcohol test was administered may become an issue in any controversies which later arise about the test result or its significance, and should be recorded as the date/time when saliva collection occurred, or when the saliva swab was inserted into the test device if manufacturer's directions or governmental regulations so require. For U. S. Department of Transportation-regulated saliva-alcohol screening tests, alcohol testing forms are prescribed by regulation *(16)*.

It is important to emphasize that any positive saliva-alcohol screening test in federally or state-regulated testing must be confirmed by a prescribed confirmatory test (quantitative evidential breath-alcohol analysis using devices on the applicable NHTSA Conforming Products List for federally [DOT]-regulated testing). In unregulated testing under employer policies or similar auspices, every positive screening test should also be followed by acceptable confirmatory testing for alcohol in blood, breath, or saliva before adverse action is taken against the tested person. Positive screening tests in clinical situations will generally lead to clinically-indicated follow-up such as blood-alcohol analysis, in accordance with the local organization's policies and practices. In clinical settings, many but not all of the quality assurance procedures described in the NCCLS Approved Guideline for Blood-Alcohol Testing in the Clinical Laboratory *(36)* will be applicable to saliva-alcohol testing. In any event, the overall general principle holds that no adverse action against an individual should occur based solely on an unconfirmed saliva-alcohol screening test result.

5.1. Testing Personnel

As with many on-site or clinical point-of-care or law enforcement field procedures there are some key qualifications and skills required of the persons who perform those tests. A particular problem is that these testers almost universally operate in the field with little, if any, technical supervision in marked contrast to the laboratory situation with its hierarchy of qualified and experienced workers and professional supervisors. In clinical settings the point-of-care testing is commonly performed by personnel already attending patients as a nurse, medical assistant or other health care specialist. In on-site workplace situations, breath or saliva-alcohol testing may occasionally occur at employer-provided medical facilities (as in association with an accident-related injury). Often, however, breath or saliva-alcohol tests on-site are coupled with collection of urine for other drug tests. Thus persons originally assigned as urine specimen collectors are also commonly designated as on-site screening testers because of their availability at the collection site. There are a few commonalities between urine collection and saliva-alcohol screening testing in workplace settings. The work involves knowledge of applicable regulations and policies, ability to follow directions and to execute the necessary paperwork, and to communicate effectively with persons subject to testing.

Persons who perform on-site alcohol screening tests on breath or saliva, most commonly for a federally regulated workforce, typically receive only one day or less of actual training and testing practice because of training costs and the deceptively simple nature of the task. Professional medical personnel and clinical laboratorians are deemed qualified as screening test technicians based on their education and professional background and experience. A person who has been qualified as a breath alcohol technician (BAT) under U. S. DOT rules (49 CFR Subpart J) and who has demonstrated proficiency in the operation of the nonevidential screening device he/she is using may act as a Screening Test Technician (STT) *(29)*. Any other individual may act as an STT under DOT rules if he/she has successfully completed a course of instruction concerning the procedures required by DOT for conducting alcohol screening tests and has demonstrated proficiency with the device in use *(29)*. The required minimum training consists of the DOT model course, or a course of instruction determined by the DOT's Office of Drug and Alcohol Policy and Compliance to be equivalent to the model course.

6. Interpretation and Use of Results

In the context of saliva-alcohol screening tests, the testing outcome of successfully completed tests should only be negative for alcohol in saliva, or positive for alcohol in saliva at the threshold concentration established by the device manufacturer, e.g., 0.02 g/dL. Positive screening test results must be followed by confirmatory evidential testing of breath-alcohol in federal and state regulated testing; and should be followed by quantitative blood, breath, or saliva-alcohol analysis in testing situations that are not governmentally regulated. Because the screening test is primarily intended to identify and eliminate further testing of alcohol free individuals, only a negative screening test result constitutes an endpoint.

There should be no interpolation of results between scale readings or color indications. The saliva-alcohol screening tests described in this chapter are not intended for forensic applications, and cannot be validly used for that purpose.

Positive saliva-alcohol test results as described herein, however analytically correct they may be, cannot be validly used to establish the presence or extent of alcoholic impairment of the tested person at the time of the test or at any other time. In particular, no attempt should be made to convert a positive individual saliva alcohol test result to a supposedly corresponding and coincident blood-alcohol concentration, in clinical or other settings. Results and testing outcomes which are incomplete or inconclusive should be so reported, with annotation of the apparent reason(s) and any subsequent action taken.

References

1. Chittenden, R. H., Mendel, L. B., and Jackson, H. C. (1898) A further study of the influence of alcohol and alcoholic drinks upon digestion, with special reference in secretion. *Amer. J. Physiol.* **1,** 164–209.
2. Bibliography on Saliva. ONR Report ACR-48. (1960) Washington, DC. Office of Naval Research, pp. 417–418.

3. DiGregorio, G. J., Piraino, A. J., and Ruch, E. (1978) Correlations of parotid saliva and blood ethanol concentrations. *Drug & Alcohol. Depend.* **3,** 43–50.
4. Jones, A. W. (1978) A rapid head-space method for ethyl alcohol determination in saliva samples. *Analyt. Biochem.* **86,** 589–596.
5. Böttger, G. and Feller, K. (1979). Konzentrationsbestimmung von Äthanol in Blut und Speichel. *Zbl. Pharm.* **118,** 328–331.
6. Jones, A. W. (1979) Assessment of an automated enzymatic method for ethanol determination in microsamples of saliva. *Scand. J. Clin. Lab. Invest.* **39,** 199–203.
7. Jones, A. W. (1979) Distribution of ethanol between saliva and blood in man. *Clin. & Exper. Pharmacol. & Physiol.* **6,** 53–59.
8. Jones, A. W. (1979) Inter- and intra-individual variations in the saliva/blood alcohol ratio during ethanol metabolism in man. *Clin. Chem.* **25,** 1394–1398.
9. McColl, K. E. L., Whiting, B., Moore, M. R., and Goldberg, A. (1979) Correlation of ethanol concentrations in blood and saliva. *Clin. Science* 56: 283–286.
10. Jones, A. W. (1981) Quantitative relationships among ethanol concentrations in blood, breath, saliva and urine during ethanol metabolism in man. In L. Goldberg (ed.), Alcohol, Drugs, and Traffic Safety, Vol. II. Stockholm. Almqvist & Wiksell International, pp. 550–569.
11. Tsukamoto, S., Karasawa, S., Sudo., T., Ueno, T., Seito, K. I., et al. (1983) Experimental study on ethanol concentration ratios of breath to body fluid. *Nihon Univ. J. Med.* **25,** 281–286.
12. Matzinger, D., Ervin, K. R., and Phillips, R. (1984) A solid state approach to alcohol testing. *Clin. Chem.* **30,** 1029–1030.
13. Ervin, K. R. and Giovannoni, A. (1985) New enzymatic test strip for alcohol in saliva: Its utility in roadside and consumer use. In Proceedings of the Section on Alcohol, Drugs and Traffic Safety, 34th International Congress on Alcoholism & Drug Dependence, Calgary, Alberta, Canada, pp. 1–14.
14. Schultz, E., Magerl, H., and Vock, R. (1986) Der Alkoholgehalt des Speichels und seine Verwertbarkeit. *Blutalkohol* **23,** 55–63.
15. Haeckel, R. and Bucklitsch, I. (1987) The comparability of ethanol concentrations in peripheral blood and saliva: The phenomenon of variation in saliva to blood concentration ratios. *J. Clin. Chem. Clin. Biochem.* **25,** 199–204.
16. National Highway Traffic Safety Administration. Highway safety programs; model specifications for screening devices to measure alcohol in bodily fluids. 59 *Federal Register* 7372–7378 (February 15, 1994).
17. National Highway Traffic Safety Administration. Highway safety programs; model specifications for screening devices to measure alcohol in bodily fluids. 59 *Federal Register* 39,382–39,390 (August 2, 1994).
18. Jones, A. W. (1993) Pharmacokinetics of ethanol in saliva: Comparison with blood and breath alcohol profiles, subjective feelings of intoxication and diminished performance. *Clin. Chem.* **39,** 1837–1844.
19. Drobitch, R. K. and Svensson, C. K. (1992) Therapeutic drug monitoring in saliva. An update. *Clinical Pharmacokinetics* **23,** 365–379.
20. Höld, K, M., et al. (1996) Saliva as an analytical tool in toxicology. *International J. of Drug Testing*, 1 (No. 1): 1–36. [Accessible via the Internet]

21. Dubowski, K. M. (1975) Studies in breath-alcohol analysis: Biological factors. *Z. Rechtsmedizin/ J. Legal Medicine* **76,** 93–117.
22. Saliva. (1981) In Geigy Scientific Tables. 8th ed., Vol. 1, ed. by C. Lentner. West Caldwell, NJ. Ciba-Geigy Corp., 114–122.
23. Linde, P. (1932) Der Übergang des Äthylalkohols in den Parotisspeichel beim Menschen. *Arch. Exp. Pharmacol.* **167,** 285–291.
24. Coldwell, B. B. and Smith, H. W. (1959) Alcohol levels in body fluids after ingestion of distilled spirits. *Canad. J. Biochem. and Physiol.* **37,** 43–52.
25. Jones, A. W. (1979) Distribution of ethanol between saliva and blood in man. *Clin. Exp. Pharmacol. Physiol.* 53–59.
26. Elbel, H. (1949) Über den Alkoholgehalt des Speichels. *Deut. Z. ges. gerichtliche Med.* **39,** 538–540.
27. Jones, A. W. (1979) Inter-and intra-individual variations in the saliva/blood alcohol ratio during ethanol metabolism in man. *Clin. Chem.* **25,** 1394–1398.
28. Q.E.D. Saliva Alcohol Test Fact Sheet. Bethlehem, PA. STC Diagnostics, 1994.
29. Office of the Secretary of Transportation, — Procedures for transportation workplace drug and alcohol testing programs. 49 Code of Federal Regulations Part 40, (August 1, 2001).
30. National Highway Traffic Safety Administration. Highway safety programs; conforming products list of screening devices to measure alcohol in bodily fluids. 60 *Federal Register* 42,214–42,215 (August 15, 1995).
31. Schwartz, R. H., et al. (1989) Evaluation of colorimetric dipstick test to detect alcohol in saliva: A pilot study. *Ann. Emergency Med.* **18,** 1001–1003.
32. ON-SITE Alcohol Assay for the Qualitative Dectection of Alcohol in Urine and Saliva. Indianapolis, IN. Roche Diagnostics, 1998.
33. Christopher, T. A. and Zeccarchi, J. A. (1992) Evaluation of the Q.E.D.™ saliva alcohol test: A new, rapid, accurate device for measuring ethanol in saliva. *Ann. Emergency Med.* **21,** 1135–1137.
34. Jones, A. W. (1995) Measuring ethanol in saliva with the Q.E.D.® enzymatic test device: Comparison of results with blood- and breath-alcohol concentrations. *J. Analyt. Toxicol.* **19,** 169–174.
35. Health Care Financing Administration. Program Memorandum - Transmittal No. AB-0980-25 Change Request #494: Tests approved by CDC as waived tests for CLIA. April 1998.
36. Dubowski, K. M., et al. (1997) Blood Alcohol Testing in the Clinical Laboratory; Approved Guideline. T/DM 6-A. Wayne, PA. National Committee for Clinical Laboratory Standards.

Chapter 8

Analysis of Drugs in Saliva

Vina Spiehler, Dene Baldwin, and Christopher Hand

1. Roadside or On-Site Saliva Drug Testing

1.1. Introduction

Investigation of the involvement of drugs in impaired driving would be facilitated by a roadside test for drugs in saliva such as currently exists for alcohol in breath. Collection of saliva is simple and noninvasive. It can be carried out by the suspect while under observation. The feasibility of detecting drugs in saliva samples obtained from impaired drivers was first investigated by Peel et al. *(1)*. They found that the presence of drugs in saliva correlated well with officer judgements of driving while intoxicated.

1.2. Saliva Collection

The greatest advantage of saliva in roadside testing is the possibility of having the sample collected by the donor under observation shortly after the time of the incident. Saliva collection is noninvasive and can be done by the donor themselves in most situations. An exception may be when the donor is unconscious or too sedated to follow instructions.

Peel et al. *(1)* asked DWI suspects to expectorate into a test tube with or without sour candy stimulus. A similar approach was taken by Cone et al. *(2)* at the Addiction Research Center (National Institute on Drug Abuse, Baltimore, MD) in controlled administration clinical studies. Modern saliva collection devices generally use an absorbent material on a stick similar to that employed for saliva alcohol tests. For example, the Epitope saliva-sampling device con-

From: *Forensic Science: On-Site Drug Testing*
Edited by: A. J. Jenkins and B. A. Goldberger © Humana Press, Inc., Totowa, NJ

sists of an absorbent paper pad impregnated with citric salt on a plastic straw. Following collection, the paper is placed in a tube with preservative liquid and shipped to the laboratory for analysis. Cozart's RapiScan (Cozart Biosciences, Abingdon, Oxfordshire, UK) uses a detachable absorbent cellulose pad on an indicator handle. After the indicator has turned from white to blue indicating that 1 mL of saliva has been collected on the pad, the pad can be detached and stored in a test tube containing preservative buffer until analysis. The Avitar (Canton, MA) collector uses a proprietary dental absorbent which absorbs saliva when placed in the mouth for a few minutes. The Draeger Securetec saliva test attempts to wipe the tongue with a wiping pin and then transfer the saliva collected by washing it onto the Drugwipe™ on-site test developed for testing surfaces for traces of drugs.

BioQuant (Irvine, CA) developed a small plastic sack (SalivaSac) composed of semi-permeable membranes which contains high molecular weight sugars. When placed in the mouth, osmotic pressure drives an ultra-filtrate of saliva into the interior of the sack *(3)*. The drawback is that the sack requires from 10 to 20 min (depending on the sack size) for collection of sufficient fluid for testing.

LifePoint (Ontario, CA) is developing an aspirator machine that will draw saliva directly from the mouth of the test subject through a tube with a disposable individual sterile mouthpiece. For on-site testing the saliva will pass directly into the analyzer, eliminating the need to elute saliva from the collector pad with buffer and transfer into an immunoassay cartridge.

1.3. Cutoff Concentrations in Saliva

The foremost question in the application of saliva testing to forensic casework is "What is the relationship of saliva positive results to blood drug concentrations?" Drug concentrations in saliva reflect the free, unbound parent drug and lipophilic metabolites circulating in the blood. Since these are the forms of the drug which cross the blood-brain barrier and effect performance and behavior, saliva is a good specimen for detecting drug involvement in driving behavior or impairment of performance. An immunoassay for drugs in saliva must be able to detect the parent drug or lipophilic metabolites. It must also be able to detect drugs at concentrations which appear in saliva.

Drug and lipophilic metabolite concentrations in saliva are a function of the drug's pKa, plasma and saliva pH and the fraction of drug bound to saliva and plasma protein as shown by the following form of the Henderson-Hasselbach equation for saliva. S/P is the saliva to plasma ratio:

$$S/P = \frac{[1 + 10\,(pKd\text{-}pHs)]}{[1 + 10(pKd\text{-}pHp)]} + \frac{fp}{fs} \qquad \text{basic drugs}$$

$$S/P = \frac{[1 + 10(pHs - pKa)]}{[1 + 10(pHp - pKa)]} + \frac{fp}{fs} \qquad \text{acidic drugs}$$

Where S is the drug concentration in saliva and P is the drug concentration in plasma, pKd is the log of the ionization constant for basic drugs, pKa is the log ionization constant for acidic drugs and pHs is the pH of saliva and pHp is the pH of the plasma. fp is the fraction of drug protein bound in plasma and fs is the fraction protein bound in saliva. Dawes and Jenkins demonstrated that saliva pH is inversely proportional to flow rate and the re-absorption of sodium in the salivary tubules *(4)*. At faster flow rates, less sodium is re-absorbed in the tubules on the way from the saliva glands to the saliva outlets in the mouth and the pH raises. For this reason unstimulated saliva has a low pH and stimulated saliva has a higher pH.

For drugs that have a pKa between 5.5 and 8.5, the saliva/plasma ratio may vary between stimulated and unstimulated saliva. This is true of many drugs of abuse. For this reason it is more conservative to use a cutoff value for drugs of abuse in saliva rather than to determine the absolute concentration.

The theoretical range of saliva/plasma ratios over a saliva pH range of 6.4–7.6 were calculated for cocaine, amphetamine, methamphetamine, 6-acetylmorphine, morphine, codeine, methadone, and diazepam and compared to published saliva/plasma ratios *(5)*. The lowest ratio values were multiplied by the lower limit plasma levels for therapeutic or recreational effects from Uges *(6)*. The resulting suggested cutoffs for saliva were: cocaine, 60 ng/mL; amphetamine, 56 ng/mL; methamphetamine, 40 ng/mL; 6-acetylmorphine, 30 ng/mL; morphine, 40 ng/mL; codeine, 66 ng/mL; methadone, 50 ng/mL; and diazepam, 3.6 ng/mL *(5)*.

1.4. Amphetamines

Amphetamine, methamphetamine, methylenedioxymethamphetamine (MDMA), methylenedioxyamphetamine (MDA) and other amphetamine class drugs have been detected in saliva. Parent drug rather than amphetamine metabolites are found in saliva. The saliva/plasma ratio for amphetamine is 2.76 and for methamphetamine is 3.98. After administration of 10 mg amphetamine, plasma levels ranged from 1 to 20 ng/mL and saliva concentrations ranged from 10 to 60 ng/mL *(7)*. Based on the therapeutic range of 20–150 ng/mL for amphetamine *(6)*, positives at a cutoff value of 56 ng/mL amphetamine or greater would indicate pharmacologically significant levels of amphetamine drugs in blood. The Cozart RapiScan cutoff is 10 ng/mL amphetamine in diluted oral fluid or 30 ng/mL amphetamine or MDA in saliva. This would correspond to a plasma concentration of approx 10 ng/mL amphetamine or MDA in plasma. The crossreactivity of the antibody is 1% for methamphetamine or MDMA so a concentration of 1000 ng/mL methamphetamine or MDMA in saliva would be required to read positive on the device. This would be equivalent to a plasma concentration of 500 ng/mL methamphetamine or MDMA. An alternative test is the single MAMP/MDMA cartridge with cutoffs of 50 ng/mL of MDMA or MAMP in the diluted sample or 150 ng/mL in the neat saliva.

1.5. Benzodiazepines

Benzodiazepines have an unfavorable saliva to plasma ratio (S/P = 0.01–0.08 *[8]*). However, cases of driving under the influence of benzodiazepines often occur with persons who, with long-term over use of benzodiazepines, have developed tolerance and present with blood levels greater than therapeutic levels. In several cases, the authors have observed diazepam blood levels greater than 1 µg/mL. This would correspond to a saliva concentration of 30 ng/mL which might not be detected by immunoassay. The current Cozart RapiScan cutoff is 20 ng/mL temazepam or 30 ng/mL diazepam in diluted oral fluid or 60 and 90 ng/mL respectively in saliva.

However, Cozart Bioscience Ltd. is about to introduce a new antibenzodiazepine antibody with broader crossreactivity and significantly lower detection limits (*see* Table 1).

1.6. Cannabinoids

Δ^9-Tetrahydrocannabinol (THC) and 11-nor-Δ^9-THC-carboxylic acid (THCA) are excreted in only trace amounts in saliva. Idowu and Caddy *(9)* calculated a theoretical saliva/plasma ratio of 0.099–0.129 for Δ^9-tetrahydrocannabiniol and of 0.060–0.099 for 11-OH-Δ^9-tetrahydrocannabinol. The measured saliva/plasma ratio after intravenous injection of labeled cannabidiol was 0.0012 *(10)*. However the measured saliva/plasma ratio for THC after smoking marijuana was 10 and was found to be a function of the time since smoking *(2)*. Cannabinoids in saliva are due to residuals left in the mouth during ingestion or smoking of marijuana or marijuana products.

A rather high cutoff concentration of 100 ng/mL THC is recommended based on literature reports *(5)*. Cone et al. *(2)* found saliva levels of greater than 100 ng/mL for an hour after smoking a 3% THC marijuana cigarette. Menkes et al. *(11)* found that saliva levels correlated with rapid heart rate and psychological feelings of "high". At a cutoff concentration of greater than 100 ng/mL, a positive saliva result for THC will correspond to blood levels which produce these common physiological symptoms which indicate recent smoking of marijuana. The Cozart RapiScan cutoff is 10 ng/mL THCA in diluted oral fluid or 30 ng/mL THCA in saliva. Since the crossreactivity of the Cozart RapiScan cartridge antibody to THC is 10% relative to THCA, this is equivalent to a cutoff of 300 ng/mL for THC in saliva. From the relationship published by Menkes *(11)*, this would indicate recent use (1–2 h) or ingestion of very potent marijuana.

1.7. Cocaine

In unstimulated saliva, cocaine is trapped in saliva and the saliva/plasma ratio may be greater than five *(3,12)*. In stimulated saliva, the saliva/plasma ratio ranges from 0.5 to 3.0 *(13–16)*. Benzoylecgonine is also found in saliva at concentrations approximately equal to those in blood. The Cozart RapiScan uses a cutoff of 10 ng/mL benzoylecgonine or 25 ng/mL cocaine in diluted oral fluid which is equivalent to 30 and 75 ng/mL respectively in saliva. If this is caused by the inactive metabolite benzoylecgonine, it is unlikely that the person was driving under the influence of cocaine. The Cozart RapiScan antibody has 40% crossreactivity with cocaine. A concentration of greater than 75 ng/mL cocaine in saliva would most likely correspond to pharmacologically significant concentrations of cocaine in blood, or in excess of approx 25 ng/mL cocaine in plasma after snorted or injected cocaine. If cocaine is smoked then, as is the case with marijuana, very high levels will be detected in saliva in the period after smoking due to deposition in the oral cavity.

1.8. Opiates

The major metabolite found in saliva after heroin use is 6-acetyl morphine (6-AM, S/P ratio of 6) *(17–19)*. After codeine administration, codeine is found in saliva with a saliva to plasma ratio of 3.3 and after morphine administration, morphine may be found in a saliva to plasma ratio of 0.2 *(17)*. The Cozart RapiScan cutoff is 10 ng/mL morphine equivalents in diluted oral fluid or 30 ng/mL morphine equivalents in saliva and the Cozart RapiScan antibody is equally cross-reactive with morphine, 6-AM, heroin, dihydrocodeine and codeine. An opiate positive in saliva with the Cozart RapiScan would indicate the recent use of heroin or codeine or the use of a large amount of dihydrocodeine, pholcodeine or morphine. For example, a saliva opiate positive due to 6-AM at a cutoff of 10 ng/mL in dilution or 30 ng/mL in saliva corresponds to a greater than 0.5 ng/mL concentration of 6-AM in plasma. A saliva morphine concentration in excess of 10 ng/mL corresponds to a plasma concentration of greater than 50 ng/mL free morphine.

If heroin is snorted or smoked, then very high levels would be detected in saliva due to deposition of drug in the oral cavity *(15–19)*.

1.9. Conclusion

Saliva drug concentrations are related to the blood concentration of the unbound, unionized parent drug or its lipophilic metabolites. Therefore saliva concentrations are a function of circulating drug levels. However, without knowing the instantaneous saliva pH, saliva drug concentrations can not be extrapolated to blood drug concentrations. Saliva concentrations can be exceptionally high when the route of administration is smoking of the drug such as occurs with marijuana, cocaine and possibly amphetamine and opiates. When appropriate cutoff concentrations are employed, saliva drug presence may be associated with recent drug use and in some cases with being under the influence of the drug.

2. Cozart RapiScan Saliva Drug Test System

2.1. Introduction

The Cozart RapiScan Saliva Drug Test is a fully integrated oral fluid testing system composed of a saliva collection system, a test cartridge and a battery-powered Cozart RapiScan instrument.

2.2. Testing Principle

The Cozart RapiScan Saliva Drug Test cassette (Fig. 1) uses lateral transfer immunoassay with colloidal gold-labeled anti-drug antibodies. The cassette result (binding of gold-labled antibody to immobilized drug in the absence of drug in sample) is monitored by the portable, battery-powered Cozart RapiScan reader (Fig. 2) and reported on the display screen. In addition, if one or more positive results are obtained, then a light on the face of the reader will appear red in color. If all results are negative the light will appear green.

The results can be printed out on an optional battery-powered Cozart RapiScan printer to provide a permanent record of results. Results are sent to the printer via the multi-functional port which also serves to charge the instrument batteries and to up-load new versions of the instrument software via an internet interface module. This access to the latest software allows new tests or drug combinations to be released and made available to any user, no matter how remote, provided they have internet access. Users will therefore always be able to run the latest software available from the manufacturer. This software upgrade facility is currently managed by Cozart field engineers, available to any Cozart RapiScan system user who has the necessary interface module.

The saliva specimen is collected from the mouth using the Cozart RapiScan collection pad and placed in a test tube containing 2 mL of assay buffer (Fig. 3). When placed in the mouth, the collection pad absorbs exactly 1 mL of saliva, which is indicated by development of a blue color in the indicator section of the handle. The pad is then placed in the tube, where it is diluted with 2 mL of assay buffer fluid. The pad is separated from the plastic

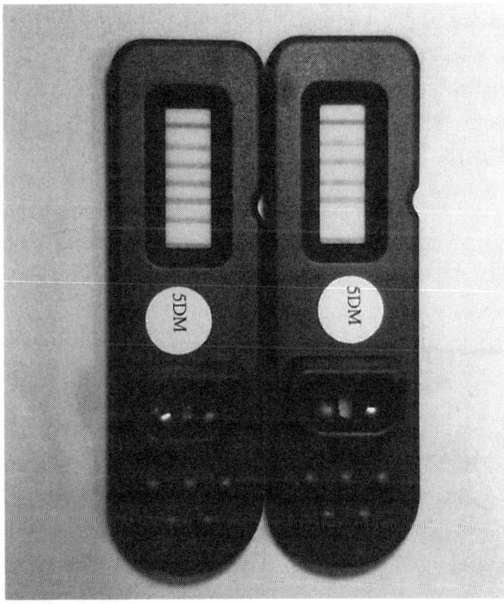

Fig. 1. Cozart RapiScan Saliva drug test cassette.

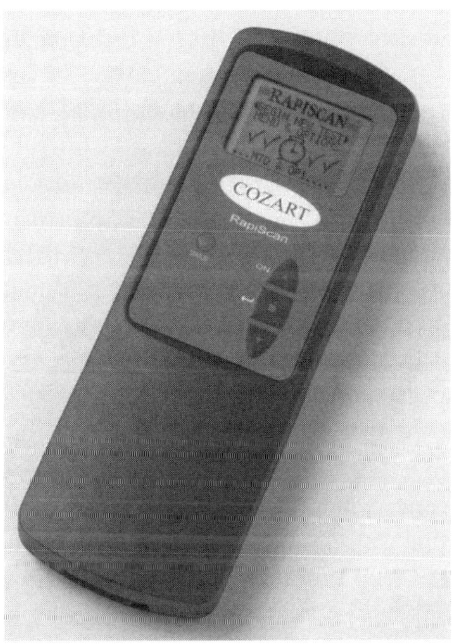

Fig. 2. Cozart RapiScan reader.

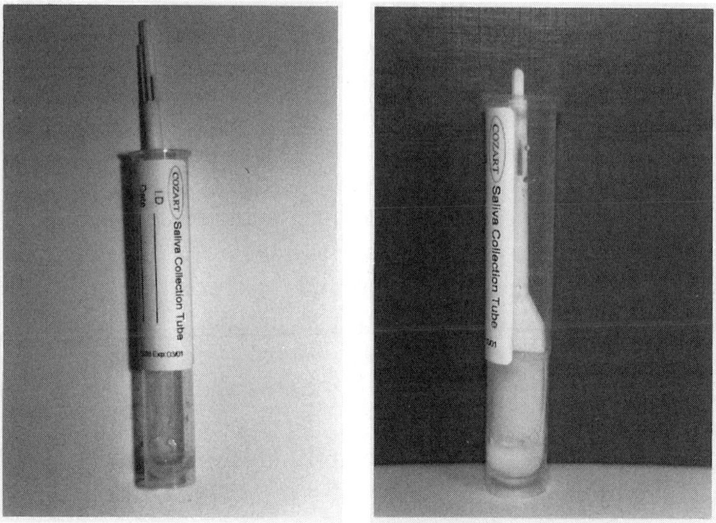

Fig. 3. Cozart RapiScan collection pad and test tube.

handle along the perforated edge. After removing the cap and plastic collector handle, the cotton pad is compressed using a dispense filter separator plunger which is used to dispense six drops of the saliva/buffer mixture on to the cassette.

For each test, a fresh disposable cassette and collection kit are used. The cassette or cartridge is inserted into the hand-held Cozart RapiScan instrument for incubation. The saliva/run fluid rehydrates gold-labeled antidrug antibodies contained within the cartridge. This mixture travels by capillary action across an array of immobilized drug sites. Absence of color development at an immobilized drug position indicates drug presence. The quality control position contains antimouse IgG to ascertain that complete lateral transfer of specimen has been achieved.

Once the reagent appears on the white membrane (this takes 2 to 30 s) the cassette can be inserted into the reader. The reader will time the incubation (12 min for a 5 panel test, between 3–5 minutes for single and two panel tests) and indicate that the countdown is complete with a buzzer. Results are shown on the display screen as a table of drug groups abbreviated with three letter codes AMP, BZO, COC, MTD, THC, OPI and the results as positive or negative ("POS" or "NEG"). The back-lit screen for reading results, timing, quality control, and error messages is similar to those used in mobile phones, on-site glucose analyzers, and hand-held computers. In addition to the message, if all results are negative, a green light appears above the power switch. If any of the results are positive a red light appears. A flashing red light indicates a new message or result is about to appear on the screen.

If the saliva screening test is positive, the remainder of the sample (1.75 mL fluid) and the whole of a second sample of saliva collected at the same time as the first or at the time of the positive reading (10 to 15 min later), are capped, tamper-proof tape is placed across the cap and the samples are sent to the designated laboratory for confirmation.

The collector pad has a dead volume of approx 1 mL and the Cozart RapiScan cartridge requires 0.12 mL for completion. The same volume is required for single, dual or multiple drug panels. The excess volume of saliva/run fluid mixture was designed to allow confirmation to be performed on the collected sample.

Alternatively, a urine or blood sample may be collected and sent with the remainder of the presumptive positive saliva to the laboratory, depending on the preference of the contracting laboratory.

2.3. *Quality Control*

The device contains internal quality control checks. These consist of the operational controls of each cassette for blank reading between the test lines and that a correct result for the IgG reference band is obtained.

At the start of each day of testing a battery check is performed and the Cozart RapiScan instrument is checked using the positive and negative quality control cassettes. These quality control cassettes contain printed results that correspond to the band intensity obtained with positive and negative samples, respectively.

It is recommended that saliva collection and testing be recorded on a checklist sheet similar to that used for saliva alcohol testing. Saliva collection and testing should be performed by technicians trained to use the Cozart RapiScan test. Collector/testers should participate in any available saliva proficiency testing survey. Training is similar to that provided for breath alcohol or saliva alcohol collection and testing by the testing agency.

2.4. *Interpretation*

The Cozart RapiScan cassettes use cutoffs that will correspond to saliva levels and blood levels of drug or time of dose which may be expected to cause impairment of human performance, specifically driving impairment. Each cassette can test for five drug classes: for example amphetamine, benzodiazepines, cannabis, cocaine, and opiates (THC 5 Panel Drug Test) or amphetamine, benzodiazepines, cocaine, methadone and opiates (MTD 5 Panel Drug Test). The cassette cutoffs are 10 ng/mL of amphetamine, 10 ng/mL of morphine equivalents, 10 ng/mL of methadone, 10 ng/mL of benzoylecgonine, 10 ng/mL of THCA, 100 ng/mL of Δ^9-THC, and 30 ng/mL of diazepam in the diluted oral fluid. The Cozart RapiScan uses 1 mL of saliva collected with the saliva collection pad and diluted 1:3 with elution buffer. With the dilution factor of three in the Cozart RapiScan procedure, this is equivalent to saliva concentrations of 30 ng/mL of amphetamine, 30 ng/mL of morphine equivalents, 30 ng/mL of methadone, 30 ng/mL of benzoylecgonine, 30 ng/mL of THCA, or 300 ng/mL of Δ^9-THC, and 90 ng/mL of diazepam respectively.

The antibody crossreactivity for each drug class is listed in Table 1. The values represent concentrations that would produce a negative or positive response in the oral fluid. Consideration of the dilution factor of three from the Cozart RapiScan specimen collection should be applied for further interpretation (i.e., an amphetamine positive of greater than 10 ng/mL in oral fluid would have an original saliva concentration of greater than 30 ng/mL). Noncrossreacting compounds are shown in Table 2.

2.5. *Performance*

Controlled dosing studies of codeine were conducted to assess the sensitivity and specificity of the Cozart RapiScan Saliva Drug Test for Opiates. Codeine concentrations have been used as a model for opiate pharmacokinetics in alternative fluids because while codeine has pharmacokinetic parameters similar to heroin, 6-AM, and morphine, its pharmacodynamics are relatively safe and benign allowing codeine to be used in clinical studies with healthy volunteers.

In this study six volunteers (four male, two female) received 16 mg codeine, 2 × 8 mg Codeine and 500 mg Paracetamol (Codamol tablets, Sterwin Medicines, Guildford, Surrey, UK). Saliva specimens were obtained and measured at 0, 15 min, 30 min, 60 min, 4 h, 6 h, 8 h, and 24 h after dosing. One mL of saliva was obtained at each time point using the Cozart saliva collection pad and indicator. The indicator in the plastic handle turned blue when 1 mL of saliva had been collected. The pad was then placed in a test tube containing 2 mL elution fluid and separated from the plastic handle. Four drops of diluted saliva were placed in the Cozart RapiScan opiate single cartridge, which was then inserted into the Cozart RapiScan hand-held reader. After a 5-min incubation the RapiScan reader indicated "Opiates Positive" or "Opiates Negative". The cutoff concentration for the RapiScan was 10 ng/mL morphine equivalents. The remainder of the diluted saliva was analyzed by Cozart Microplate EIA. A Cozart RapiScan Opiates Positive response was present in

Table 1
Drugs and Drug Metabolite Concentrations Together With the Cozart RapiScan Response at These Concentrations

Drug/Metabolite	ng/mL	Cozart RapiScan Response
Amphetamines[a]		
d-Amphetamine	10	AMP Positive
Methylenedioxyamphetamine	10	AMP Positive
d-Methamphetamine	1,000	AMP Positive
Methylenedioxymeth-amphetamine	1,000	AMP Positive
Imipramine	1,000	AMP Positive
MBDB	10,000	AMP Positive
MDEA	10,000	AMP Positive
Ephedrine	10,000	AMP Negative
Fenfluramine	10,000	AMP Negative
Tyramine	10,000	AMP Positive
Cannabinoids[a]		
Δ^9-THC	100	THC Positive
THC-COOH	10	THC Positive
11-OH-Δ^9-THC	200	THC Positive
Cocaine[a]		
Cocaine	25	COC Positive
Benzoylecgonine	10	COC Positive
Methadone[b]	10	MTD Positive
Opiates[a]		
Morphine	10	OPI Positive
6-Acetylmorphine	10	OPI Positive
Heroin (Diacetylmorphine)	10	OPI Positive
Dihydrocodeine	5	OPI Positive
Codeine	10	OPI Positive
Morphine-3-glucuronide	15	OPI Positive
Pholcodeine	10	OPI Positive
Nalorphine	15	OPI Positive

(continued)

[a]These derivatives have been tested at 10,000 ng/mL and found not to cause a positive for the other Cozart RapiScan drug tests.

[b]Methadone has been tested at 10,000 ng/mL and found not to cause a positive for the Opiates RapiScan drug test.

Table 1 (continued)
Drugs and Drug Metabolite Concentrations Together With the Cozart RapiScan Response at These Concentrations

	Current		New	
Drug/Metabolite	ng/mL	Cozart RapiScan Response	ng/mL	Cozart RapiScan Response
Benzodiazepines[c]				
Temazepam	20	BZO Positive	10	BZO Positive
Oxazepam	1,000	BZO Positive	20	BZO Positive
Diazepam	30	BZO Positive	20	BZO Positive
Desmethyldiazepam	2,000	BZO Negative	10	BZO Positive
Alprazolam	500	BZO Negative	20	BZO Positive
Nitrazepam	10,000	BZO Negative	20	BZO Positive
Prazepam	10,000	BZO Negative	10,000	BZO Positive
Triazolam	10,000	BZO Negative	50	BZO Positive
Lorazepam	—	—	50	BZO Positive
Flunitrazepam	—	—	20	BZO Positive
Clobazam	—	—	10	BZO Positive
7-Aminoflunitrazepam	—	—	250	BZO Positive

[c]These derivatives have been tested at 10,000 ng/mL and found not to cause a positive for the other Cozart RapiScan drug tests.

Table 2
Noncrossreacting Compounds

Noncrossreacting	Cozart RapiScan Response
Amitriptyline	AMP, BZO, THC, COC, OPI Negative
Amobarbital	AMP, BZO, THC, COC, OPI Negative
Buprenorphine	AMP, BZO, THC, COC, OPI Negative
Cotinine	AMP, BZO, THC, COC, OPI Negative
Chlorothiazide	AMP, BZO, THC, COC, OPI Negative
Dextromethorphan	AMP, BZO, THC, COC, OPI Negative
Gentamycin	AMP, BZO, THC, COC, OPI Negative
LSD	AMP, BZO, THC, COC, OPI Negative
Paracetamol	AMP, BZO, THC, COC, OPI Negative
Phencyclidine	AMP, BZO, THC, COC, OPI Negative
Phenobarbital	AMP, BZO, THC, COC, OPI Negative
Ranitidine	AMP, BZO, THC, COC, OPI Negative
Quinalbarbitone	AMP, BZO, THC, COC, OPI Negative

These compounds have been tested at 10,000 ng/mL and found not to cause a positive for any Cozart RapiScan drug tests.

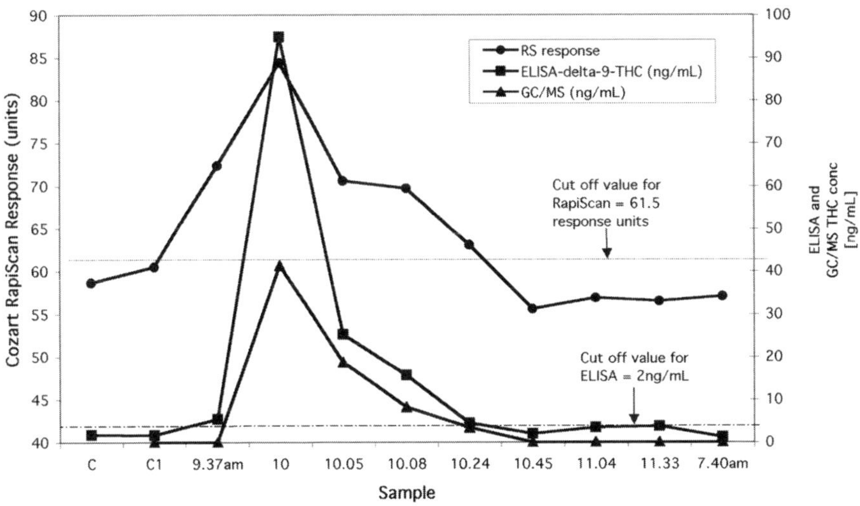

Fig. 4. Cannabis levels in saliva following smoking marijuana. Comparison of Cozart RapiScan vs ELISA vs GC/MS results.

all subjects at the first 15 min specimen and persisted as long as the saliva codeine concentrations were greater than 15 ng/mL by Cozart Microplate EIA. The saliva of volunteers not taking codeine (n = 23) all displayed "Opiates Negative".

Clinical studies with the Cozart RapiScan in controlled administration of marijuana are currently underway. Figure 4 shows the test response for a person who has smoked a single marijuana cigarette.

It should be noted that many of the publications in the field of saliva drug testing have focused on giving small one-off doses to volunteers. The use of the Cozart Rapiscan in a number of drug dependency clinics has detected a significant number of positives for all drug groups which have been confirmed by GC/MS (data being compiled for publication). This indicates that the street doses taken are both higher than those used in other publications and with more frequency. Testing of clinical samples from drug dependency clinics and prisons has confirmed the validity of the Cozart Rapiscan System.

2.6. Adulteration

The manufacturer recommends a 10 min observation period in which the donor does not smoke, consume food or drink before collection of the saliva sample. In the authors' experiences, a person cannot retain saliva, especially saliva containing liquid or solids, in the mouth for more than three minutes without swallowing or dribbling. Rinsing of the mouth is not required.

2.7. Unique Features

The unique features of the Cozart RapiScan are that it can be read as a written report displayed on a screen, or be printed by a battery-powered printer to create a permanent record of the results. The immunoassays have antibodies with crossreactivity to drug analytes found in saliva. The cutoff concentrations have been set for use in DUI or DWI testing. The size and configuration of the instrument resulted from specifications for roadside testing by law enforcement.

References

1. Peel, H. W., Perrigo B. J., and Mikhael N. Z. (1984), Detection of drugs in saliva of impaired drivers. *J. Forensic Sci.* **29,** 185–189.
2. Cone, E. J. (1993) Saliva Testing for Drugs of Abuse. *Ann. New York Acad. Sci.* **694,** 91–127.
3. Schraum, W. Smith R. H., Craig, P. A., and Kidwell, D. A., (1992) Drugs of abuse in saliva: A Review. *J. Anal. Toxicology.* **16,** 1–9.
4. Dawes, C. and Jenkins, G. N. (1964) The effects of different stimuli on the composition of saliva in man. *J. Physiol.* **170,** 86–100.
5. Spiehler, V. R (2000) Cutoff Concentrations for Drugs of Abuse in Saliva for DUI, DWI or other Driving-Related Crimes. (M. Kala ed.) *1999 TIAFT Proceedings.* Cracow, Poland.
6. Uges, D. (1996) Tables of Therapeutic, Toxic and Fatal Drug Concentrations *TIAFT Bulletin.* **26(1),** 1–75.
7. Wan S. H., Matin S. B., Azarnoff, D.L., (1974) Kinetics, salivary excretion of amphetamine isomers and effect of urinary pH. *Clin. Pharmacol. Ther.* **23,** 585–590.
8. DiGregorio, G. H., Piraino, A. J., and Ruch, E. (1978) Diazepam concentrations in parotid saliva, mixed saliva and plasma. *Clin. Pharmacol. Ther.* **24,** 720–725.
9. Idowu, O. R. and Caddy, B. (1982) A review of the use of saliva in the forensic detection of drugs and other chemicals. *J. Forensic Sci. Soc.* **22,** 123–135.
10. Ohlsson, A. et al, (1986) Single dose kinetics of deuterium-labeled cannabidiol in man after smoking and intravenous administration. *Biomed. Environ. Mass Spectrom.* **13,** 77–83.
11. Menkes, D. B. et al, (1991) "Salivary THC following cannabis smoking correlates with subjective intoxication and heart rate," *Psychopharmacol.* **103,** 277–279.
12. Schramm, W., Craig, P. A., Smith R. H., and Berger, G. E., (1992) Cocaine and benzoylecgonine in saliva, serum and urine. *Clin. Chem.* **39,** 481–487.
13. Cone, E. J., Kumor, K, Thompson, L. K. and Sherer, M., (1988) Correlation of saliva cocaine levels with plasma levels and with pharmacologic effects after intravenous cocaine administration in human subjects. *J. Anal. Toxicol.* **12,** 200–206.
14. Cone, E. J. and Weddington, W. W., (1989) Prolonged occurrence of cocaine in human saliva and urine after chronic use. *J. Anal. Toxicol.* **13,** 65–68.

15. Jenkins, A. J., Oyler, J. M., and Cone, E. E., (1995) Comparison of heroin and cocaine concentrations in saliva with concentrations in blood and plasma. *J. Anal. Toxicol.* **19,** 359–374.
16. Cone, E. J., Oyler, J., and Darwin, W. D., (1997) Cocaine disposition in saliva following intravenous, intranasal and smoked administration. *J. Anal. Toxicol.* **21,** 465–475.
17. Cone, E. J. (1990) Testing Human Hair for Drugs of Abuse, I. Individual dose and time profiles of morphine and codeine in plasma, saliva, urine and beard compared to drug induced effects on pupils and behavior. *J. Anal Toxicol.* **14,** 1–7.
18. Cone, E. J., Holicky, B. A., Grant, T. M., Darwin, W. D., and Goldberger, B. A., (1993) Pharmacokinetics and pharmacodynamics of intranasal "snorted" heroin. *J. Anal Toxicol.* **17,** 327–337.
19. Jenkins, A. J., Keenan, R. M., Henningfield, J. E., and Cone, E. J., (1994) Pharmacokinetics and pharmacodynamics of smoked heroin. *J. Anal. Toxicol.* **18,** 317–330.

Chapter 9

AccuSign Drugs of Abuse Test

Johannes J. W. Ros and Marinus G. Pelders

1. Introduction

Several methods are available for screening drugs of abuse including fluorescence polarization immunoassay (FPIA), enzyme immunoassay (EMIT) and radioimmunoassay (RIA). In addition, assays are available that allow visual and timely detection (e.g., within 10 min) performed by individuals with minimal training and without the need for expensive equipment.

In this chapter information is presented concerning the principle of the AccuSign test, how it is performed, and discussion of problems of interpretation. Finally, a summary of studies which have evaluated the device is presented. It should be noted that there is little published information about the performance of the AccuSign slide tests.

2. The AccuSign Test Slide

In Fig. 1 the device to perform the AccuSign test is shown. The test comprises a 7 × 3.5 cm slide. The slide contains a sample well (S), in which three drops of urine are added. In the reading (T) zone the test result is read. The Control (C) zone measures the validity of the test result.

Single drugs tests are available in addition to several multiple drugs tests (Table 1).

The AccuSign, drugs of abuse test is a competitive immunoassay. During incubation, the three drops of urine move through the membrame in the slide and migrate to the reading and control zone. This reading zone contains an

From: *Forensic Science: On-Site Drug Testing*
Edited by: A. J. Jenkins and B. A. Goldberger © Humana Press, Inc., Totowa, NJ

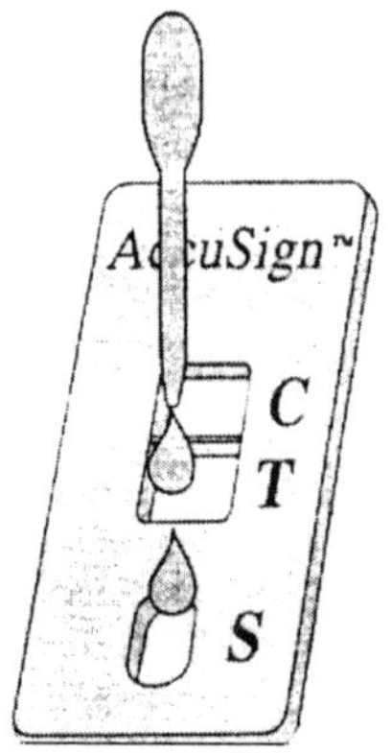

Fig. 1. AccuSign test-slide.

Table 1
List of Drug-of-Abuse Slide Tests of AccuSign

Device name	Target analyte	Cutoff concentration (ng/mL)
COC (cocaine)	benzoylecgonine	300
THC (cannabinoids)	11-nor-Δ^9-THC-COOH	50
mAMP (methamphetamine)	*d*-methamphetamine	1000
OPI (opiates)	morphine	300
AMP (amphetamines)	*d*-amphetamine	1000
PCP (phencyclidine)	phencyclidine	25
BAR (barbiturates)	secobarbital	300
BZO (benzodiazepines)	oxazepam	300
MDN (methadone)	methadone	300
TCA (tricyclic antidepressants)	nortriptyline	1000
d.a.u. 2 panel	11-nor-Δ^9-THC-COOH	50
THC/COC	benzoylecgonine	300
d.a.u. 2 panel	secobarbital	300
BAR/BZO	oxazepam	300
d.a.u. 3 panel	11-nor-Δ^9-THC-COOH	50
THC/COC/OPI	benzoylecgonine	300
	morphine	300
d.a.u. 3 panel	secobarbital	300
BAR/BZO/PCP	oxazepam	300
	phencyclidine	25
d.a.u. 3 panel	secobarbital	300
BAR/BZO/MDN	oxazepam	300
	methadone	300

Table 1 (continued)
List of Drug-of-Abuse Slide Tests of AccuSign

Device name	Target analyte	Cutoff concentration (ng/mL)
d.a.u. 4 panel THC/COC/OPI/mAMP	11-nor-Δ^9-THC-COOH	50
	benzoylecgonine	300
	morphine	300
	d-methamphetamine	1000
d.a.u. 4 panel THC/COC/OPI/AMP	11-nor-Δ^9-THC-COOH	50
	benzoylecgonine	300
	morphine	300
	d-amphetamine	1000
d.a.u. 5 panel THC/COC/OPI/AMP/PCP	11-nor-Δ^9-THC-COOH	50
	benzoylecgonine	300
	morphine	300
	d-amphetamine	1000
	phencyclidine	25
d.a.u. 5 panel THC/COC/OPI/mAMP/PCP	11-nor-Δ^9-THC-COOH	50
	benzoylecgonine	300
	morphine	300
	d-methamphetamine	1000
	phencyclidine	25
d.a.u. 10 panel	11-nor-Δ^9-THC-COOH	50
	benzoylecgonine	300
	morphine	300
	amphetamines	1000
	d-methamphetamine	1000
	phencyclidine	25
	secobarbital	300
	oxazepam	300
	methadone	300
	nortriptyline	1000

antibody–dye conjugate specific to the drugs tested. If a drug is present in the urine, it will bind to the antibody–dye conjugate. If the amount of drug present in the urine is higher than the cutoff concentration, all the antibody–dye conjugate will bind to the drug and be unable to bind to the immobilized drug in the reading zone: no pink line should appear. If there is no drug present in the urine, or if the concentration of the drug is below the cutoff concentration, some of the nonbound antibody–dye conjugate will bind to the immobilized drug in the reading zone: a pink line should become visible. A pink line

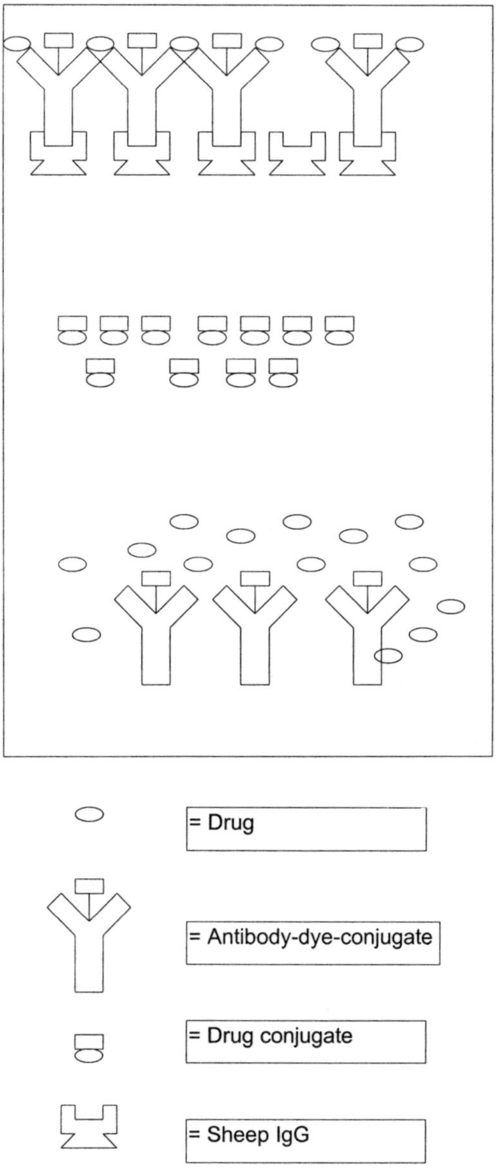

Fig. 2. Drug Positive Sample.

should always appear in the control zone, since it contains a special immobilized antibody. This antibody consists of sheep immunoglobulin G. If no pink line appears in the control zone, the test result is invalid. According to

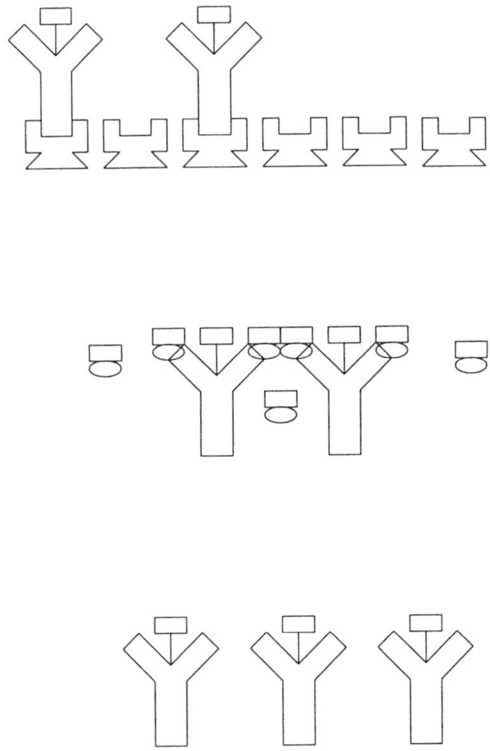

Fig. 3. Drug Negative Sample.

the manufacturer the result should be read between 3 and 10 min after the urine is added to the slide. In Figs. 2 and 3 the principle of a positive and negative urine sample is presented.

It should be noted that the First Check and Syva Rapid tests contain the same test strip and function in a similar way.

3. Summary of Studies

3.1. Nonpublished Pilot Study

According to the distributor, several studies with the AccuSign test have been performed. However, most of the studies have not been published in peer review journals.

In a Dutch pilot-study, Mostert *(1)* compared the AccuSign test with an EMIT™ immunoassay (data on file with the manufacturer). Only the single drug tests for opiates, cocaine, cannabinoids, and amphetamines were investi-

Table 2
Test Results of the Pilot Study of Mostert (1)

Test	EMIT positive AccuSign negative	EMIT negative AccuSign positive	Number of urine specimens tested
Opiates	2	1	112
Cocaine	0	1	106
Cannabinoids	0	10	172
Amphetamines	15	2	80

gated. The study was divided into two parts. In the first part, the test results of a series of urine samples obtained from the EMIT immunoassay were compared with the test results obtained with the AccuSign test. Table 2 shows the discrepancies between the two methods. It can be concluded that the results of the tests for opiates and cocaine were comparable, but for cannabinoids and amphetamines there were a large number of discordant results. The significance of these findings is questionable since no confirmation data (by gas chromatography/mass spectrometry) were reported.

In the second part of the study, the cutoff value of the AccuSign tests was investigated. A range samples with drug concentrations varying from 50% below the cutoff to 50% above the cutoff were analyzed. The concentrations at which 50% and 100% of the samples gave a positive test result were determined. The difference between these two concentrations should be small in order to rate the test as highly discriminating between positive and negative urine samples. Mostert concluded that the concentration gradient from 50% positive to 100% positive samples was quite large. For morphine 50% of samples were positive at a concentration of 520 µg/L, 100% became positive at 670 µg/L. For benzoylecgonine (cocaine) these concentrations were 420 and 900 µg/L, for marijuana 62 and 112 µg/L, for *d*-amphetamine 1195 and 1700 µg/L and for *d*-methamphetamine 390 and 710 µg/L, respectively. According to Mostert these large differences may lead to a large number of false positive and false negative samples with concentrations of drugs near the cutoff.

3.2. Duo Research Report

In September, 1997 at the Scientific Meeting on Drug Testing of Alternative Specimens and Technologies, Dr. Robert Willette of Duo Research presented a report entitled "An evaluation of non-instumental drug test devices: Summary report for workplace programs and recommendations for purchasing non-instrumental drug test devices" *(2)*. Duo Research Inc. performed an evalu-

Table 3
Test results of the study of Willette (2)

Test	Device	PPV[a]	NPV[a]	Accuracy[a]
Amphetamines, cocaine, opiates, cannabinoids	AccuSign DOA 4	0.64	0.92	0.79
	AccuSign single	0.61	0.90	0.77
	First Check	0.57	0.95	0.74
Amphetamines	AccuSign DOA 4	0.41	0.96	0.85
	AccuSign single	0.35	0.94	0.82
	First Check	0.33	0.94	0.81
Cannabinoids	AccuSign DOA 4	0.85	0.77	0.81
	AccuSign single	0.83	0.76	0.80
	First Check	0.70	0.91	0.76
Opiates	AccuSign DOA 4	0.41	1.0	0.66
	AccuSign single	0.35	0.97	0.59
	First Check	0.38	1.0	0.63
All drugs	AccuSign DOA 4	0.64	0.92	0.79
	AccuSign single	0.61	0.90	0.77
	First Check	0.59	0.94	0.74

[a] The maximum score is 1.0.
PPV, Positive Predictive Value.
NPV, Negative Predictive Value.

ation of 15 different single and multiple non-instrumental drug test devices. The results were compared with an EMIT immunoassay as a reference method. Correct results were assessed in terms of "Positive Predictive Values" (PPV) and "Negative Predictive Values" (NPV). GC/MS was used as the gold standard. In Table 3 illustrates the results of this study. It was concluded that no single product was ideally suited for all applications. The EMIT immunoassay gave the best test results, but even with this technique, the average PPV and NPV values did not exceed 0.95.

3.3. Performance of AccuSign Slide Test Near the Cutoff

Ros, Pelders, and Egberts *(3)* evaluated five different AccuSign test slides: cocaine (cutoff 300 ng/mL benzoylecgonine), opiates (cutoff 300 ng/mL), cannabinoids (cutoff 50 ng/mL), cannabinoids (cutoff 100 ng/mL) and a panel test for 4 drugs. The latter tests simultaneously for the presence of amphetamine (cutoff 1000 ng/mL amphetamine), opiates (cutoff 300 ng/mL morphine), cannabinoids (cutoff 100 ng/mL 11-nor-Δ^9-THC-9-COOH) and cocaine (cutoff 300 ng/mL benzoylecgonine).

Urine samples were selected with screening results obtained with FPIA-ADx within the 75–125% range of the AccuSign cutoff value. For each type of slide test, approx 35 samples were selected, except for the slide test for cannabinoids. For this test 104 samples were selected. Also, a few samples with a concentration of the drug exceeding the cutoff were selected to serve as positive controls. The samples were analyzed with AccuSign slide tests and confirmed immediately by gas chromatography/mass spectrometry (GC/MS).

The performance of the AccuSign, slide tests were assessed in several ways. First, the inter individual agreement was asessed for the five slide tests as well as the consistency of the observation made by the same person in time. Four individuals were asked to read the slides 3, 5, and 10 min after the urine was added to the slide and to write the result (positive or negative) on a standard form. They read the results independently of each other. Table 4 shows the agreement between different observers and the agreement per observer in time for the five different slide tests. In the third column the number of unequivocal observations at t = 5 min, which reflected agreement between different observers, is shown. An observation was called unequivocal when all 4 persons reading the test arrived at the result. The percentage of unequivocal observations for the cannabinoid test and the panel test was low. In the last four columns, the intra-individual agreement in observation with increasing observation time is shown.

With the AccuSign panel test, two randomly chosen samples were analyzed twice and independently assessed by two observers. Both volunteers had different observations for the second analysis for the presence of cannabinoids when compared to the first analysis of one sample. This also occurred when one of the volunteers judged the presence of cannabinoids for the second time in the second sample.

Finally, sensitivity and specificity of the slide test for cannabinoids (cutoff 50 ng/mL) was assessed using GC/MS as the gold standard. The results were compared with the sensitivity and specificity of FPIA-ADx. A sample was considered positive if the concentration measured with GC/MS was higher than 15 ng/mL in accordance with SAMSHA guidelines. A sample was considered positive for FPIA-ADx if the result was > 50 ng/mL and for the AccuSign drugs test if at least three persons read the test as positive at t = 5 min. In comparison with FPIA-ADx, the AccuSign test slide had a higher sensitivity (87% vs 46%) but a lower specificity (51% vs 95%). The AccuSign slide test had a higher false-positive rate than FPIA-ADx (49% vs 5%) and a lower false-negative rate (13% vs 54%).

Table 4

Results of AccuSign Drugs of Abuse Slide Test (3)

Test (Cutoff ng/mL)	Number of samples	Unequivocal observations by all persons at $t = 5$ min	Number of changing observation/sample between $t = 3$, $t = 5$, and $t = 10$ min			
			Person 1	Person 2	Person 3	Person 4
Cannabinoids (100 ng/mL)	35	15 (43 %)	8 (23 %)	7 (20 %)	10 (29 %)	5 (14 %)
Cannabinoids (50 ng/mL)	104	36 (35 %)	33 (31 %)	29 (28 %)	20 (19 %)	15 (14%)
Opiates (300 ng/mL)	35	17 (50 %)	13 (37 %)	3 (9 %)	7 (20 %)	6 (17 %)
Cocaine metabolite (300 ng/mL)	35	21 (60 %)	2 (6 %)	6 (17 %)	5 (14 %)	6 (17 %)
*Cannabinoids (100 ng/mL)	34	23 (68 %)	4 (12 %)	5 (15 %)	3 (9 %)	1 (3 %)
*Opiates (300 ng/mL)	34	23 (68 %)	8 (24 %)	1 (3 %)	2 (6 %)	2 (6 %)
*Cocaine metabolite (300 ng/mL)	34	31 (91 %)	2 (6 %)	0 (0 %)	2 (6 %)	0 (0 %)
*Amphetamines (1000 ng/mL)	34	23 (68 %)	3 (9 %)	3 (6 %)	3 (9 %)	6 (18 %)
DOA-panel* all 4 tests	34	12 (35 %)	11 (32 %)	8 (24 %)	10 (29 %)	8 (24 %)

*A DOA-4 panel has been tested. The test results of the four individual drugs are marked with an asterisk; the results of all four tests together are also presented and marked with an asterisk.

It was found that intensely colored or turbid urine samples interfered with the interpretation of the test. Centrifugation of the urine sample prior to performing the test is recommended.

4. Discussion

The study of Ros, Pelders, and Egberts demonstrated that near the cutoff value there is considerable variability in reading the test result between observers as well as for one observer over time. In addition, the test slide for cannabinoids had a higher sensitivity but a lower specificity than FPIA-ADx. The results from the study of Mostert predicted a large number of false-positive results. Mostert also expected a large number of false-negative samples; although the AccuSign test showed fewer false-negative test results than FPIA-Adx, 13% is still a fair number. The study of Willette showed that the AccuSign test scored relatively well in comparison with other slide tests and with EMIT. FPIA-ADx was not tested by Willette.

The results of the study of Ros et.al. suggests that it is advisable to use the AccuSign slide test when a strict protocol (i.e., always at the same time after incubation) is available and when the test is conducted by more than one individual with experience in reading the test *(3)*. However, this situation is less economical. The experience of the reader is important because the majority of the individuals reading the results in the evaluation of Ros et al. had difficulty interpreting the test result. This meant that expertise in performing the AccuSign slide test is necessary in order to minimize error. In addition, the inconvenient shade cast on the result-window, the poor quality of the reading zone that was sometimes pink and sometimes colorless, and the presence of vertical pink lines in the result-window were disadvantages of the test. The high rate of false-positive test results is unacceptable in daily practice since it necessitates costly confirmation procedures.

5. Conclusions

The AccuSign test slides should not be used without further testing in situations where a reliable test result is needed. The test result depends much on the observer and the time of reading the slide. In addition, the specificity is low. The test may be of value for use in emergency toxicology when a rapid result is needed and when an answer to the question of whether large quantities of a drug-of-abuse are present is the only purpose of the testing. The test is also suitable in a drug rehabilitation program or in prisons or detoxification centers in order to get a first impression of the absence of drugs-of-abuse: a positive test result should always be confirmed.

A pre-requisite for a proper use of the AccuSign slide test is adequately educated personnel to perform the test and to interprete the test result. The study of Ros et al. demonstrated that training and experience is necessary in order to conduct the test and interpret the results appropriately *(3)*. Like all slide tests, the AccuSign slide test is suitable as an individual test; it is not adapted to work in series. The test is not presented with standards, and has no place for recording case number or individual name, and no hardcopy of the result is provided unless the slide is photocopied. The used AccuSign slide cannot be stored long term since the color band dissipates.

6. Product Contact Information

The AccuSign® slide test is manufactured by:

Princeton BioMeditech Corporation
P.O. Box 7139, Princeton, NJ 08543-7139 USA
4242 U.S. Route 1, Monmouth Junction, NJ 08852-1905 USA
Internet adress: www.pbmc.com
Internet E-mail: prinbiomed@aol.com

References

1. Mostert, L. J. (1993) Rapport vergelyking EMIT dav—Abusign. Deltalab, Poortugaal, The Netherlands. Data on file at manufacturer, not published.
2. Willette, R. (1997) An evaluation of non-instumental drug test devices: Summary report for workplace programs and recommendations for purchasing non-instrumental drug test devices. Presented at the Scientific Meeting on Drug Testing of Alternative Specimens and Technologies, Washington, DC.
3. Ros, J. J. W., Pelders, M. G., and Egberts, A. C. G. (1998) Performance of Abusign, Drugs-of-Abuse Slide Tests with Particular Emphasis on Concentrations Near the Cutoff: Comparison with FPIA-ADx and Confirmation of Results with GC-MS. *J. Analyt. Toxicol.* **22,** 40–44.

Chapter 10

The EZ-SCREEN and RapidTest Devices for Drugs of Abuse

*Santo Davide Ferrara, Luciano Tedeschi,
and Franca Castagna*

1. Introduction

Many on-site drug-testing devices (OTD) have been described in the literature *(1–7)*. Although the first of these (KDI Quick Test), marketed at the end of the 1980s, turned out to be inaccurate and unacceptable *(8)*, improved devices have been developed and are now in use for analysis of drugs in urine *(9–11)*.

After more than ten years of experience in assessing screening tests based on immunochemical techniques *(12–15)*, an evaluation of EZ-SCREEN (Environmental Diagnostics, Burlington, NC) and Syva RAPIDTEST (Behring Diagnostics) is described here.

2. EZ-SCREEN

EZ-SCREEN appeared on the market in 1988, available both as a single test for cannabinoids, cocaine, opiates, barbiturates, amphetamines and phencyclidine, and as a multiple test for cannabinoids/cocaine and cannabinoids/cocaine/opiate combinations (*see* Fig. 1).

2.1. Principle

EZ-SCREEN is a competitive sequential immunoassay testing system. An analyte present in the sample or control competes with an analyte coupled to an enzyme for an antibody applied to the QUIK-CARD. In this type of assay, the specimen, positive control and negative control are added to the indicated QUIK-CARD test ports. After absorption, the enzyme conjugate is

From: *Forensic Science: On-Site Drug Testing*
Edited by: A. J. Jenkins and B. A. Goldberger © Humana Press, Inc., Totowa, NJ

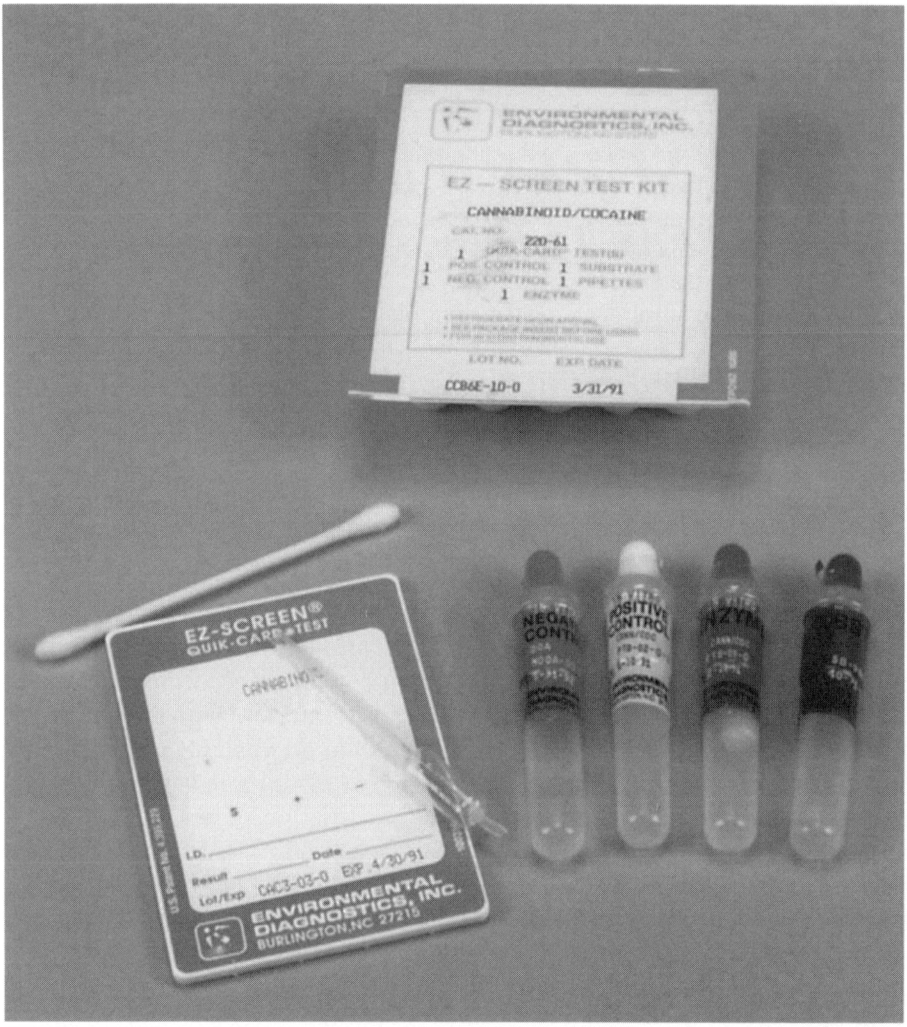

Fig. 1. EZ-SCREEN card and reagents.

added to the test ports, followed by the wash reagent and substrate reagent. The analyte in the sample or positive control competes with the enzyme-bound analyte for attachment to the antibody already in the reactive area of the card. Results can be interpreted after three minutes. The presence of the analyte in the sample causes a reduction in color development after the substrate has been added.

2.2. Materials and Reagents

Each EZ-SCREEN test kit contains the following materials necessary to conduct one test:

1. The Quik-Card serves as a solid support for the assay. On the "drug" section of the card, the reaction sites are coated with specific antibodies, mechanically trapped within a fiber matrix which allows for wicking of the sample and all reagents.
2. The enzyme conjugate contains a lyophilized mixture of horseradish peroxidase conjugated to the drug to be tested.
3. The positive control contains the drug dissolved in phosphate-buffered saline solution, pH 7.2 ± 0.2 at a concentration which varies according to drug tested.
4. The negative control.
5. The substrate, containing 4-chloro-1-naphthol and a urea peroxide substrate that has been tableted with inert fillers.
6. One disposable plastic sample pipet.
7. One cotton swab.

2.3. Procedure and Interpretation

For optimal test results, specimens should be tested within one day of collection. If refrigerated or frozen specimens are used, they should be brought to room temperature before testing. Testing is conducted according to the steps illustrated in Fig. 2. Since particulate matter will interfere with the wicking of the specimen into the card, it may be necessary to pretreat the urine specimen by centrifugation or to allow particulate matter to settle out, leaving a clear liquid layer.

The test is Not Valid if the negative control port or the positive control port develops the same degree of color, or if neither port develops any color. The test is Valid if color differentiation can be seen between the darker negative control port and the lighter positive control port.

The specimen is considered to be NEGATIVE when the blue-gray color in sample site S of the test card is darker than the adjacent positive control site. The specimen is considered to be POSITIVE when the color in the sample site is equal to or lighter than the adjacent positive control site.

2.4. Performance Characteristics

In a comparative assessment *(15)* of nine different types of immunochemical and chromatographic techniques typically employed for analysis of drugs in urine, the authors evaluated the capability and degree of reliability of EZ-SCREEN in selecting positive and negative samples in terms of sensitivity, specificity, false-positive rates, and false negative rates (Tables 1–4).

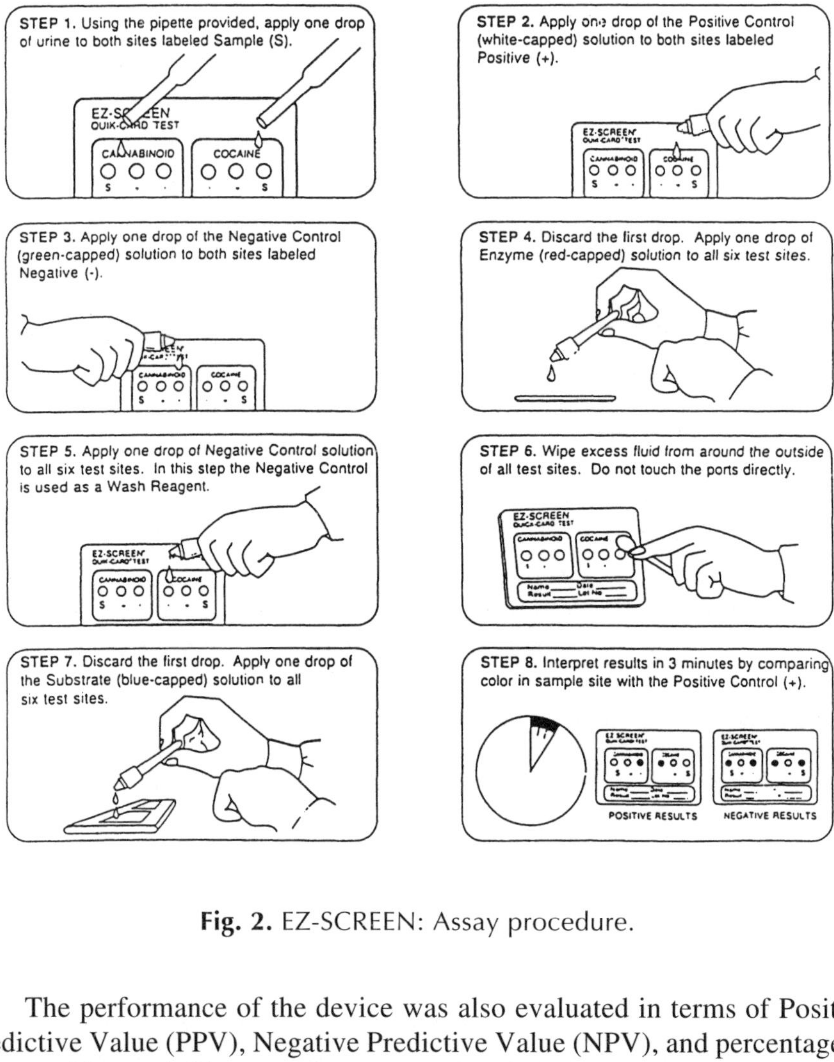

Fig. 2. EZ-SCREEN: Assay procedure.

The performance of the device was also evaluated in terms of Positive Predictive Value (PPV), Negative Predictive Value (NPV), and percentage of false positive and false negative test results. A low percentage or high PPV indicated that there was high certainty that a positive result from the test would be confirmed as positive, or as negative for high NPV.

In the sample population, EZ-SCREEN, like other OTD, revealed low sensitivity for several classes of drugs. In particular, for amphetamines, the probability of confirming a positive result was 54.8%. Again for amphetamines, specificity was equally low, and the probability that a negative sample would be identified as such was 83.6%. For cocaine and amphetamines, unacceptably low PPV values were found: 61.6% and 22.5%, respectively.

Table 1
Definitions

TP (True positive)	Results obtained using GC/MS and another analytical technique are both positive.
TN (True negative)	Results obtained using GC/MS and another analytical technique are both negative
FP (False positive)	Result obtained using GC/MS is negative but that obtained using another analytical technique is positive.
FN (False negative)	Result obtained using GC/MS is positive but that obtained using another analytical technique is negative.
False-positive rate	Percentage of samples identified as positive by a certain analytical technique when they are in fact negative.
False-negative rate	Percentage of samples identified as negative by a certain analytical technique when they are in fact positive.
PPV (Positive predictive value)	Incidence of correct positive results supplied by a given analytical technique when it is applied to a population, including both positive and negative samples.
NPV (Negative predictive value)	Incidence of correct negative results supplied by a given analytical technique when it is applied to a population, including both positive and negative samples.

The same three on-site urinalysis drug-testing devices (EZ-SCREEN, ONTRAK, and TRIAGE) were assessed by Crouch et al. *(16)* using current U. S. Department of Health and Human Services (DHHS) testing guidelines. The highest percentage of false-positive samples was found to be that of EZ-SCREEN, with 38.3% and 15% for THC-COOH and cocaine, respectively. Several samples tested positive by the on-site test devices containing less than the current DHHS amount required GC/MS confirmation of the target drug. When the confirmation cut-offs in GC/MS were lowered to 7.5 ng/mL for THC-COOH and 75 ng/mL for benzoylecgonine, potential false positives fell to 8.3% for THC-COOH and zero for cocaine. For amphetamines, benzodiazepines and opiates, the same authors found data which turned out to be complex and difficult to present in a practical manner. Conversely, for THC-COOH, EZ-SCREEN revealed a potential false negative rate which was better than that of ONTRAK and TRIAGE. This high sensitivity for

Table 2
Results of Immunochemical and Chromatographic Analyses

	Opiates				Cocaine				Cannabinoids				Amphetamines				Barbiturates			
Technique	E	P	TP	TN	E	P	TP	TN	E	P	TP	TN	E	P	TP	TN	E	P	TP	TN
ONTRAK	414	206	193	198	383	91	79	265	389	119	115	228	390	37	23	327	390	48	43	326
EZ-SCREEN	284	175	163	101	214	69	53	125	275	115	107	140	237	55	23	163	261	43	31	199
TRIAGE	202	59	58	132	202	39	38	161	202	29	25	154	202	10	4	187	202	13	12	182

E, Number of samples tested.
P, Number of positive samples.
TP, Number of true positive samples.
TN, Number of true negative samples.

Table 3
Sensitivity, Specificity, and False-Positive and False-Negative Rates (%)

Technique	Opiates	Cocaine	Cannabinoids	Amphetamines	Barbiturates
	$n = 283$	$n = 214$	$n = 275$	$n = 237$	$n = 261$
Sensitivity					
EZ-SCREEN	95.3	72.6	84.3	54.8	62.0
TRIAGE	84.1	95.0	56.8	44.4	66.7
ONTRAK	95.1	74.5	73.2	46.9	72.9
Specificity					
EZ-SCREEN	89.4	88.7	94.6	83.6	94.3
TRIAGE	99.2	99.4	97.5	96.9	99.5
ONTRAK	93.8	95.7	98.3	95.9	98.5
FP rate					
EZ-SCREEN	10.6	11.3	5.4	16.4	5.7
TRIAGE	0.8	0.6	2.5	3.1	0.5
ONTRAK	6.2	4.3	1.7	4.1	1.5
FN rate					
EZ-SCREEN	4.7	27.4	15.7	45.2	38.0
TRIAGE	15.9	5.0	43.2	55.6	33.3
ONTRAK	4.9	25.5	26.8	53.1	27.1

Table 4
Positive (PPV) and Negative (NPV) Predictive Values

Technique	Opiates	Cocaine	Cannabinoids	Amphetamines	Barbiturates
PPV					
ONTRAK	92.3	81.2	94.6	49.9	85.7
EZ-SCREEN	87.6	61.6	86.4	22.5	57.3
TRIAGE	98.8	97.5	90.3	55.5	94.3
NPV					
ONTRAK	96.1	93.8	90.0	95.4	96.7
EZ-SCREEN	96.0	92.8	93.7	95.5	95.3
TRIAGE	88.8	98.8	84.7	95.2	96.0

THC COOH had already been reported by Jenkins et al. *(3)*, who found that a standard concentration of 5 ng/mL of THC-COOH was enough to produce a positive result. If the assay is very sensitive, as EZ-SCREEN is for cannabinoids, some presumptive positive test results will not be confirmed by GC/MS.

Re-analysis of EZ-SCREEN using 107 clinical specimens, of which 36 were positive for 9-carboxy-THC by GC/MS, Schwartz et al. *(17)* reported 92% and 89% of sensitivity and specificity respectively; similarly, 38 clinical specimens positive for benzoylecgonine resulted in 95% and 67% of sensitivity and specificity. Faced with this evident discrepancy between specificity for benzoylecgonine in their study (67%) and that stated by the manufacturer in the product information (95%), the above authors concluded that additional investigations in independent laboratories were required.

In conclusion, the disadvantages of EZ-SCREEN include the limited number of classes of substances that can be tested; complicated packing of reagents; the possibility of breaking the glass pipet and consequent danger of accident to the operator; the relatively time-consuming procedure; need to time the test; testing difficulties for nontechnical personnel; subjective color comparisons; no stated cut-offs; and no data on test interferences and crossreactivity by other compounds.

3. RapidTest

The Syva RapidTest (SRT) is a one-step, solid-phase immunoassay for single or multiple simultaneous detection of drugs in human urine (Fig. 3). It is currently available for AMP (amphetamines), m-AMP (methamphetamine), CAN (cannabinoids), COC (benzoylecgonine), OPI (opiates), PCP (phencyclidine), BAR (barbiturates), BZO (benzodiazepines), MDN (methadone), and TCA (tricyclic antidepressants).

The SRT, made by Behring Diagnostics Inc., is identical to Accusign (Princeton Biomeditech), Status DS (Lifesign L.L.C), Mahsan (Mahsan Diagnostika), and Dako (Veda Lab). The number of parameters per device varies from one to ten.

3.1. Principle

The SRT device contains a membrane strip on which the drug conjugated to bovine serum albumin (BSA) is immobilized at a specific location. The panel is based on the principle of highly specific immunochemical reactions between antigens and antibodies, which are used to analyze specific substances in biological fluids. The test relies on the competition for binding to antibodies between drug conjugates and drugs which may be present in the urine specimen.

In the test procedure, an aliquot of urine is placed in the sample well (S) of the device. If the drug is present in the urine specimen, it forms a complex with the antibody-dye conjugate specific for that drug. The drug in the specimen

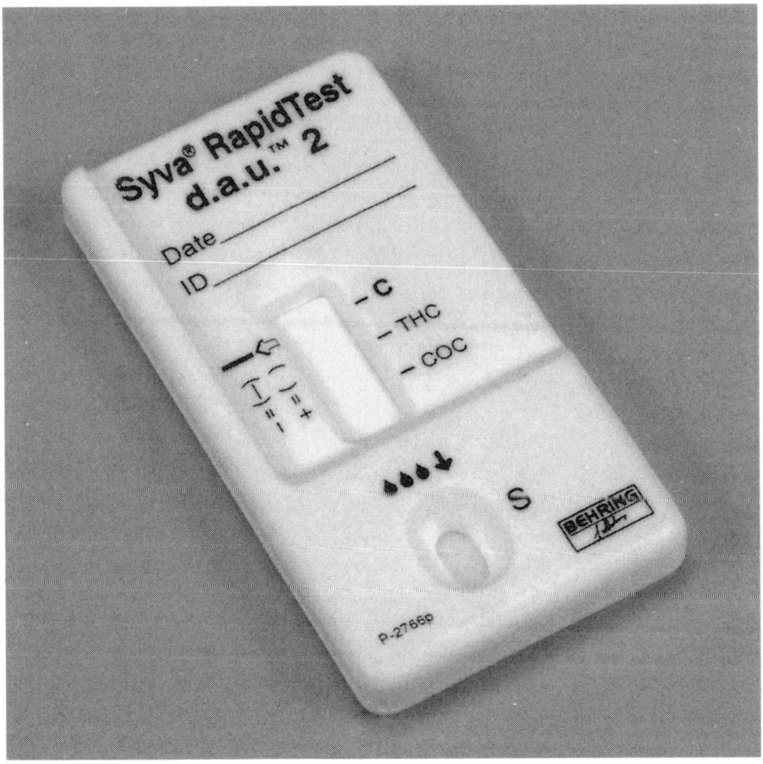

Fig. 3. SRT: Test card.

competes with the drug conjugate for the limited antibodies present in the form of antibody-dye conjugate. Therefore, a drug-positive urine specimen will not generate a line at the specific drug position in the result window, indicating a positive result due to positive drug competition. Conversely, if a particular drug is absent in the urine specimen, the antibody on the antibody-dye conjugate will bind the membrane-bound drug, in which case, a drug-negative urine specimen will generate a line at the specific drug position in the result window.

In addition to the line which may appear in the specific drug position in the result window, a Control line must appear at the Control validation position (C), and also in the result window, in order to confirm the viability of the test. This control line is always visible if the test is conducted properly. The control line is immobilized with polyclonal antimouse antibody, and will therefore capture monoclonal antibody–dye conjugates that pass the region, causing a colored line to show in position C (Fig. 4).

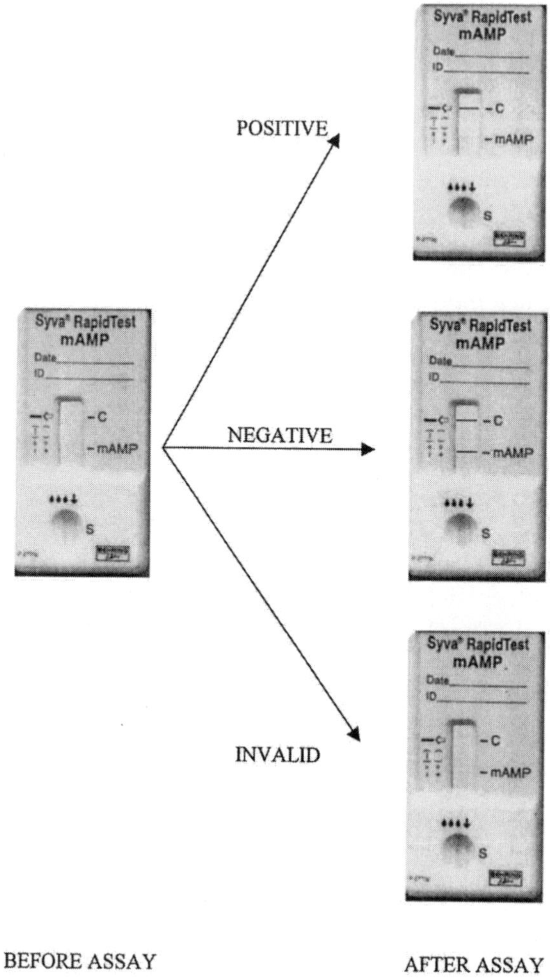

Fig. 4. Appearance of test card before and after assay.

3.2. Materials and Reagents

The SRT panel contains the following materials necessary to conduct one test:

1. Instructions for use.
2. A membrane strip coated with drug conjugates and a pad containing dye-conjugated antibodies (according to the drug(s) to be tested, mouse monoclonal, rabbit or sheep polyclonal) in a protein matrix.
3. One disposable sample dropper.

3.3. Procedure and Interpretation

The procedure consists of the following steps:

1. If test cards have been refrigerated or frozen, allow them to warm up to room temperature before conducting any testing. Specimens containing large amounts of particulate matter may give inconsistent test results. These specimens should be clarified by centrifuging or allowing them to settle before testing.
2. Remove the test card from the pouch. Fill out name and date.
3. Place 3 full drops (150 µL) of the urine specimen into the sample well (S) of the device and watch for the appearance of colored lines in the result window after 3 min, and within 10 min of sample application.

As Fig. 4 shows, interpretation of results involves three possibilities: Negative, Positive, Invalid.

3.3.1. Negative: the appearance of a reddish-purple Control (C) line and a line for a specific drug.

3.3.2. Positive: the appearance of the reddish-purple Control (C) line only, and no line next to a specific drug name.

3.3.3. Invalid: A Control (C) line should always appear. The test is invalid if no Control line forms at the C position and the test should be repeated with a new device.

There are several reasons a test may be invalid; for example, insufficient sample volume may have been applied, the reagents are not wicking on the membrane, or the test reagents are not working.

3.4. Performance Characteristics

A summation of the results of an evaluation performed by Behring Diagnostics on various SRT panels is as follows:

- Sensitivity: equal to the cut-offs recommended by the U.S. Substance Abuse Mental Health Service Administration (SAMHSA) and listed in Table 5 for the various drug classes.
- Accuracy, the SRT for eight classes of drugs was compared with a commercially available immunoassay (EMIT II) on random clinical samples and samples with drug concentrations above the cut-off level. Table 6 shows the results of this assessment. The most significant differences regard the sensitivity of the SRT m-AMP vs the EMIT II monoclonal amphetamine/methamphetamine assay. The accuracy of the SRT was also separately assessed on specimens confirmed to be drug-positive by GC/MS, with sample percentages in complete agreement, and in every case higher than 98%, with a minimum value for amphetamines of 98.2%.
- Precision and reproducibility: minimum values of 95% and 100%, respectively.

Table 5
Syva RapidTest Sensitivity

Compounds	ng/mL
*THC (11-nor-Δ^9-THC-9-COOH)	50
*OPI (Morphine)	300
*COC (Benzoylecgonine)	300
*AMP (*d*-Amphetamine)	1000
*MAMP (*d*-Methamphetamine)	1000
BZO (Benzodiazepines-Oxazepam)	300
BAR (Barbiturates-secobarbital)	300
MDN (Methadone)	300
TCA (Tricyclic Antidepressants-Nortriptyline)	1000
*PCP (Phencyclidine)	25

*Similar to DHHS-SAMHSA screening cut-off concentrations.

Table 6
Accuracy: Syva RapidTest compared with EMIT II

Compounds	With agreement	Relative sensitivity	Relative specificity
	%	%	%
AMP	99.0	97.8	99.9
	(n=480)	185/189	291/291
mAMP	91.3	79.4	99.9
	(n=320)	108/136	184/184
THC	98.0	96.5	99.2
	(n=1001)	305/316	680/685
BZO	98.7	98.8	98.6
	(n=223)	84/85	136/138
BAR	98.8	97.1	99.9
	(n=248)	102/105	143/143
COC	97.0	96.3	99.8
	(n=1021)	362/376	644/645
MDN	98.0	95.8	99.9
	(n=89)	23/24	65/65
OPI	99.0	99.6	99.9
	(n=966)	(249/259)	716/716

- Specificity: Tables 7 and 8 list the compounds detected by the SRT and the concentrations at which they produced positive results for the various drug classes tested.

Table 7
Syva RapidTest Specificity

Compounds	SRT µg/mL	Compounds	SRT µg/mL
COCAINE		***BARBITURATES***	
Benzoylecgonine	**0.3**	Allobarbital	0.2
Cocaine	0.5	Alphenal	1
METHADONE		Amobarbital	2
Diphenhydramine	50	Aprobarbital	0.2
Doxylamine Succinate	100	Barbital	2
Imipramine	100	Butabarbital	0.5
Meperidine	50	Butalbital	0.2
Methadone	0.3	Cyclopentobarbital	0.5
BENZODIAZEPINES		Pentobarbital	1
Alprazolam	6	Phenobarbital	5
Bromazepam	0.1	**Secobarbital**	**0.3**
Chlordiazepoxide	1	Thiopental	>10
Clobazam	3.3	***OPIATES***	
Clonazepam	>30	Codeine	0.3
Clorazepate	0.015	Hydrocodone	0.5
Delorazepam	2	Hydromorphone	0.6
N-Desmethyldiazepam	0.075	Levorphanol	5
Diazepam	0.1	Meperidine	80
Estrazolam	0.05	**Morphine**	**0.3**
Flunitrazepam	0.1	Morphine-3-glucuronide	0.5
Flurazepam	0.2	Nalorphine	1
α-Hydroxyalprazolam	0.2	Naloxone	100
α-Hydroxytriazolam	0.2	Norcodeine	60
Lorazepam	5	Oxycodone	20
Lormetazepam	5	Oxymorphone	60
Medazepam	1	Procaine HCl	100
Midazolam	1	Thebaine	5
Nitrazepam	1	***CANNABINOIDS***	
Oxazepam	**0.3**	11 Hydroxy-Δ^8-THC	25
Prazepam	0.3	11-Hydroxy-Δ^9-THC	1
Temazepam	0.05	**11-nor-Δ^9-THC-9-COOH**	**0.05**
Triazolam	1		

Regarding barbiturates, the sensitivity of phenobarbital is much greater than that of the reference compound, secobarbital. For benzodiazepines, the SRT presents a crossreactivity favorable for some benzodiazepines used by drug addicts such as flunitrazepam and diazepam, but less favorable for others, very popular on the international market, such as alprazolam and lorazepam.

Table 8
Syva RapidTest Specificity

Compounds	SRT AMP μg/mL	SRT mAMP μg/mL
d-Amphetamine	1	30
d,l-Amphetamine	1.5	100
l-Amphetamine	60	nt
MDA	0.7	100
MDMA	100*	7
**Ephedrine	nt	100
l-Ephedrine	nt	75
d-Methamphetamine	nt	1
p-OH-methamphetamine	100*	10
Phenethylamine	60	100*
Phentermine	0.35	150*
Tryptamine	50	nt
Tyramine	70	100*

*, tested negative at this concentration.
nt, not tested.

For amphetamines, the two available OTD both have marked crossreactivity unfavorable for identifying amphetamine analogs, favorable for MDMA using SRT/AMP (mouse monoclonal antibodies) and for MDA using SRT/mAMP (rabbit polyclonal antibodies).

For various substances contained in the eight classes of drugs, Tables 9 and 10 list crossreactivity data supplied with the SRT and other widely used Syva tests such as EMIT® d.a.u. and EMIT II®. It should be noted that SRT-COC differs from EMIT d.a.u. and EMIT II in that the crossreactivity value for the parent cocaine is similar to that of the metabolite, benzoylecgonine. In some cases, this may be a disadvantage unless contamination is carefully avoided in the laboratory.

The Division of Workplace Programs (DWP) of SAMHSA *(18)*, which has begun a review of the testing of alternative specimens and the use of on-site devices, has included the SRT in a study of 15 on-site test devices. Specimens clustered above and below the cut-offs and along with known quality control samples specimens that were clearly either negative or positive, are part of the evaluation. This assessment of non-instrumental drug test devices is being carried out in terms of PPV, NPV, sensitivity and specificity. Codes are used

Table 9
Syva RapidTest, EMIT d.a.u. and EMIT II Crossreactivity Data

Compounds	SRT AMP μg/mL	SRT mAMP μg/mL	EMIT d.a.u. Class μg/mL	EMIT d.a.u. MAMA μg/mL	EMIT II MAMA μg/mL
d-Amphetamine	1	30	300	0.4	1
d.l-Amphetamine	1.5	100	300	1	1.5
Chloroquine	100*	100*	500*	3.6	380
l-Ephedrine	nt	75	nt	50*	180
Fluoxetine	nt	100*	555	5920	500*
Isoxsuprine	100*	100*	6	500*	500*
Labetolol	100*	100*	2.9	750*	750*
d-Methamphetamine	nt	1	0.2	1	1
Methoxyphenamine	100*	100*	56.5	17.4	25
MDA	0.7	100	25	1	3
MDMA	100*	7	10	3	6
Nylidrin	100*	100*	2	750*	750*
Phendimetrazine	100*	100*	1	332	400*
Phenelzine	100*	100*	17.4	100*	100*
Phenethylamine	60	100*	1.6	10*	30*
Phentermine	0.35	150*	0.4	0.35	2
Phenylpropanolamine	100*	100*	1	75*	290
Propanolol	100*	100*	339	1000*	160
Pseudephedrine	100*	100*	10.3	180	670
Ranitidine	100*	100*	125*	62	900*
Tyramine	70	100*	450*	100*	200

MAMA, Monoclonal Amphetamine Methamphetamine Assay.
*, test negative at this concentration.
nt, not tested.

to conceal personal identities and relative results are only communicated to the manufacturers. In general, the study states that "the favorable performance of the devices was encouraging considering the simplicity of their design and operational requirements".

In 1998, the European Commission Directorate-General VII Transport approved and financed the "Rosita Project" (RoadSide Testing Assessment), to study and identify requirements for roadside testing equipment, and to make an international comparative assessment of existing equipment or pro-

Table 10

Syva RapidTest, EMIT d.a.u. and EMIT II Crossreactivity Data

Compounds	SRT µg/mL	EMIT d.a.u. µg/mL	EMIT II µg/mL	Compounds	SRT µg/mL	EMIT d.a.u. µg/mL	EMIT II µg/mL
COCAINE				***OPIATES***			
Benzoylecgonine	**0.3**	**0.3**	**0.3**	Amitriptyline	100*	338	1000*
Cocaine	0.5	100	80	Codeine	0.3	0.2	0.24
METHADONE				Hydrocodone	0.5	0.4	0.4
Diphenhydramine	50	100*	nt	Hydromorphone	0.6	0.5	0.5
Doxylamine Succinate	100	50	500*	Levorphanol	5	0.9	1.25
Meperidine	50	200*	200*	Meperidine	80	50	90
Methadone	**0.3**	**0.3**	**0.3**	**Morphine**	**0.3**	**0.3**	**0.3**
BENZODIAZEPINES				Morphine-3-glucuronide	0.5	0.9	0.8
Alprazolam	6	100	0.15	Nalorphine	1	90	4
Bromazepam	0.1	0.55	0.8	Oxycodone	20	4.5	4
Chlordiazepoxide	1	1.4	1.89	Oxymorphone	60	30	32
Clobazam	3.3	0.27	0.29	***CANNABINOIDS***			
Clonazepam	>30	0.64	1	11-Hydroxy-Δ^8-THC	25	0.08	0.06
Clorazepate	0.015	6.15	0.3	11-Hydroxy-Δ^9-THC	1	0.9	0.05
N-Desmethyldiazepam	0.075	nt	0.15	**11-nor-Δ^9-THC-9-COOH**	**0.05**	**0.05**	**0.05**
Diazepam	0.1	0.8	0.15	***BARBITURATES***			
Flunitrazepam	0.1	0.23	0.45	Alphenal	1	0.5	0.8
Flurazepam	0.2	0.13	0.23	Amobarbital	2	0.7	0.4
α-Hydroxyalprazolam	0.2	0.1	0.16	Aprobarbital	0.2	0.35	0.4
α-Hydroxytriazolam	0.2	0.14	0.22	Barbital	2	3.5	4.7
Lorazepam	5	1.3	1.4	Butabarbital	0.5	0.5	1.4
Lormetazepam	5	0.28	0.35	Butalbital	0.2	0.4	0.45
Medazepam	1	0.14	0.18	Cyclopentobarbital	0.5	0.35	0.4
Midazolam	1	0.18	0.2	Pentobarbital	1	0.4	0.4
Nitrazepam	1	0.26	0.35	Phenobarbital	5	2.5*	0.65
Oxazepam	**0.3**	**0.3**	**0.3**	**Secobarbital**	**0.3**	**0.3**	**0.3**
Prazepam	0.3	0.1	0.17	Thiopental	>10	45	44

totypes. The assessment will address roadside testing result validity, equipment reliability, usability (practicality) and usage costs. These evaluations are being conducted in Belgium (NICC), Finland (KTL), France (IMLS), Germany (ILMH), Italy (CBFT), Norway (NIFT), Scotland (FMS) and Spain (USDC, IML).

The inventory will focus on: the number and types of immunoassays available; cut-offs used; test specificity and crossreactivity for related medications and illicit drugs; ease of use; published and unpublished evaluation reports; information from patent offices, U.S. Food and Drug Administration; and similar studies performed in the United States.

The SRT is currently being assessed at the Centre of Behavioral and Forensic Toxicology (CBFT) of the University of Padova on 300 urine specimens collected at the roadside. Independently of the Rosita Project, the SRT d.a.u 4 (THC/OPI/COC/AMP) was assessed at the CBFT on 96 clinical specimens, with the results listed in Table 11.

Of the 96 analyzed samples, 15 were found to be positive for cannabinoids, 35 for opiates, 6 for cocaine and 4 for amphetamines. Confirmatory analyses on samples positive for cannabinoids, opiates and cocaine showed that, in two cases of opiates, positivity was due to the presence in one sample of dihydrocodeine and in one of folcodine. Of the 4 samples positive for amphetamines, 3 were confirmed by GC/MS; and in the 2 samples positive for MDA, MDMA was also present at a concentration exceeding 2000 ng/mL. Of the 44 negative results with the SRT assessed using the EMIT d.a.u. monoclonal amphetamine/methamphetamine assay, there was only one sample positive for MBDB, in GC/MS, providing a value of 1540 ng/mL.

Using an identical Accusign test, Kintz and Giraud. *(19)* reported that the PPV and NPV for opiates are excellent and noted some false positives for cocaine, whereas greater problems were found with designer amphetamines, on both AMP and m-AMP tests. In particular, with m-AMP, false negatives were found for MDMA, MDEA and MBDB. In an assessment of the accuracy and reliability of five on-site tests (including Accusign) compared with conventional laboratory testing processes, Taylor et al. *(20)* found that the devices gave discrepant results when challenged by quality-control material prepared at 25% over and 25% under the standard SAMHSA cut-off values (especially with amphetamines).

In conclusion, a comprehensive evaluation of the studies performed indicate that the SRT has the following advantages: it incorporates an internal check (Control C); a number or name may be applied to identify the test device; results are provided easily and quickly in 3–5 minutes and can be photocopied; only a few drops of the sample (about 150 μL) are needed for the test,

Table 11
GC/MS results of 60 positive samples with Syva RapidTest

Compounds	SRT Positive results *n*	GC/MS Positive results *n*	GC/MS Concentration range (ng/mL)
CANNABINOIDS	15		
Δ^9-THC-COOH		15	75–350
OPIATES	35		
Morphine		33	280–1920
Dihydrocodeine		1	450
Folcodine		1	5400
COCAINE	6		
Benzoylecgonine		6	350–980
AMPHETAMINES	4		
Amphetamine		1	1450
MDA		2	450-980

even when a multi-panel device is used, without the need for single tests of each single class of drugs; and tests may be carried out on single substances or on many combinations at the same time (up to 10).

References

1. Armbruster, D. A. and Krolak, J. M. (1992) Screening for drugs of abuse with the Roche ONTRAK assays. *J. Anal. Toxicol.* **16,** 172–175.
2. Buechler, K. F., Moi, S., Noar, B., McGrath, D., Villela, J., Clancy, M., et al. (1992) Simultaneous detection of seven drugs of abuse by Triage panel for drugs of abuse. *Clinical Chemistry* **38,** 1678–1684.
3. Jenkins, A. J., Mills, L. C., Darwin, W. D., Huestis, M. A., and Cone, E. J. (1993) Validity testing of the EZ-SCREEN Cannabinoid test. *J. Anal. Toxicol.* **17,** 292–298.
4. Hwang, S. M., Huang, S. H., and Huang, B. C. (1994) Evaluation of five commercial amphetamines and opiates immunoassay test kits inTaiwan. *J. Food Drug Analy.* **2,** 89–96.
5. Poklis, A. and O'Neal, C. (1996) Potential for false-positive results by TRIAGE panel of drugs-of-abuse immunoassay. *J. Anal. Toxicol.* **20,** 209–210.
6. Beck, O., Goerlach, A. G., Iten, P. X., Kraft, M., Moeller, M., Meyer, L., et al. (1998) Evaluation of three immunochromatographic rapid tests for screening of amphetamines/methamphetamines, benzodiazepines and cocaine in urine. Poster presented at TIAFT/SOFT Joint Congress, October, Albuquerque, New Mexico.

7. Wennig, R., Moeller, M. R., Haguenoer, J. M., Marocchi, A., Zoppi, F., Smith, B. L., et al. (1998) Development and evaluation of immunochromatographic rapid tests for screening of cannabinoids, cocaine, and opiates in urine. *J. Anal. Toxicol.* **22,** 148–155.
8. Schwartz, R. H., Bogema, S., and Thorne, M. M. (1989) Evaluation of the Keystone Diagnostic Quik Test. *Archives of Pathology and Laboratory Medicine* **113,** 363–364.
9. Malcolm, C., Oliver, J. S., Hand, C. W., and Baldwin, D. (1998) Evaluation of on-site method for the detection of drugs of abuse in saliva. Poster presented at TIAFT/SOFT Joint Congress, October, Albuquerque, New Mexico.
10. Kintz, P., Cirimele, V., and Ludes, B. (1998) Codeine testing in sweat and saliva with the drugwipe. *Intl. J. Legal Med.* **111,** 82–84.
11. Mura, P., Kintz, P., Papet, Y., and Piriou, A. (1999) Evaluation of six rapid tests for screening of cannabis in sweat, saliva and tears. *Acta Clinical Belgica* **1,** 35–38.
12. Ferrara, S. D., Tedeschi, L., Castagna, F., and Marigo, M. (1978) Comparison of GLC-EMIT analysis for the assay of methadone and its major metabolites in urine. *Forensic Sci. Intl.* **11,** 181–188.
13. Ferrara, S. D. and Tedeschi, L. (1982) Droghe d'abuso - Programma di controllo di qualita' - *Annuario Istituto Superiore della Sanita* 18, **4,** 727–734.
14. Ferrara, S. D., Tedeschi, L., Frison, G., and Castagna, F. (1992) Screening of psychoactive substances in traffic accidents – A comprehensive analytical approach. Proc. XII Int. Conf. Alcohol, Drugs, Traffic Saf., Cologne, September 28–October 2, pp. 465–479.
15. Ferrara, S. D., Tedeschi, L., Frison, G., Brusini, G., Castagna, F., Bernardelli, B., et al. (1994) Drugs-of-abuse testing in urine: Statistical approach and experimental comparison of immunochemical and chromatographic techniques. *J. Anal. Toxicol.* **18,** 278–291.
16. Crouch, D. J., Frank, J. F., Farrell, L. J., Karsch, H. M., and Klaunig, J. E. (1998) A multiple-site laboratory evaluation of three on-site urinalysis drug-testing devices. *J. Anal. Toxicol.* **22,** 493–502.
17. Schwartz, R. H., Bogema, S., and Thorne, M. M. (1990) Evaluation of the EZ-SCREEN enzyme immunoassay test for detection of cocaine and marijuana metabolites in urine specimens. *Pediatric Emergency Care* Vol. 6, **2,** 147–149.
18. An evaluation of Non Instrumental Drug Test Devices – Report of the Substance Abuse and Mental Health Services Administration, Center for Substance Abuse Prevention. Division of Workplace Programs; e-mail: Wogl@samhsa. gov.
19. Kintz, P. and Giroud, C. (1997) Immunoassay responses of MBDB. *J. Anal. Toxicol.* **21,** 589–590.
20. Taylor, E. H., Oertli, E. H., Wolfgang, J. W., and Mueller, E. (1999) Evaluation of five on-site immunoassay drugs-of-abuse testing devices. *J. Anal. Toxicol.* **23,** 119–124.

Chapter 11

Frontline Testing for Drugs of Abuse

Serge Schneider and Robert Wennig

1. Introduction

Many non-instrument based immunoassays have been developed and commercialized due their ease of use and rapid results. At least 15 different tests are available, such as the Frontline rapid screen for drugs of abuse. Since the early 1990s Boehringer Mannheim (now Roche Diagnostics) has developed and commercialized these single parameter test strips for qualitative and semiquantitative analysis of cannabinoids, cocaine, opiates, benzodiazepines and amphetamines in urine specimens. The test for methadone is currently under development (1999). The test principle and an evaluation of the different Frontline tests will be presented in this chapter.

2. Test Principle and Test Instructions

The Frontline test strips are available in 10 or 30 sample packages. Each test strip (size: 12 cm × 0.5 cm) (Fig. 1) bears the name of the drug to be analyzed and has an unique color code: green for cannabis (marijuana), yellow for cocaine, purple for opiates, brown for benzodiazepines and grey for amphetamines. A color scale for visual reading of the test results is included with the test kit.

2.1. Test Principle

The test principle is the so called GLORIA technique (Gold Labeled Optically-read Rapid Immuno Assay) *(1)*. Each test strip (Fig. 2) consists of a carrier foil, an absorbent fleece, a conjugate fleece, a collection matrix and a detection area (color identification).

From: *Forensic Science: On-Site Drug Testing*
Edited by: A. J. Jenkins and B. A. Goldberger © Humana Press, Inc., Totowa, NJ

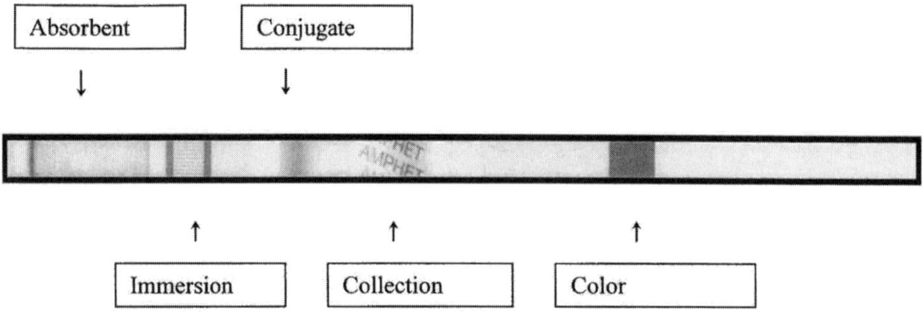

Fig. 1. The Frontline test strip for amphetamines (for an explanation of the different parts of the test strip, *see* Subheading 2.2.).

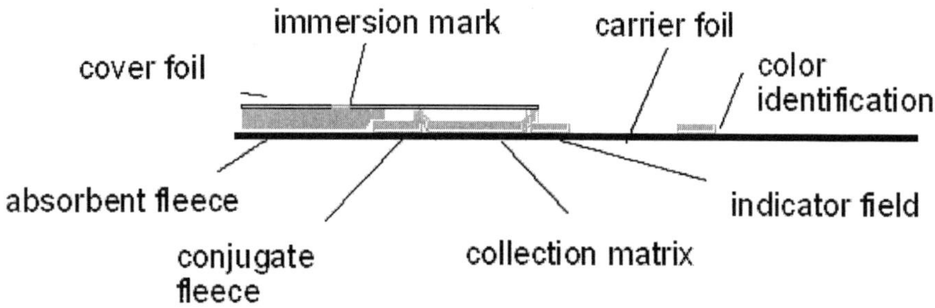

Fig. 2. Principle of the Frontline test (GLORIA technique).

The absorbent fleece (lower end of the test strip) is dipped into the urine to absorb a sufficient volume for analysis. The conjugate fleece holds gold-labeled monoclonal antibodies specific for the drugs to be analyzed. Drugs in the urine react with the conjugate and form a red-colored antibody-analyte complex. By capillary force the reaction mixture then reaches a collection matrix, which contains a drug analogue. The fraction of the antibody gold conjugate, which has not reacted with any drug in the urine specimen, will be immobilized by a specific binding agent (polyhapten) in the collection matrix. The fraction containing the gold antibodies conjugates with a sufficient amount of analyte will pass through to the detection area and give a positive signal. The results of the tests are read against a color code. The cutoff values for some of the drugs of the Frontline test strips have been set according to former recommendations of the U.S. Department of Health and Human Services (DHHS) Substance Abuse and Mental Health Services Administration (SAMSHA) (Table 1) *(2)*.

Table 1
Main Metabolites of the Test Parameters, Cutoff Values, and Full Signal Concentration of the Frontline Tests for Cannabis, Cocaine, Opiates, and Amphetamines

Analyte	Target drug	Cutoff (ng/mL)	Full signal (ng/mL)
Cannabinoids	11-nor-Δ^9-THC-COOH	50	200
Cocaine	benzoylecgonine	300	3000
Opiates	morphine	200	1000
Amphetamines	*d*-amphetamine	300	1000
Benzodiazepines	bromazepam	50	?

2.2. Test Instructions

The handling of the test strips is identical for all tests. Before performing the tests the temperature of the urine specimens has to be checked. In order to obtain reliable results the specimen must be > 10°C (50°F). Thus, urine specimens removed from the refrigerator should be allowed to warm up before analysis.

The strips are dipped into the urine and thoroughly drained for 3–5 s. They are then placed on a horizontal surface for approximately 2 min. The reaction colors are estimated by comparison with a color scale, intermediate colors have to be allocated to the next lower color. A white or slightly yellowish color indicates a negative result. A red color indicates a positive result ("+" on the color scale). The intensity of the red signal correlates approximately with the drug concentrations in the specimen. At high concentrations the test strip will show an intense red color ("++" on the scale). The reaction colors are stable for approximately 10 min.

Erroneous results may be obtained by dipping the test strips too deep into the urine specimen so sediment is collected on the strips, and also with dark colored urine. Adding detergents to drug free urine may give false positive results. Adding high amounts of salts slows down the time needed for analysis. Finally it should be noted that the use of glucuronidase for cleaving conjugated benzodiazepines is possible, since the presence of glucuronidase in the urine does not interfere with the test.

3. Evaluation of the Frontline Tests

Several authors have evaluated the Frontline tests and compared the performance to other immunological technologies and/or to GC/MS analysis. A

Table 2
Crossreactivities of Several Metabolites and Similar Substances of Cannabis, Cocaine and Opiates for their Respective Tests

Test parameter	Compounds tested	Concentrations giving a positive result (ng/mL)
Cannabis	11-nor-Δ^8-THC-COOH	50
	11-hydroxy-Δ^9-THC	500
	Δ^8-THC	700
	Δ^9-THC	1,000
	cannabinol	1,000
	cannabidiol	> 5,000
Cocaine	cocaine	100
	ecgonine methyl ester	> 50,000
	ecgonine	> 100,000
	EDDP	> 100,000
Opiates	morphine-3-glucuronide	300
	codeine	200
	ethylmorphine	200
	heroin	300
	hydromorphone	500
	hydrocodone	300
	oxymorphone	> 20,000
	oxycodone	> 10,000
	N-normorphine	> 20,000
	N-norcodeine	20,000
	thebaine	300
	dihydrocodeine	200
	levorphanol	2,500
	nalorphine	20,000
	naloxone	> 20,000
	buprenorphine	> 20,000
Amphetamines	*d*-methamphetamine	300
	methylenedioxyamphetamine	250
	methylenedioxymethamphetamine	250
	methylenedioxyethylamphetamine	750

(*continued*)

Table 2 (continued)
Crossreactivities of Several Metabolites and Similar Substances of Cannabis, Cocaine and Opiates for their Respective Tests

Test parameter	Compounds tested	Concentrations giving a positive result (ng/mL)
	l-amphetamine	100,000
	p-hydroxymethamphetamine	500
	N-hydroxymethylenedioxyamphetamine	25,000
	p-methoxyamphetamine	200
	dimethoxybromoamphetamine	> 100,000
	dimethoxymethylamphetamine	100,000
	p-chloroamphetamine	100
	D,L-ephedrine	25,000
	phentermine	5,000
	phenylethylamine	50,000
	tyramine	50,000
	3-methoxypyramine	100,000
Benzodiazepines[a]	7-amino-clonazepam	75
	lorazepam	100
	7-aminonitrazepam	75
	oxazepam	100
	prazepam	150
	α-hydroxy-triazolam	75
	oxazolam	> 100 mg/L
	carbamazepine	> 100 mg/L

[a]The following benzodiazepines gave a positive result at 50 μg/L: α-hydroxy-alprazolam, clobazam, oxazepam, nordiazepam, flurazepam, desalkylflurazepam, flunitrazepam, 7-amino-flunitrazepam, lormetazepam, delorazepam, midazepam, nitrazepam, temazepam, triazolam.

critical overview of many of the so-called "non instrumental immunoassays" including the Frontline test has been published by Scholer *(3)*

3.1. Crossreactivity and Cutoff Concentrations

The crossreactivity of the main metabolites and similar compounds of cannabis, cocaine and opiates have been determined *(1,4)*. The results are summarized in Table 2.

Cutoff determination has been performed by spiking urine specimens with benzoylecgonine, THC-carboxylic acid and morphine and performing

Table 3
Cutoff Determination of Cocaine, Cannabis, and Opiates (n=5)

conc (ng/mL)	traces[a]	negative %	positive %	high %
Cocaine test (spiked with benzoylecgonine)[b]				
0		100	0	0
100		100	0	0
150		100	0	0
200		76	24	0
250		36	64	0
300		20	80	0
350		16	84	0
400		0	100	0
1000		0	13	87
5000		0	0	100
Cannabis test (spiked with THC carboxylic acid)[c]				
0		100	0	0
17		94	6	0
35		79	21	0
41		53	47	0
47		53	47	0
65		0	88	13
78		0	63	37
Opiates test (spiked with morphine)				
0	0	100	0	0
50	0	100	0	0
100	93	7	0	0
150	93	0	7	0
200	33	0	67	0
2501	0	0	100	0
300	0	0	73	27
400	0	0	67	33
1000	0	0	40	60
2000	0	0	0	100

[a]Traces = result between negative and positive
[b]Concentration of weight.
[c]Concentration by FPIA.

the Frontline tests by four individuals *(1)*. Consensus was generally good at very low and very high concentrations but discordance was apparent in the intermediate concentration range (Table 3).

Table 4
Sensitivity and Specificity Results for the Different Frontline Tests

	Test	Comparison Method	n =	Sensitivity (%)	Specificity (%)
1	Cannabinoids	EMIT DAU	374	98	97
	Cocaine	EMIT DAU	385	100	94
	Opiates	EMIT DAU	373	99	100
2	Cannabinoids	EMIT ST	120	100	100
	Cocaine	EMIT ST	97	100	98
	Opiates	EMIT ST	102	100	100
3	Cannabinoids	RIA	203	92	99
	Cocaine	RIA	235	100	100
	Opiates	RIA	231	100	92
4	Cannabinoids	FPIA	284	98	98
	Cocaine	FPIA	289	100	99
	Opiates	FPIA	286	100	99
5	Cannabinoids	EMIT DAU	261	100	96
	Cocaine	EMIT DAU	264	100	85
	Opiates	EMIT DAU	253	100	99
6	Cannabinoids	FPIA	261	99	100
	Cocaine	FPIA	264	100	99
	Opiates	FPIA	253	100	99
7	Amphetamines	GC/MS	658	93	98

During the initial evaluation process, false positive results were observed with methadone and clozapine metabolites (cocaine test), bezafibrate (cannabis test), carbochromen (cannabis, opiate and cocaine tests), procaine (opiate and cocaine tests) and trimethoprim (opiate test) *(5,6)*. Nitrofurantoin gave a false negative result for the cocaine test *(6)*.

3.2. Influence of Temperature

The influence of low temperatures on the opiates and cocaine tests has been evaluated *(6)*. The tests failed if the urine temperature was 4°C. More intense color reactions were observed for both opiates and cocaine, resulting in false positive results. At a urine temperature of 10°C, false negative results were obtained for 20% of the opiate tests and for 50% of the cocaine tests. The optimal working temperature resulting in the lowest rate of false positive or negative results was found to be 20°C.

3.3. Evaluation of Frontline Tests

A description of the test development and a multicenter evaluation has been published by Wennig et al. *(7)* for the cannabis, cocaine and opiate tests and by Beck et al. *(8)* for the amphetamine test. In both reviews, the Frontline results were compared with other immunoassays and GC/MS. Sensitivity and specificity (Table 4) were > 90 % for all compounds. These parameters were defined as follows:

$$\text{Sensitivity} = \frac{\text{Frontline positive specimens} \times 100}{\text{Total number of positive specimens by comparison method}}$$

$$\text{Specificity} = \frac{\text{Frontline negative specimens} \times 100}{\text{Total number of negative specimens by comparison method}}$$

The results overall demonstrated good performance of the four tests with authentic clinical and forensic specimens. The relatively low sensitivity of the amphetamine test may be explained by the selectivity of the test for the *d*-enantiomers. A low number of specimens (3 out of 755) were not suited for evaluation by Frontline and by the other immunoassays because of the very dark color of the urine.

In another investigation, Mura et al. *(9)* evaluated several rapid tests including the Frontline test for detection of cannabis in saliva. Unfortunately, all the tests studied (Biomedix, Dako, Syva RapidTest, Crotez, and Frontline) showed a high number of false positive and false negative results. None of these tests is reliable enough to be used with saliva as the testing matrix.

4. Conclusions

The Frontline test was developed in order to obtain semi-quantitative results of the major drugs and drugs of abuse in 2 min. However, the rapidity of the test is possible while sacrificing flexibility. The manufacturer imposes the cutoff values (which vary from one country to another) and as with all immunoassays, no information about the exact nature of the compound(s) giving a positive result is obtained. Confirmation of positive results should be conducted, preferably by GC/MS.

When using the Frontline test, the investigator should be aware of the benefits and pitfalls of the methodology. When handled by untrained individuals there is a risk of misinterpretation of the test results. False negative as well as false positive results are rare but possible.

References

1. Goerlach-Graw, A. and Carstensen, C. A. (1994) Rapid Screening Test for the Detection of Drugs of Abuse in Urine, in *Abstract Book TIAFT/SOFT Joint Congress*, October 31–November 4, 1994, Tampa, FL, p 95.

2. NIDA. (1988) Mandatory Guidelines for Federal Workplace Drug Testing Programs. *Federal Register* **53,** 11,970–11,989.
3. Scholer, A. (1999) Nicht-instrumentelle Immunoassays in der Suchtmittelanalytik (Drogenanalytik). *Toxichem. and Krimtech.* **66 (1),** 27–44.
4. Frontline Benzodiazepines. Test zum immunologischen semiquantitativen Nachweis von Benzodiazepinen im Urin. Application instructions in the manufacturers notice provided by Boehringer (Roche Diagnostics) with the benzodiazepines test.
5. Geib, D., Wennig, R., Kraemer, T., and Maurer, H. H. (1995) Evaluation of the New Immunoassay Frontline, in *Proceedings of the 33rd TIAFT meeting*, Tessaloniki, Greece, pp. 339–341.
6. Carstensen, C. A., Goerlach-Graw, A., Haguenoer, J. M., Marocchi, A., Zoppi, F., Möller, M. R., et al. (1995) Multicenter Evaluation of Frontline Tests. New Immunological Tests for the Screening of Cannabis, Opiates and Cocaine in Urine. Poster presented at the 33rd International Congress of Forensic (TIAFT) and 1st on Environmental Toxicology (ENVIR) "Gretox 1995", Tessaloniki, August 27–31, 1995.
7. Wennig, R., Moeller, M. R., Haguenoer, J. M., Marocchi, A., Zoppi, F., Smith, B. L., et al. (1998) Development and Evaluation of Immunochromatographic Rapid Tests for Screening of Cannabinoids, Cocaine, and Opiates in Urine. *J. Anal. Toxicol.* **22,** 148–155.
8. Beck, O., Kraft, M., Moeller, M. R., Smith, B. L., Schneider, S., Wennig, R. Frontline Immunochromatographic Device for On-site Urine Testing of Amphetamines: Laboratory Validation Using Authentic Specimens. *Ann. Clin. Biochem.* **37,** 199–204.
9. Mura, P., Kintz, P., Papet, Y., Ruesch, G., and Piriou, A. (1999) Evaluation of Six Rapid Tests for Screeening of Cannabinoids in Sweat, Saliva and Urine. *Acta Clinica Belgica* **Supplement 1999-1,** 35–38.

Chapter 12

Abuscreen ONTRAK Tests for Drugs of Abuse

Laurel J. Farrell

1. Introduction

The desire to have noninstrument on-site immunodiagnostic assays for drugs of abuse was fulfilled by the Abuscreen ONTRAK® assays manufactured by Roche Diagnostics Systems. Launched in the spring of 1989, this product was the first to allow non-technical, trained personnel to analyze a urine specimen for drugs of abuse at the site of collection. The list cost of an ONTRAK assay was $385.00 for a 100 test kit. Pricing was dependent upon purchasing contracts and volume purchased *(1)*.

Table 1 details the Abuscreen ONTRAK Kits that were available, the cutoff concentrations, and the target compounds. Table 2 provides crossreactivity data listed for each ONTRAK assay taken from the individual package inserts *(2)*.

2. Principle of Abuscreen ONTRAK

All Abuscreen ONTRAK assays were based on the principle of latex agglutination-inhibition. This involved competition for antibody binding sites between drug in the urine and latex-drug conjugate reagent supplied in the kits (Fig. 1). If drug was not present in the urine specimen, agglutination occurred. The large particles formed by the binding of the latex drug conjugate and the antibody, appeared in the viewing area as a grainy, white mixture. If drug was present in the urine specimen at a concentration greater than the cutoff for the assay, then drug bound with the antibody, preventing aggregate formation. In this case a milky, white reaction mixture filled the viewing area. The expected results for both a positive and a negative test were shown on each black plastic ONTRAK reaction slide (Fig. 2)

From: *Forensic Science: On-Site Drug Testing*
Edited by: A. J. Jenkins and B. A. Goldberger © Humana Press, Inc., Totowa, NJ

Table 1
Abuscreen ONTRAK Kits

ONTRAK Kit	Cutoff (ng/mL)	Target compound
Amphetamines	1000	Amphetamine
Barbiturates	200	Secobarbital
Benzodiazepines	100	Nordiazepam
Cocaine	300	Benzoylecgonine
Methadone	300	Methadone
Morphine	300	Morphine
PCP	25	Phencyclidine
Cannabinoids	100	11-nor-Δ^9-THC-9-carboxylic acid
Cannabinoids	50	11-nor-Δ^9-THC-9-carboxylic acid

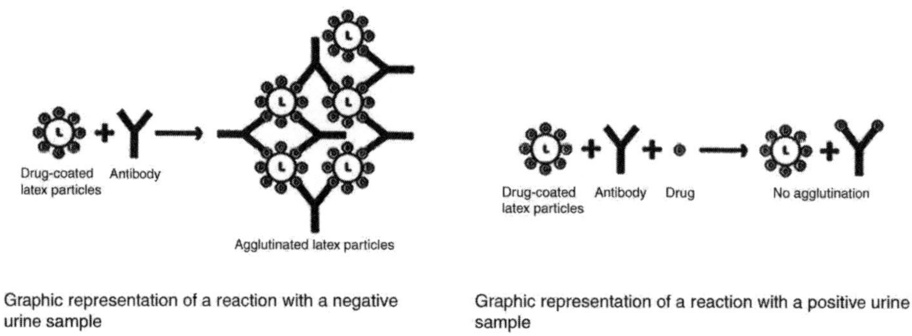

Fig. 1

2.1. Procedure

Each Abuscreen ONTRAK kit included the assay plastic reaction slides, the appropriate Reagents A, B, and C in dropper squeeze bottles, pipet tips, plastic stirrers, and a negative control. Reagent A contained the antibody for the drug, Reagent B contained a reaction buffer, and Reagent C contained the latex drug conjugate. The package inserts all provided guidelines for upright, refrigerated storage of all reagents and warnings, advising technicians that reagents from different lots of kits may not be interchanged and kit expiration dates must be adhered to *(2)*.

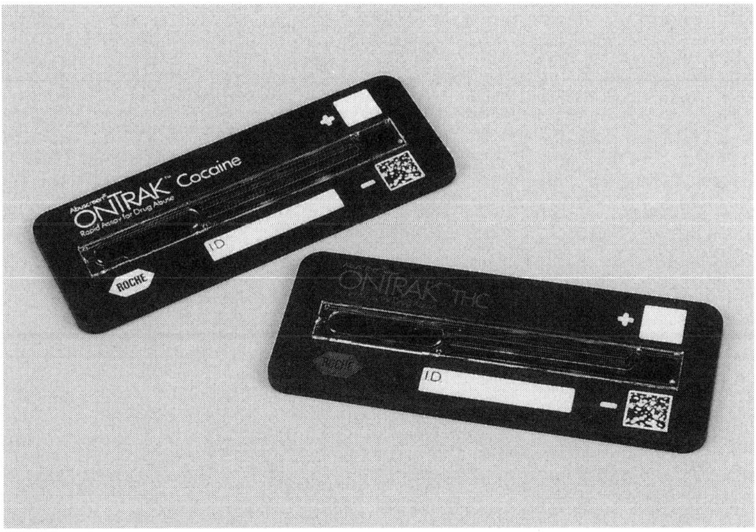

Fig. 2. The Abuscreen ONTRAK® assays manufactured by Roche Diagnostics Systems.

The step by step assay procedure (Fig. 3):

1. All reagents and slides were brought to room temperature.
2. 11 µL of the urine specimen to be tested was transferred to the slide mixing well using one of the new pipet tips supplied.
3. Reagent C was inverted approx 8 to 10× before use. If excessive foam was observed, the technician was to allow the reagent to settle.
4. A single drop of each reagent was then added to the mixing well. They were added in order A, B, C. In each case, the reagent bottle was held at a 45° angle during dispensing. Care was taken to avoid contact between the dropper tip and the urine specimen. Care needed to be taken to avoid addition of more than one drop of each reagent as this could invalidate the test results.
5. Using the stirrer provided, the mixture was stirred gently for approx 8 to 10 s.
6. The stirrer was then used to push the reaction mixture into the track opening. Once started, the mixture would proceed down the track to the viewing area by capillary action.
7. Interpretation of the test results occurred when the mixture completely filled the viewing window (approx 3 to 5 min).

A negative urine specimen resulted in the formation of the white agglutination particles. A positive urine specimen resulted in a reaction mixture

Table 2
Structurally Related Compounds

Assay	Concentration (ng/mL)	% Crossreactivity (ng/mL)
Amphetamines		
p-Hydroxyamphetamine	2000	50
β-Phenethylamine	25,000	4.0
Tyramine HCl	100,000	1.0
Barbiturates		
Allobarbital	200	100
Allycyclopentylbarbituric acid	25	800
Amobarbital	200	100
Aprobarbital	200	100
Barbital	100	200
Butabarbital	250	80
Butalbital	250	80
p-Hydroxyphenobarbital	700	29
Mephobarbital	25,000	0.8
Pentobarbital	500	40
Phenobarbital	700	29
Benzodiazepines		
7-Acetamidonitrazepam	25,000	0.4
Alprazolam	188	53
7-Aminonitrazepam	250	40
Chlordiazepoxide	375	27
Clonazepam	188	53
Clorazepate	300	33
Demoxepam	375	27
Desalkylflurazepam	250	40
Desmethylchlordiazepoxide	375	27
Desmethylflunitrazepam	170	59
Desmethylmedazepam	375	27
Diazepam	170	59
Didesethylflurazepam	188	53
Flunitrazepam	125	80
Flurazepam	375	27
Halazepam	500	20
α-Hydroxyalprazolam	150	67
4-Hydroxyalprazolam	150	67
3-Hydroxyflunitrazepam	375	27
α-Hydroxytriazolam	188	53
4-Hydroxytriazolam	375	27
Lorazepam	250	40
Medazepam	375	27

(*Contintued*)

Table 2 (continued)
Structurally Related Compounds

Assay	Concentration (ng/mL)	% Crossreactivity (ng/mL)
Midazolam	250	40
n-Methyloxazepam (Temazepam)	188	53
Nitrazepam	150	67
Oxazepam	200	50
Pinazepam	225	44
Prazepam	250	40
Morphine		
Codeine	250	120
Dihydrocodeine bitartrate	500	60
Dihydromorphine	400	75
Ethyl morphine HCl	400	75
Hydrocodone bitartrate	800	38
Hydromorphone HCl	800	38
Meperidine	50,000	<0.06
Morphine-3-glucuronide	800	38
N-Norcodeine HCl	100,000	<0.3
Oxycodone	50,000	<0.06
Thebaine	1600	19
Cocaine		
Cocaine HCl	1500	20
Ecgonine HC1	50,000	0.6
Ecgonine methyl ester HCl	>100,000	<0.01
PCP		
N-(*N*-Butyl)-1-phencyclohexlyamine	10,000	<0.25
Dextromethorphan	30,000	<0.1
2-*N*,*N*-Diethyl-l-phencyclohexylamine	150	17
3-*N*,*N*-Dimethyl-l-phencyclohexylamine	2500	1
1-(1-Phenylcyclohexyl)-4-hydroxypiperidine	10,000	<0.01
1-(1-[2-Thienyl]cyclohexyl)-piperidine	25	100
1-(1-Phencyclohexyl)-pyrrolidine	50	50
THC (100 ng/mL)		
11-Hydroxy-cannabinol	875	1.1
Cannabidiol	100,000	0.1
Cannabinol	1250	8
Δ^9-THC	1000	10
11-Hydroxy-Δ^9-THC	875	11
8-β-11-Dihydroxy-Δ^9-THC	400	25
8-α-Hydroxy-Δ^9-THC	400	25

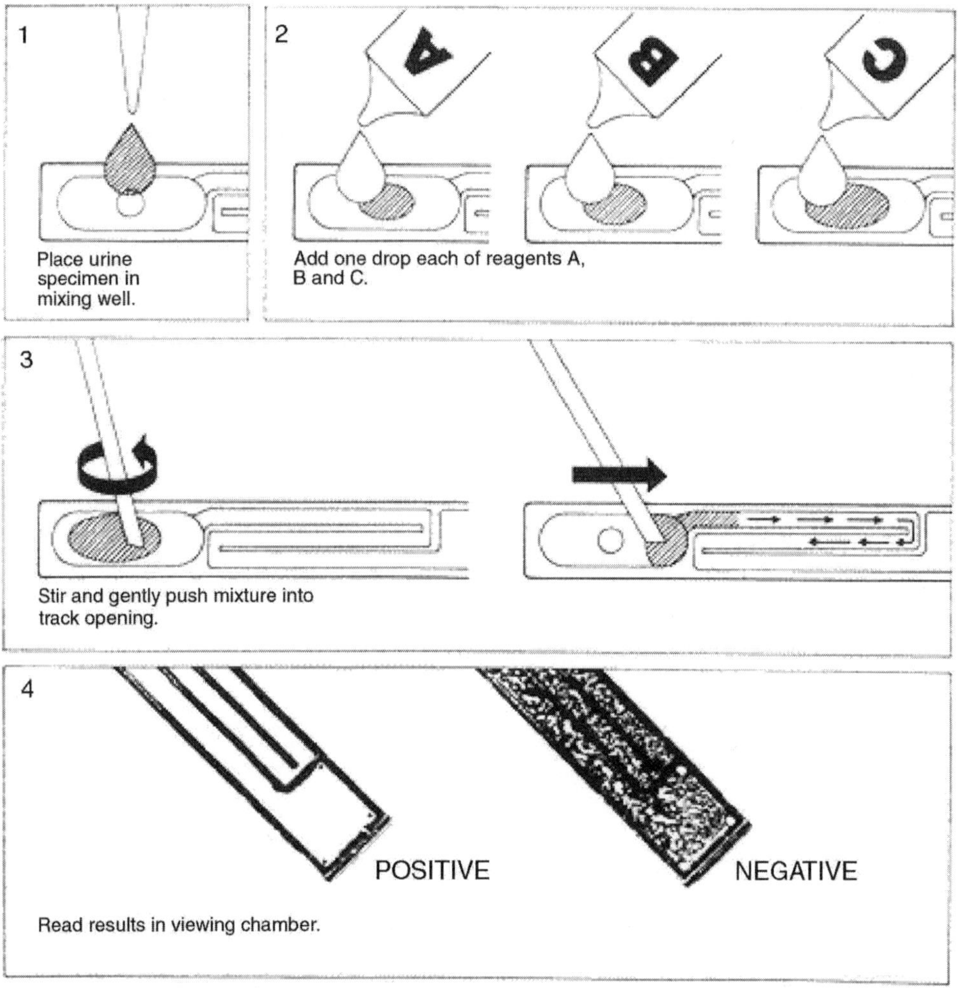

Fig. 3.

that was smooth, milky white in appearance. A specimen that contained drug in a concentration near the cutoff resulted in a viewing area that contained some particles because of agglutination but one that also had some degree of milky white background (Fig. 2). These specimens were to be called negative but the package insert did suggest that follow-up testing should be considered for specimens that gave a result that was near the cutoff or difficult to interpret.

2.2. Quality Control

A negative control was provided with all kits. This negative control was formulated to contain the target drug at approximately one half the cutoff concentration. All package inserts advised that this control should always read negative. If it did not, the test should be repeated. If a second positive result was obtained with a negative control, no patient specimens were to be analyzed. The use of a positive control was advised as a way to improve the quality control and was available from the manufacturer. The use of a positive control was required if this product was used for diagnostic purposes that would be regulated by CLIA.

2.3. Performance

Abuscreen ONTRAK represented a new direction in urine drug testing. The sensitivity and specificity of this product was evaluated rigorously over the ten years that it was available. Evaluations typically involved comparison of ONTRAK performance to that of other instrumented and non-instrument immunoassay screening methods such as FPIA *(3–6)*, RIA *(3,4,7,8)*, EMIT *(4,6,9–14)* ONLINE *(15–17)*, EZSCREEN *(4,9)*, TRIAGE *(4,9)*, TESTCUP *(15,16)*, Toxi-Lab *(4)*, high-performance liquid chromatography (HPLC) *(4)* and gas chromatography-mass spectrometry (GC/MS) *(4–6,9,12,15–20)*. These evaluations involved both drug fortified negative urine specimens and actual clinical and/or forensic specimens. The ONTRAK assays performed well in all of these evaluations. The reported sensitivity and specificity did vary slightly but these differences were explained by problems with analyte stability, differences in reactivity to a specific drug or metabolite, and the selected GC/MS cutoff concentration.

The Abuscreen ONTRAK assays were also evaluated in performance studies that investigated use of this product in a wide variety of applications. Baker et al. *(8)* documented that nonclinically trained personnel in multiple sites were able to accurately screen urine specimens when compared to clinically trained personnel. This high correlation (98.6%) was achieved even though the difficulty of visual interpretation at or near the cutoff was noted by these authors and later by Armbruster et al. *(3)*. Armbruster et al. further demonstrated that the volume of specimen used could effect the accuracy of results. The manufacturer did offer a fixed volume 11 μL pipet with the kits. This recognized that many non-laboratorians, less familiar with verifying pipet accuracy, would be using this product. Tsai et al. *(18)* evaluated the amphetamine, cocaine, opiate, PCP, and THC assays for susceptability to nitrite adulteration. No effects of nitrite were observed on the results of the Abuscreen ONTRAK assays. Salamone et al.

(17) evaluated the ONTRAK Benzodiazepine assay's ability to detect flunitrazepam and its metabolites in human urine. The ONTRAK assay was found to have an increased sensitivity to flunitrazepam and its metabolites when compared to the ONLINE immunoassay. This increased sensitivity was present without β-glucuronidase treatment of the specimens prior to testing.

The Abuscreen ONTRAK assays overall were shown to be a product that produced results in an on-site testing environment that later would be verified by a typical instrumented immunoassay method and by GC/MS in a clinical or forensic laboratory. The ONTRAK assays were available for ten years. During this time they were used in a variety of applications in clinical and medicolegal settings. The last ONTRAK assays were sold in June 1999.

References

1. Phillips, J. (1999) *Personal Communication*, Marketing, Roche Diagnostics Systems, Inc.
2. Roche Diagnostic Systems, I., Somerville, NJ, *ONTRAK package inserts.*
3. Armbruster, D. A. and J. M. Krolak (1992) Screening for drugs of abuse with the Roche ONTRAK assays. *J. Anal. Toxicol.* **16,** 172–175.
4. Ferrara, S. D., et al. (1994) Drugs-of-abuse testing in urine: statistical approach and experimental comparison of immunochemical and chromatographic techniques. *J. Anal. Toxicol.* **18,** 278–291.
5. Belfer, R. A., et al. (1996) Emergency department evaluation of a rapid assay for detection of cocaine metabolites in urine specimens. *Pediatr. Emerg. Care* **12,** 113–115.
6. Schwartz, J. G., et al. (1991) Accuracy of common drug screen tests. *Am. J. Emerg. Med.* **9,** 166–170.
7. Baker, D. P., et al. (1991) Evaluation of Abuscreen ONTRAK Assays: Correlation with RIA and GC/MS, in *American Academy of Forensic Sciences Annual Meeting Program,* New Orleans, LA.
8. Baker, D. P., et al. (1991) Evaluation of Abuscreen ONTRAK assays: Correlation between clinically trained personnel and non-clinical personnel in the field, in *American Academy of Forensic Sciences Annual Meeting Program*, New Orleans, LA.
9. Crouch, D. J., et al. (1998) A multiple-site laboratory evaluation of three on-site urinalysis drug-testing devices. *J. Anal. Toxicol.* **22,** 493–502.
10. Welch, E., et al. (1993) Rapid cocaine screening of urine in a newborn nursery. *J. Pediatr.* **123,** 468–470.
11. Birnbach, D. J., et al. (1997) Cocaine screening of parturients without prenatal care: an evaluation of a rapid screening assay. *Anesth. Analg.* **84,** 76–79.
12. Kaferstein, H. and G. Sticht (1990) (Comparative studies of drug detection using recent immunologic methods). *Beitr. Gerichtl. Med.* **48,** 51–56.
13. Robinson, C. A., M. Morrison, and C. H. Ketchum (1990) Evaluation of on-site THC Screening Products. *Clin. Chem.* **36,** 1027.

14. Zettl, J. R., T. L. Curry, and D. M. Durfee. (1990) Comparative Study of the Roche Abuscreen ONTRAK System, in *Society of Forensic Toxicologists Annual Meeting Program*.
15. Crouch, D. J., et al. (1998) A comparison of ONTRAK TESTCUP, Abuscreen ONTRAK, Abuscreen ONLINE, and GC/MS urinalysis test results. *J. Foren. Sci.* **43,** 35–40.
16. Towt, J., et al. (1995) ONTRAK TESTCUP: a novel, on-site, multi-analyte screen for the detection of abused drugs. *J. Anal. Toxicol.* **19,** 504–510.
17. Salamone, S. J., et al. (1997) Flunitrazepam excretion patterns using the Abuscreen OnTrak and OnLine immunoassays: comparison with GC-MS. *J. Anal. Toxicol.* **21,** 341–345.
18. Tsai, S. C., et al. (1998) Determination of five abused drugs in nitrite-adulterated urine by immunoassays and gas chromatography-mass spectrometry. *J. Anal. Toxicol.* **22,** 474–80.
19. Cone, E. J., W. D. Darwin, and S. L. Dickerson (1991) Evaluation of the Abuscreen ONTRAK assay for cocaine (metabolite). *Clin. Chem. News* **17,** 40.
20. Schwartz, R. H., S. Bogema, and M. M. Thorne (1990) Evaluation of a rapid latex-particle agglutination-inhibition screening assay for cocaine in urine. *J. Pediatr.* **117,** 670–672.

Chapter 13

The OnTrak TesTcup® Systems

Dennis J. Crouch

1. Introduction

OnTrak TesTcup® was introduced in 1995 and was one of the first products of the second-generation on-site drug testing devices. The second generation of devices incorporated innovative features designed to make the products easier to use and to eliminate many of the procedural steps where testing errors might be introduced into the analysis. No dispensing of reagents, mixing of reagents or transferring of the urine is required. With OnTrak TesTcup®, the urine is collected in the testing container or cup. Testing is initiated by tilting the cup to wet an absorbent pad. The urine migrates from the pad through a testing area where the immuno-chemical reaction(s) designed to detect the drugs occurs. Within approximately 5 min, the drug test results are visually read. For each drug tested, the device also has a second visually interpreted area designed to indicate whether the drug test was valid or invalid. After the analysis is completed, the OnTrak TesTcup® can then be used as a long-term storage or shipment container.

OnTrak TesTcup® was initially designed to test for three drugs/drug classes. These were cocaine metabolite (benzoylecgonine, BZE), opiates (morphine) and marijuana metabolite (THC-COOH) *(1)*. The original OnTrak TesTcup® has evolved into three products that are currently marketed as the OnTrak TesTcup®, OnTrak TesTcup® -5 and OnTrak TesTcup® -er *(2–5)*. The OnTrak TesTcup® and the OnTrak TesTcup® -5 were introduced 1996 and 1997, respectively. In addition to the three drugs detected by the original OnTrak TesTcup®, the revised 1996 product also tests for amphetamines *(3)*. The OnTrak TesTcup® -5 tests for the original three drugs plus amphetamines and phencyclidine (PCP) *(4)*. This expanded testing capability encompasses

From: *Forensic Science: On-Site Drug Testing*
Edited by: A. J. Jenkins and B. A. Goldberger © Humana Press, Inc., Totowa, NJ

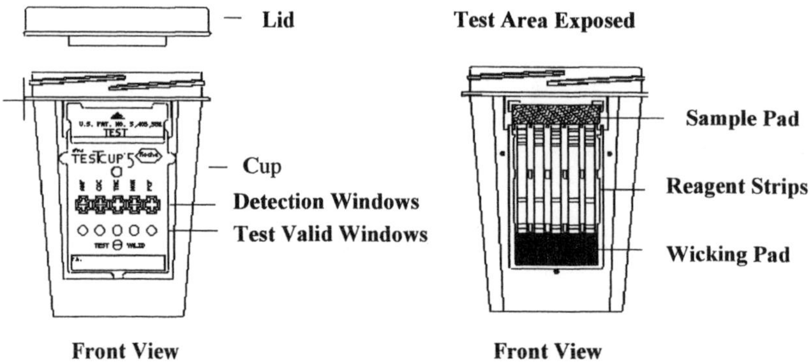

Fig. 1. Expanded Membrane of Reagent Test Strip (courtesy of Roche Diagnostics). AMP, amphetamines; COC, cocaine metabolite; THC, marijuana metabolite; MOR, opiates; PCP, phencyclidine.

the standard 5-drug workplace panel *(6)*. In 1999, the OnTrak TesTcup® -er, was introduced *(5)*. This product has the same collection and testing features that the original OnTrak TesTcup® and the expanded OnTrak TesTcup® -5, but is designed to test for amphetamines, barbiturates, benzodiazepines, BZE and opiates. All three products are available to test for opiates using either a 300 ng/mL or a 2000 ng/mL detection cutoff.

OnTrak TesTcup®, OnTrak TesTcup® -5 and OnTrak TesTcup® -er are self-contained devices designed to serve as specimen collection containers, shipment and storage containers and as drug testing devices. The cups are approx 3 and 3/4" (9.5 cm) in height, 3" (7.5 cm) in diameter and have a capacity in excess of 120 mL. The size of the cup and the wide-mouth design allow for easy collection of urine specimens from male or female donors. The cups are shipped from the manufacturer in individually sealed foil bags. However, they are generally supplied in kits containing 25 cups. The products can be obtained by contacting Roche, Diagnostics at 9115 Hague Road, Indianapolis, IN 46250 USA (1-800-737-9667) *(3–5)*.

The U.S. federal guidelines for workplace drug testing have established the following testing cutoff concentrations for drug screening and GC/MS confirmation, respectively: amphetamines (1000 ng/mL and 500 ng/mL); BZE (300 ng/mL and 150 ng/mL); opiates (300 ng/mL and 300 ng/mL)*; THC-COOH (50 ng/mL and 15 ng/mL) and PCP (25 ng/mL and 25 ng/mL) *(6)*.

*Recently changed to 2,000 ng/mL and 2,000 ng/mL.

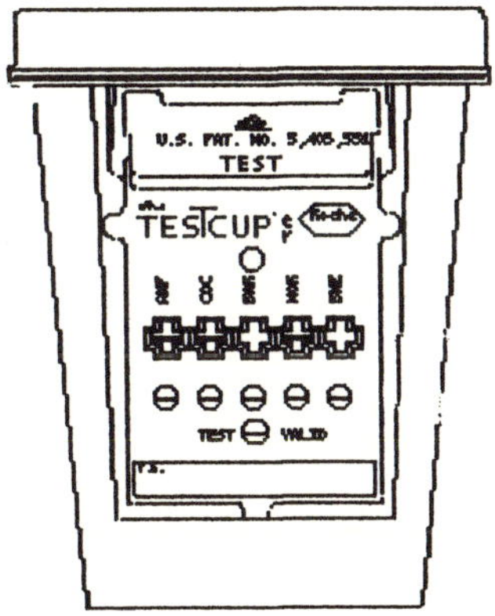

Fig. 2. TesTcup® -er (courtesy of Roche Diagnostics). AMP, amphetamines; COC, cocaine metabolite; BAR, barbiturates; MOR, opiates; BZP, benzodiazepines.

These cutoff concentrations apply to all of the drug tests discussed in this chapter unless other cutoffs are specified.

2. Product Design and Theory of Drug Detection

The basic design of OnTrak TesTcup®, OnTrak TesTcup® -5 and OnTrak TesTcup® -er is shown in Figs. 1 and 2. After collection of the urine, an analysis is initiated by turning the lid to the test position. The cup is then tilted forward to allow the urine to enter the sample reservoir and contact the sample pad (Figs. 1 and 3). For each of the drug/drug classes tested, a reagent strip is in contact with the sample pad. Urine travels down the reagent strip (membrane) by capillary action and interacts with antibody-coated microparticles and with drug conjugates that are immobilized on the membrane (Fig. 3). The immunoreaction is based on competitive interactions between the target drug or drug metabolite in the urine and the drug conjugate immobilized on the membrane. If no drug is present in the urine, the antibody-microparticle complex interacts with the immobilized drug conjugate and a horizontal blue band appears in the detection window (Figs. 1 and 2). This band is demonstrated in the detection windows for amphetamines, cocaine, and morphine in the OnTrak TesTcup® -5 and the OnTrak TesTcup® -er examples shown in the Figs. 1 and 2. If drug is present in the urine at a concentration in excess of the detection cutoff, the drug binds to the antibody-microparticle complex. Therefore, the complex is not available to bind with the drug conjugate immobilize on the reagent strip

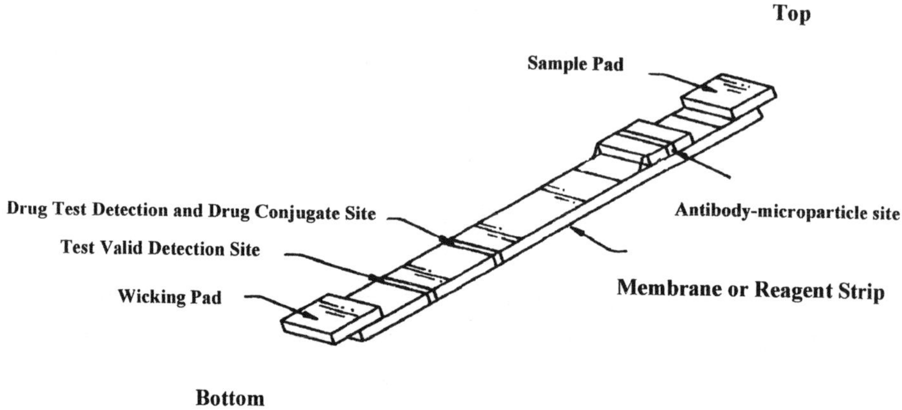

Fig. 3. TesTcup® system drug testing reagent strips (courtesy of Roche Diagnostics).

and no color is observed in the detection window. As a result, a white "+" sign appears in the detection window indicating that the urine tested positive for that drug/drug class. Positive results are shown in the detection windows for THC and PCP in the OnTrak TesTcup® -5 example and for barbiturates and benzodiazepines in the OnTrak TesTcup® -er example (Figs. 1 and 2). Also shown in the Figs. 1 and 2 is the "test valid" window. This window is used to determine if the urine and associated testing reagents have properly migrated down the test strips. In addition to the reagents used to detect drugs, bovine serum albumin with an associated blue dye is also placed on the membrane. Antibodies to the bovine serum albumin are immobilized on the reagent strip at the test valid window. If the urine and testing reagents migrate properly, a horizontal blue band will appear in the test valid window for each of the five drugs tested. This band is shown in the test valid windows for OnTrak TesTcup® -5 and the OnTrak TesTcup® -er in Figs. 1 and 2. If the urine does not migrate properly, for example because of the presence of an adulterant, no color is observed in the test valid window and the analysis must be repeated or another urine specimen collected and the analysis repeated.

3. Analysis Method and Analysis Precautions

3.1. Method

As stated, OnTrak TesTcup®, OnTrak TesTcup® -5 and OnTrak TesTcup® -er are designed to serve as specimen collection containers, shipment and storage containers and as drug testing devices. The cups are shipped in individually sealed foil bags and should be stored in the bags. Specimens collected in the cups should be within the acceptable testing temperature range for optimal performance of the device (see precautions below). The lid of the cup is designed with a small tab that indicates whether the cup is in the test or the fully sealed position. This tab should be aligned with the arrow (Fig. 1) indicating that the lid is in the "TEST" position before an analysis can be performed. To initiate an analysis, the cup is tilted forward, toward the testing area, until urine covers approx 1/2 of the lid. The cup should be held in that position for approx 5 to 10 s. This allows urine to enter a sample reservoir, to wet the sample pad and to be absorbed onto the reagent strips where the analysis and detection take place. The cup is then return to its upright position. In approx 3 to 5 min, a blue band should appear for each test in the test valid window and the drug test results may be read. A "Results Label" is fixed by an adhesive to the testing area and covers the drug testing detection window. This label is removed and the test results are visible in the detection window (Fig. 1 and 2). If the urine contains drug/metabolites at a concentration ≥ the cutoff, no color is observed in the detection window and a positive urine drug test is recorded. If no drug is present in the urine, a blue horizontal bar "negative" sign appears in the detection window for that drug. After the results have been read and recorded, the lid should be rotated clockwise to the stop position. In the stop position, the tab will no longer be aligned with the TEST indicator and the lid completely seals the cup. The results label should be used to cover the pinhole-sized vent on the upper-back portion of the cup. The cup may now be used for sample storage or sample shipment.

3.2. Precautions

To ensure optimum device performance, the cups should be used within 8 h of removal from their shipping bags. This is particularly true in humid environments where environmental conditions may affect the testing characteristics. The minimum recommended urine collection volume is 30 mL. This is to ensure proper wetting of the sample pad and sufficient sample for confirmation testing. Refrigerated urine samples should be allowed to equilibrate to room temperature (≥ 65°F or 17°C) to ensure that the urine migrates properly on the test strip. Specimen temperatures should not exceed 99°F or 37°C because immunoassay reactions are temperature sensitive. The manufacturer provides no minimum or maximum migration times. However, the normal migration time is < 5 min and analysis times in excess of 10 min are unusual.

The lack of a blue band in any test valid window is an indication of a testing problem for that drug. An invalid test may be the result of a simple procedural error such as not tilting the cup for the recommend period of time, or it may be the result of a more serious problem such as having an adulterated specimen or a cup that was not performing properly. If it is suspected that the invalid test was the result of insufficient wetting of the sample pad, the lid may be returned to the test position and the testing procedure maybe repeated. Samples that do not pass urine validity tests should be treated as diluted, substituted or adulterated and must be recollected according to the client's drug testing policy *(7,8)*. Cup performance should not be a problem if it is used prior to the expiration date that is stamped on each cup's shipping bag and if the 8-h time limit is observed. Cup performance may be evaluated by testing positive and negative quality control (control) samples to evaluate each new shipment or new lot number of devices. Originally, the cup had a small built-in venting area. There were reports that this vent was sometimes not effective and that it was possible to tilt the cup without urine entering the sample reservoir. This author has not had that experience using the OnTak TesTcup®. However, to address this potential problem, later designs of the OnTrak TesTcup®, OnTrak TesTcup® -5 and OnTrak TesTcup® -er have been modified to include a vent hole. This hole must be sealed to prevent leakage, especially during specimen storage or shipment.

4. Interpretation of Results

Interpreting any drug test result requires knowledge of the testing technology, the testing device, its procedural limitations and its accuracy, precision and specificity. Also, the test must be valid before accepting the drug test results. As discussed, the lack of a blue band in the test valid window is indicative of an invalid test for that drug. Any blue color in the drug detection window should be interpreted as a negative drug test result. Positive test results should be considered "presumptive positive" and a confirmation using a more specific analytic technique such as mass spectrometry should be performed if the analysis has significant medicolegal implications. The manufacturer reports two studies designed to assess the accuracy of OnTrak TesTcup® -5 *(4)*. In the first study an instrument-based immunoassay screen and GC/MS confirmation testing was used to select between 38 and 109 positive samples/drug class. These samples were used to challenge OnTrak TesTcup® -5. No discrepancies between the expected and observed results were found for any of the drugs tested. In the second study, OnTrak TesTcup® -5 was challenged with 307 samples that tested negative using the standard workplace screen testing cutoff concentrations. Of the negative samples, one tested positive for amphetamines and two tested positive for opiates using OnTrak TesTcup® -5. Both discrepant opiate samples contained measurable concentrations of morphine that were ≤ the screening cutoff. All other test results were consistent between OnTrak TesTcup® -5 and the laboratory-based immunoassay. For precision, the manufacturer states that discrimination between positive and negative samples with OnTrak TesTcup® -5 at drug concentrations ≥ 150% of the Substance Abuse and Mental Health Services Administration (SAMHSA) cutoffs can be performed with 95% confidence *(4)*.

The manufacturer used the studies discussed above to demonstrate the performance characteristics of OnTrak TesTcup® -er for the detection of amphetamines, BZE and opiates. In an additional study, 50 samples that tested positive for either barbiturates or benzodiazepines using immunoassay screening and GC/MS confirmation were selected to challenge the OnTrak TesTcup® -er. No discrepancies between the laboratory results and OnTrak TesTcup® -er results were found for any of the samples tested. In a second study, OnTrak TesTcup® -er was challenged with 100 samples that tested negative for barbiturates and benzodiazepines using a laboratory based immunoassay. Again, no discrepancies were found for any of the tested samples. As an assessment of precision, the manufacturer states that discrimination between a positive and negative sample using OnTrak TesTcup® er at drug concentrations ≥150 % of the testing cutoff can be done with 95% confidence. Also, a negative test result can be expected with OnTrak TesTcup® -er (95% confidence) at drug concentrations ≤ 25 % of the testing cutoff *(5)*.

Knowledge of the specificity of an analytical technique is needed when reporting and interpreting drug test results. Table 1 shows the antibody cross reactivity of the OnTrak TesTcup® -5 tests to structurally related drugs and drug metabolites. Antibody target drugs for OnTrak TesTcup® -5 and OnTrak TesTcup® -er are as follows:

Test	**Target Analyte**
Amphetamines	*d,l*-amphetamine
Opiates	Morphine
Cocaine	Benzoylecgonine
Cannabinoids	11-nor-delta-9-THC- carboxylic acid (THC-COOH)
Phencyclidine	PCP
Benzodiazepines	Oxazepam
Barbiturates	Secobarbital

Using the information provided above and that shown in Table 1, one would predict that a positive opiate test result would be obtained if a urine sample contained ≥300 ng/mL of morphine or codeine. Nearly twice that concentration of hydrocodone or 6-acetylmorphine would be needed to produce a positive opiate test.

5. Review and Discussion of the Literature

Each of the studies discussed below evaluated the performance of the OnTrak TesTcup® or OnTrak TesTcup® -5. To date, there have been no published studies that have assessed the performance of the OnTrak TesTcup® -er.

5.1. *Study #1* (1)

5.1.1. *Methods*

This study evaluated the performance of OnTrak TesTcup® for the detection of BZE, opiates and THC-COOH. Control samples were prepared for each drug at 25%, 50%, 100%, 120% and 150% and 200% of the cutoff concentration. The precision of each test was determined by analyzing (n = 20) replicates of the control samples on five separate days. Donor samples were selected as positive or negative by an instrument-based immunoassay and by GC/MS confirmation. The specificity of each test was evaluated using a variety of drugs and metabolites at concentrations up to 1,000,000 ng/mL. The stability of the target analytes in the OnTrak TesTcup® was assessed using samples fortified with drug at 50% and 120% the immunoassay cutoff concentration. The storage conditions for the stability study were room temperature, 4° and –20°C and the samples were analyzed at time 0, 1, 3 and 6 months.

5.1.2. *Results*

In the precision experiments, there were no negative (or 25% of cutoff concentration samples) that tested positive for any of the three drugs. Of those control samples containing target drug at 50% of the cutoff (n = 100 tests), four tested positive for BZE and THC-COOH and two tested positive for morphine. Good assay discrimination was demonstrated near the cutoff for the three drugs. Of those control samples fortified with drug at 120% of the cutoff ≥ 97% tested positive. Only two samples (each) that were fortified with drug at 150% of the cutoff tested negative for BZE and THC-COOH.

In one experiment, 301 donor samples that had previously tested positive by an instrument-based immunoassay and by GC/MS were selected to challenge OnTrak TesTcup®. All donor samples tested positive. In a second experiment, OnTrak TesTcup® results were compared to those obtained using an alternate on-site testing device. Approximately 100 positive and 300 negative samples were tested for BZE, morphine, and THC-COOH using both kits. A single discrepancy was found in which one sample that tested positive by OnTrak TesTcup® for morphine tested negative using the other device. In a third experiment, a comparison was made with results from an instrument-based immu-

Table 1
Crossreactivity of the Drug Test Antibodies

Test (Cutoff)	Target analyte	Tested analyte	% Crossreactivity
Amphetamines (1,000 ng/mL)	*d,l*-Amphetamine	*d*-Amphetamine	200
		l-Amphetamine	4
		p-Hydroxyamphetamine	50
		All others listed	≤ 1
Barbiturates (200 ng/mL)	Secobarbital	Amobarbital	40
		Barbital	20
		Butabarbital	50
		Butalbital	100
		Pentobarbital	50
		Phenobarbital	40
Benzodiazepines (200 ng/mL)	Oxazepam	Alprazolam	22
		α-Hydroxyalprazolam	160
		4-Hydroxyalprazolam	133
		Chlordiazepoxide	22
		Demoxepam	50
		Temazepam	200
		7-Aminoflunitrazepam	200
		Flurazepam	33
		Desalkylflurazepam	50
		Hydroxyethylflurazepam	133
		Lorazepam	50
		Triazolam	4
		α-Hydroxytriazolam	100
		4-Hyroxytriazolam	50
		Nordiazepam	22
Cannabinoids (50 ng/mL)	THC-COOH	8-11-Dihydroxy-THC	20
		8-Hydroxy-THC	12.5
		11-Hydroxy-THC	5
		11-Hydroxy-cannabinol	2.5
		All others listed	≤ 1
Cocaine (300 ng/mL)	Benzoylecgonine	Cocaine	< 1
		Ecgonine	< 1
		Ecgonine methyl ester	< 1
Opiates (300 ng/mL)	Morphine	Codeine	100
		Morphine-3-glucuronide	86
		Hydromorphone	43
		Hydrocodone	60
		6-Acetylmorphine	60
		Oxycodone	2.5
		Meperidine	1.2
		Norcodeine	1.2

Source: Roche Diagnostics, 1997, 1999.

noassay. Approx 100 positive and 300 negative samples were tested for the three drugs using both kits. Ninety-nine per cent agreement was obtained.

The results of the specificity experiments were similar to those shown in Table 1. None of the tested cocaine metabolites cross-reacted with OnTrak TesTcup® at > 0.4%. Several opiates were significantly cross-reactive. Codeine and ethylmorphine (100%), morphine-3-Glucuronide (86%), dihydrocodeine and dihydromorphine (75%), 6-acetylmorphine and hydrocodone (60%), and hydromorphone (43%). Hydroxylated metabolites of delta-9-THC had cross reactivity that varied from 2.5% to 20%.

The results of the stability experiments demonstrated that BZE, morphine, and THC-COOH were stable in urine stored in the OnTrak TesTcup® for up to 6 months if the temperature was ≤ 4°C. BZE was relatively stable in the cup at room temperature for six months. At room temperature, the morphine concentration had decreased by < 10% at one month, and declined more precipitously for the duration of the study. At room temperature, the concentration of THC-COOH decreased by > 10% in the first month and continued to decline for the duration of the study. The morphine and THC-COOH degradation observed when samples were stored in the cup was similar to that observed when samples were stored in plastic and glass bottles.

5.1.3. Discussion

This was one of the first published studies that described the OnTrak TesTcup® and its performance. As such, it contains a thorough physical description of the product and a comprehensive discussion of the immunochemical principles used by the device. The study was designed to challenge the OnTrak TesTcup® around the reporting cutoff where performance is very important. This is also an important study because it evaluated the stability of the tested drugs when stored in the cup. Unfortunately, this study was performed when OnTrak TesTcup® was only available as a product to test for three drug classes and contains no information about the detection of amphetamines or PCP.

5.2. Study #2 (2)

5.2.1. Methods

This study is similar to the study of Towt et al., 1995 described earlier *(1)*. However, it evaluated the performance of OnTrak TesTcup® -5 for the detection of amphetamines and PCP in addition to BZE, opiates and THC-COOH. Control samples were prepared for each drug at 25%, 50%, 100%, 120% and 150% of the cutoff concentration. These samples were used to determine the precision of each test by analyzing $n = 20$ replicates of the controls each day for 5 days. Donor samples were selected as positive or negative by an instrument-based immunoassay and by GC/MS confirmation as described above *(1)*. Amphetamines were confirmed to 500 ng/mL and PCP to 25 ng/mL.

5.2.2. Results

In the precision experiment, there were no negative or 25% of cutoff concentration samples that tested positive for any of the five drugs. Of the 100 control samples tested that contained target drug at 50% of the cutoff, four tested positive for BZE and THC-COOH and two tested positive for morphine. Of those control samples fortified with drug at 120% of the cutoff ≥ 97% tested positive for BZE, morphine, and THC-COOH, 87% tested positive for amphetamine and 83% tested positive for PCP. Of those control samples fortified with drug at 150% of the cutoff, ≥ 98% tested positive in each drug group.

In one experiment, donor samples were selected to challenge OnTrak TesTcup® -5 that had previously tested positive by an instrument-based immunoassay and by GC/MS. All tested positive using OnTrak TesTcup® -5. In a second experiment, OnTrak TesTcup® -5 results were compared to those obtained using an alternate on-site testing device. The results between the two devices agreed 100% for the BZE, PCP and THC-COOH negative samples. One sample tested positive for morphine and one for amphetamines using OnTrak TesTcup® -5 that tested negative using the alternate on-site device. There was 100% agreement between the devices for positive donor samples.

5.2.3. Discussion

This was one of the first published studies that described the performance of OnTrak TesTcup® -5. Therefore, it contains performance data for the analysis of PCP and amphetamines. Like the 1995 Towt study, this study was designed to challenge the OnTrak TesTcup® around the testing cutoff where discrimination between positive and negative samples is critical *(1)*. Good analytical performance was demonstrated near the screening cutoff (≥ 97%) for BZE, opiates and THC-COOH. Of those control samples fortified with drug at 150% of the cutoff, ≥ 98% tested positive in each of the 5 drug classes. Testing of donor samples compared favorably with laboratory based testing and with a second on-site device. Unfortunately, this study was not published in the peer-reviewed literature and is not widely available.

5.3. Study #3 (9)

5.3.1. Methods

This study was designed to compare results obtained from two separate on-site drug testing devices with those obtained from an instrument-based immunoassay and GC/MS. The laboratory testing were used to select 250 negative and 100 positive urine samples each for BZE, opiates and THC-COOH. The workplace urinalysis drug testing cutoff concentrations described above were used for sample selection. Samples were submitted in a random and blind fashion to trained laboratory personnel for the OnTrak TesTcup® analyses.

5.3.2. Results

OnTrak TesTcup® had a 100% agreement with GC/MS and a >99% agreement with the instrument-based immunoassay when testing negative donor samples. The agreement between OnTrak TesTcup® and the instrument-based immunoassay results for samples containing opiates was 100%, BZE was 98% and for THC-COOH was 92%. All discrepant THC-COOH samples had GC/MS determined concentrations < the 50 ng/mL screening cutoff and the discrepant BZE samples had a mean BZE concentration of 186.5 ng/mL. OnTrak® (the second on-site device) had a similar agreement with both GC/MS and the instrument-based immunoassay when testing negative samples and samples that contained opiates. A 91% agreement was found for testing of samples that contained BZE and 89% when testing samples that contained THC-COOH. The authors concluded that obtaining a positive test result, when a negative result was obtained by an instrument-based technique for the detection of BZE, opiates or THC-COOH using either on-site testing device, was a rare event. Obtaining any type of discrepant opiate results was also rare. When negative results were obtained using the on-site devices for BZE, and positive laboratory results were reported, the mean concentration of BZE by GC/MS was close to the cutoff (344.1 ng/mL). Also, most discrepant samples contained ≤300 ng/mL of BZE by GC/MS. Both OnTrak® and OnTrak TesTcup® obtained negative results for six samples that had positive instrument-based immunoassay results for THC-COOH. The GC/MS analyses of these six samples showed that no sample contained more than 36 ng/mL of THC-COOH (mean 26.8 ng/mL). Therefore, all were less than the 50 ng/mL screening cutoff concentration.

5.3.3. Discussion

This study compared OnTrak TesTcup® results those of an established first generation on-site device (OnTrak®), to an instrument-based immunoassay and to GC/MS results. All samples were tested "blindly" by the on-site testing analysts to ensure unbiased results. Additional GC/MS testing was performed at cutoffs much lower than the typical workplace concentrations to investigate all discrepant results. A thorough discussion of the impact of cross-reactive substances on the OnTrak TesTcup® and how this can affect reporting and data interpretation is provided. Like the 1995 Towt study, this study was performed when OnTrak TesTcup® was only available as a product to test for three drug classes and contains no information on its the detection of amphetamines or PCP (1).

5.4. Study #4 (10)

5.4.1. Methods

This study evaluated the performance of three on-site devices (OnTrak TesTcup® -5, Rapid Drug Screen® and AccuSign® DOA) for the analysis of amphetamines, BZE, opiates, PCP and THC-COOH. The devices were evaluated on their ability to discriminate between positive and negative samples around the cutoff and to properly identify negative and positive donor samples. The effect of adulterants on each test was also assessed. Control samples were prepared that contained drugs at 50%, 75%, 125% and 150% of the workplace immunoassay cutoff concentrations. These samples contained *d,l*-amphetamine, BZE, morphine, PCP, and THC-COOH. Donor samples were selected as positive or negative by instrument based immunoassay and by GC/MS. One hundred negative samples and positive samples (between 20 and 134/drug) were selected to challenge each device. Effects from the following commercial products were tested: dry bleach, liquid detergent, table salt, a drain opener, and Visine®. In addition, commercially available urine adulterants with the following ingredients were tested: glutaraldehyde, nitrites and a strong inorganic acid.

5.4.2. Results

Results of the experiments designed to assess the precision and discrimination of the devices at drug concentrations around the cutoff are shown in Table 2. The results show that OnTrak TesTcup® -5 had fewer errors than Rapid Drug Screen® for the detection of all of the drug classes and at all concentrations. The table also shows that, when the sample concentrations were less than the cutoff, OnTrak TesTcup® -5 had fewer errors than AccuSign® for all of the drugs tested except PCP. At sample concentrations of 125% of the cutoff, OnTrak TesTcup® -5 had < 10% errors for all drugs except THC-COOH. Results were mixed with AccuSign®, but the magnitude of the error was generally less with OnTrak TesTcup® -5. At sample concentration of 150% of the cutoff, OnTrak TesTcup® -5 had < 10% errors for all drugs. Performance of the three devices when testing donor samples is also shown in the table. When testing negative donor samples, OnTrak TesTcup® -5 had no errors, AccuSign® had < 2.0% errors for all drug classes and the Rapid Drug Screen® errors varied by drug, but were between 0% and 12%. OnTrak TesTcup® -5 had no errors when testing positive donor samples for amphetamine and PCP and < 5.0 for the other drugs. The AccuSign® error rates for positive donor samples varied between 0.8 and 30%. Rapid Drug Screen® error rates varied between 0 and 33% when testing these samples.

A complete discussion of the effect(s) of each adulterant on the individual drug tests for each device is beyond the scope of this chapter. All devices were affected to some extent. However, the author concluded that with the exception of strong acids (that caused invalid test results) the adulterants had little effect on the three devices. The addition of dry bleach, drain cleaner or table salt to urine samples had no effect on OnTrak Testcup® -5 results. The addition of liquid detergent, Visine®, glutaraldehyde and nitrites showed variable effects on the ability of OnTrak Testcup® -5 to detect THC-COOH and BZE in positive samples.

5.4.3. Discussion

This study compared results obtained from three popular on-site devices for the analysis of five commonly encountered drug classes. The study also evaluated the performance of each device near the reporting cutoff concentration where discrimination between positive samples and negative samples is most problematic. Sample dilution, substitution and adulteration are significant problems in urinalysis workplace drug testing *(7,8)*. This study contains some of the only available data describing the effects of the various potential adulterants on the devices. This study has not been published in the peer-reviewed literature. Also, the GC/MS data are not presented so it is not possible to thoroughly critique the data and fully understand the performance of each device when testing donor samples.

5.5. *Study #5* (11)

5.5.1. Methods

Results from five on-site drug testing devices (PharmScreen®, OnTrak TesTcup® -5, Status® DS, Rapid Drug Screen® and AccuSign® DOA) were compared. Each device was used to test for the standard five drugs, except AccuSign® that tested for BZE and THC-COOH only. The devices were evaluated for their ability to discriminate between positive and negative samples around the cutoff and their ability to correctly identify negative and positive donor samples. Commercial controls ($n = 10$) were prepared at 75% and 125%

Table 2

Percent Errors When Testing Samples Containing Target Drug Concentration Near the Cutoff with Three On-Site Devices

DRUG/Concentration	50% of Cutoff			75% of Cutoff			125% of Cutoff			150% of Cutoff		
	TesTcup	Rapid Drug Screen	AccuSign	TesTcup	Rapid Drug Screen	AccuSign	TesTcup	Rapid Drug Screen	AccuSign	TesTcup	Rapid Drug Screen	AccuSign
Amphetamine	0	10	30	10	20	60	7.5	90	0	2.5	80	0
Benzoylecgonine	0	0	0	0	0	40	5	100	0	2.5	100	0
THC-COOH	0	30	10	0	20	20	20	30	20	7.5	10	30
Morphine	0	10	0	10	40	10	5	80	0	0	20	0
Phencyclidine	0	40	10	10	40	0	2.5	40	50	2.5	10	20

Data presented as % errors

	Negative donor samples			Positive donor samples		
	TesTcup	Rapid Drug Screen	AccuSign	TesTcup	Rapid Drug Screen	AccuSign
Amphetamine	0	8.6	0	0	0	8.3
Benzoylecgonine	0	0	3	0.7	21.1	2.2
THC-COOH	0	12	0	4.4	21	11.4
Morphine	0	4	1	0.8	9.8	0.8
Phencyclidine	0	6.4	0	0	33.3	30

of the standard immunoassay cutoff concentrations. The controls contained methamphetamine, BZE, morphine, PCP and THC-COOH. Donor samples were selected as positive or negative by instrument-based immunoassay screening and GC/MS confirmation.

5.5.2. Results

No errors occurred with any of the devices for the analyses of BZE and opiates in the precision experiment at analyte concentrations of 125% of the cutoff. Only OnTrak Testcup® -5 tested positive for 100% of the control challenges that contained PCP. All devices failed to detect methamphetamine in this experiment and OnTrak Testcup® -5 tested positive for only 4 of 10 control samples that contained THC-COOH. The other devices tested positive for at least 90% of the THC-COOH control samples. At control sample concentration of 75% of the cutoff (where negative results were predicted), no errors were observed for amphetamine testing with any of the devices. Essentially, the devices uniformly tested positive for BZE. Only OnTrak Testcup® -5 tested negative (correctly) for 100% of the THC-COOH challenges and only OnTrak Testcup® -5 and PharmScreen® tested negative for all PCP challenges. Results were mixed when testing for opiates. However, OnTrak Testcup® -5 demonstrated the best performance of the five devices

In the experiment with donor samples, each device was challenged with 22 negative samples. OnTrak Testcup® -5, PharmScreen®, AccuSign®, and Status® DS had no testing errors. Each device was also challenged with 20 positive donor samples. No testing errors were reported using any of the devices when testing for BZE, THC-COOH or opiates (with the exception that a single error each with OnTrak Testcup® -5 and Status® DS when testing for opiates). PCP results were quite variable with all of the devices. Amphetamine results were also quite variable because some positive donor samples contained amphetamine, some methamphetamine, some amphetamine and methamphetamine, and others contained sympathomimetic amines.

5.5.3. Discussion

This study compared results from five popular on-site devices. The study evaluated the performance of each device with actual donor samples as well as near the reporting cutoff concentration. The authors reached the following conclusions: No on-site device performed as well as the instrument-based immunoassay. However, this criticism seems unwarranted since only six of the 20 positive amphetamine challenges contained amphetamine or methamphetamine when analyzed by GC/MS. The authors also concluded that this study demonstrated that GC/MS confirmation of all positive on-site results is needed. Further, because of the poor performance of the devices around the reporting cutoff concentration, the authors concluded that there may be more false positive and false negative test results using on-site devices than with instrument-based immunoassay testing. A limitation of this study was its use of a relatively small number of experimental challenges. Only ten challenges were used in each precision experiment and only 20 negative and 20 positive donor challenges were used.

5.6. Study #6 (12)

5.6.1. Methods

In this study, results obtained from fifteen on-site devices were compared. The instrument-based immunoassay response was used to categorize donor samples as negative, below the cutoff, above the cutoff or as high (>25% above the cutoff) *(13)*. GC/MS confirmation testing was performed on all samples at the conclusion of the study.

5.6.2. Results

All devices were rated by their ability to detect true negative and true positive samples and by their calculated positive and negative predictive values. These data are presented in an extensive set of tables and figures. Using the GC/MS results as the standard for performance, OnTrak Testcup® -5 was at least equivalent to the other top performing on-site devices. The authors concluded that no single product was ideally suited for all applications and that each might have a niche given the variety of drug testing needs.

5.6.3. Discussion

This study presents a comprehensive comparison of several on-site devices. It contains summaries that discuss each device, the procedure used by the device and has vendor contact information. It also presents the findings in tabular and graphic form and in great detail. However, the study has several limitations. The study has not been published in the peer-reviewed scientific literature. Not all devices were challenged with the same set of donor samples. For example, only 30% of the amphetamines challenges to OnTrak Testcup® -5 were used to challenge the other devices. Therefore, it is difficult to compare results between devices. The authors do not present the GC/MS data. These data are needed to assess the performance of the instrument-based immunoassay and to determine if an apparent error can be explained based on the cutoff concentrations used or by differences in antibody specificity *(13,14)*. In addition, some of the GC/MS confirmation analyses were performed up to 90 d after the on-site testing was performed. This can adversely affect the results, since some drugs, such as THC-COOH, are not stable in urine for extended periods of time.

5.7. *Study #7* (14)

5.7.1. *Methods*

In this study, results from four on-site drug testing devices (OnTrak Testcup® -5, Triage®, OnTrak® and Abu-Sign®) were compared. The devices were evaluated for their accuracy and efficiency in detecting BZE, opiates, and THC-COOH using samples selected from 303 drivers arrested for driving-under-the-influence (DUI). Samples were verified as positive or negative by instrument-based immunoassay and GC/MS. The authors also made a subjective assessment of the ease of use, analysis time required, and objectivity of the test results. The negative predictive value, positive predictive value, sensitivity, and specificity of each device were calculated.

5.7.2. *Results*

For ease of use and reliability, the analysts ranked the devices in this order: OnTrak TesTcup® > Abu-Sign® > Triage® > OnTrak®. The positive predictive value (PPV) is the likelihood that a positive test result is a true positive. OnTrak TesTcup® had a PPV less than the device mean for BZE and greater than the device mean for THC-COOH. There were only two opiate positive samples. Therefore, these data were not summarized. The negative predictive value (NPV) is the likelihood that a negative result is a true negative. OnTrak TesTcup® had a NPV greater than the device mean for BZE and equal to the device mean for THC-COOH. The sensitivity of the device is the likelihood that the device will detect a positive urine from the population of samples containing that drug. OnTrak TesTcup® had a sensitivity greater than the device mean for BZE and equal to the device mean for THC-COOH. The specificity of the device is the likelihood that the device will detect a negative urine from the population of samples that do not contain the drug. OnTrak TesTcup® had a specificity less than the device mean for BZE and greater than the device mean for THC-COOH.

5.7.3. *Discussion*

This study demonstrated that on-site devices could be used to test urine collected from DUI suspects. The authors concluded that all of the devices performed well and were reliable. The authors believed that nontechnical people could be trained to effectively use the devices. They recommended that positive results from on-site devices be confirmed by GC/MS. They also thought that if confirmation testing was not practical, users should choose the device that had the highest calculated specificity, because this device had the lowest probability of producing a false positive result.

6. Conclusions

OnTrak TesTcup® remains an important product for drug testing in many situations where PCP analysis is not indicated. OnTrak Testcup® -5 has been advocated for urinalysis drug testing in clinical, workplace and forensic toxicology. OnTrak TesTcup® -er has utility in the medicolegal test area, but was specifically designed for clinical testing because it can detect benzodiazepines and barbiturates. All products were designed to eliminate many of the technical barriers often encountered when using on-site drug testing devices. Because the cup acts as a collection and testing vessel, no sample transfer, no reagent dispensing, and no reagent mixing is required. A drug test for a panel of five drugs takes approximately 5 min.

Numerous studies designed to determine the accuracy of on-site devices have been presented at scientific meetings and reported in the scientific literature. However, OnTrak TesTcup® -er is a sufficiently new product and no such scientific studies have been reported. Seven studies were discussed above that have assessed the accuracy of OnTrak Testcup® -5. Usually, these studies were designed to compare OnTrak Testcup® -5 results to those obtained from an instrument-based immunoassay, GC/MS, from one or more alternate on-site devices or from a combination of these analytical techniques. Each study has limitations. Several factors are important to consider when evaluating a study. Is the study published in the peer-reviewed scientific literature? Weight should be given to those studies that have been published. How large is the study population? Generally, larger is better. What was used as the reference method? Selection of the reference method is important since drug screen and GC/MS confirmation tests usually use different cutoff concentrations. The author should provide reference method(s), data and a discussion of actual and apparent discrepant samples. What was the target drug for the antibody? This is important since device antibodies may target different drugs in a drug class. For example OnTrak Testcup® -5 and OnTrak TesTcup® -er target amphetamine, while many other on-site devices target methamphetamine. Therefore, selection of donor samples and preparation of control challenges will affect the results *(11,12)*.

In the evaluations presented, OnTrak TesTcup® and OnTrak TesTcup®-5 performed quite well. The devices were shown to be precise around the cutoff *(1,2,10,11)*. The devices were also shown to discriminate between positive and negative donor samples *(1,2,9–11)*. All immunoassay tests are subject to interferences. However, OnTrak Testcup® -5 assays performed well when testing samples adulterated with various commercial products and known testing interferants *(10)*. In a number of studies, the performance of OnTrak Testcup® -5 has been equivalent to the laboratory-based immunoassay *(1,2,9)*. In studies comparing on-site devices, OnTrak Testcup® -5 also performed very well *(9–14)*. Given this information, users should expect accurate and reliable urinalysis drug test results when using OnTrak Testcup® -5.

7. Acknowledgment

The author would like to acknowledge the contribution of Jane Tsai, Ph.D., Director of Research and Development, Roche Diagnostic Corporation, Indianapolis, IN for providing Figs. 1, 2, and 3 and for her factual review of this chapter.

References

1. Towt, J., Tsai, J. S. -C., Hernandez, M. R., Klimov, A. D., Kravec, C. V., Rouse, S. L., et al. (1995) ONTRAK TESTCUP: A novel, On-site, Multi-Analyte screen for the detection of abused drugs. *J. Analyt. Tox.* **19,** 504–510.
2. Tsai, J. S. -C., Towt, J., Kravec, D., Oades, B., Rashid, F., Talbot, L., et al. (1997) ONTRAK TESTCUP®-5: A Multi-analyte immunoassay device for On-site drug testing. *TIAFT Proccedings XXXV Annual meeting.*
3. Roche Diagnostics. (1996) ONTRAK TESTCUP® Collection/Urinalysis Panel for Amphetamines, Cocaine, THC, and Morphine—25 cup kit. Roche Diagnostics, Indianapolis, IN.
4. Roche Diagnostics. (1998) ONTRAK TESTCUP® -5 Collection/Urinalysis Panel for Amphetamines, Cocaine, THC, PCP, and Morphine—25 cup kit. Roche Diagnostics, Indianapolis, IN.
5. Roche Diagnostics. (1999) ONTRAK TESTCUP® -er Collection/Urinalysis Panel for Amphetamines, Barbiturates, Benzodiazepines, Cocaine, and Morphine—25 cup kit. Roche Diagnostics, Indianapolis, IN.
6. Dept. of Health & Human Services. (1996) Mandatory Guidelines for Fedreal Workplace Drug Testing Programs; Notice. Federal Register.
7. Dept.of Health & Human Services. (1998) Notice to HHS Certified and Applicant Laboratories, Subject: Guidance for Reporting Specimen Validity Test Results. PD 035.
8. Dept.of Health & Human Services. (1999) Notice to HHS Certified and Applicant Laboratories, Subject: Specimen Validity Testing. PD 037.
9. Crouch. D. J., Cheever, M. L., Andrenyak, D. M., Kuntz, D. J., and Loughmiller, B. S. (1998) A comparison of ONTRAK TESTCUP™, Abuscreen ONTRAK®, Abuscreen ONLINE®, and GC/MS urinialysis test results. *J. For. Sci.* **43,** 35–40.
10. Bogema, S. C. (1997) Evaluation of three rapid immunoassay devices for screening of DHHS five drugs in urine. Presented Annual Meeting of the Society of Forensic Toxicologists., Salt Lake City, UT.
11. Taylor, H. E., Oertli, E. H., and Wolfgang, J. W. (1999) Accuracy of five on-site immunoassay drugs-of-abuse testing devices. *J. Analyt. Tox.* **23,** 119–124.

12. Willette, R. E. (1997) Administrative Office of the U. S. Courts (report to). An Evaluation of Non-Instrumented Drug Tests. Duo Research, Denver, CO.
13. Crouch, D. J., Frank, J. F., Farrell L. J., Karsch, H. M., and Klaunig, J. E. (1998) A multiple-site laboratory evaluation of three on-site urinialysis drug-testing devices. *J. Analyt. Tox.* **22,** 493–514.
14. Buchan, B. J., Walsh, J. M., and Leaverton, P. E. (1998) Evaluation of the accuracy of on-site multi-analyte drug testing devices in the determination of the prevalence of illicit drugs in drivers. *J. For. Sci.* **43,** 395–399.

Chapter 14

OnTrak TesTstik Device

Salvatore J. Salamone and Jane S-C. Tsai

1. Introduction

The OnTrak TesTstik represents a second generation point-of-care device for the testing of drugs in urine (Fig. 1). It was launched in November 1997 and was developed as a replacement product for the Abuscreen OnTrak line *(1–5)* of drug testing products. The Abuscreen OnTrak line was launched in 1989 and was the first full product line that tested for drugs in urine without the need of instrumentation or the need to have highly trained technical personnel. The OnTrak technology was based on latex agglutination and when compared to instrument based immunoassays and gas chromatography/mass spectroscopy (GC/MS) was shown to be a reliable testing method for on–site testing. OnTrak gained wide Market acceptance especially in the fields of Criminal Justice and Drug Treatment. OnTrak TesTstik was developed in response to market forces, which required on-site drug tests with a minimum amount of manipulation. While OnTrak was shown to give accurate results within three minutes, the addition of sample followed by one drop each of three different reagents, followed by a quick stir, was seen as too labor intensive. In the mid 1990s one step tests were commercialized that were based on immunochromatography. These tests involved the addition of sample and reading the colored result within three to ten minutes. Other types of tests also appeared during this time that analyzed for multiple drugs within the same device. A number of these devices were reported in the literature under various product names Triage *(5–10)*, EZ-Screen *(5,11)*, Verdict *(12)*, AbuSign *(12)*, Biosign *(12)*, I.D.Block *(12)*, MachIV *(12)*, AccuPinch *(13)*, and TesTcup *(14,15)*. This chapter will describe the TesTstik device and show the performance of five TesTstik assays for the detection of amphetamines, cocaine

From: *Forensic Science: On-Site Drug Testing*
Edited by: A. J. Jenkins and B. A. Goldberger © Humana Press, Inc., Totowa, NJ

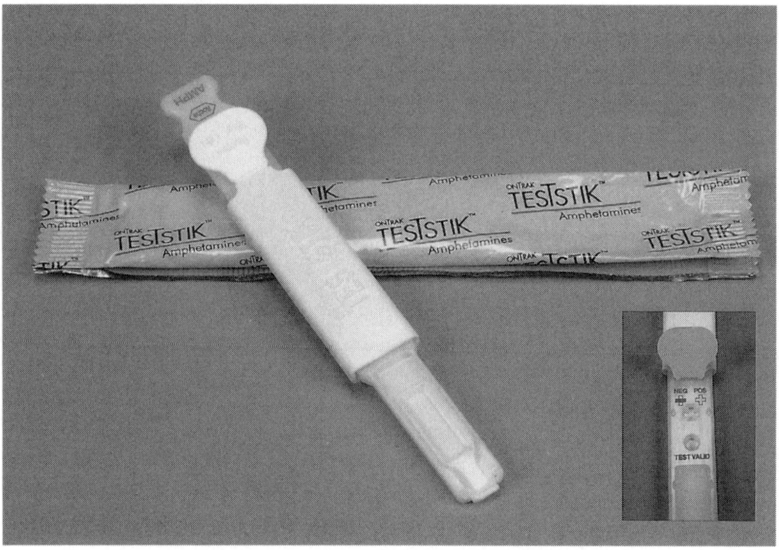

Fig. 1. OnTrak TesTstik device with packaging.

metabolite (benzoylecgonine), morphine, phencyclidine (PCP), and cannabinoids. The performance was compared to the performance of Abuscreen OnTrak, Abuscreen OnLine, and GC/MS using drug spiked urine standards and human urine specimens.

2. *Materials and Methods*

2.1. *Instrumentation and Reagents*

Abuscreen OnLine reagents and calibrators, Abuscreen OnTrak reagents and the OnTrak TesTstik assays were obtained from Roche Diagnostics Corporation (Indianapolis, IN). OnLine assays were performed on a COBAS MIRA analyzer, and OnTrak assays were performed according to the manufacturer's instructions.

2.2. *Precision Study Methods*

Standards at 0, 0.25, 0.75, 1.25, and 1.5 times the cutoff were each assayed by 20 individual TesTstiks each day for 5 d for each of the five drug types (In total: 100 replicate tests for each drug type at each standard drug concentration). Standard (300 µL) was added directly to the sample pad of each TesTstik. Each TesTstik was evaluated randomly by two individuals who were blind as to the origin of the sample. These two individuals were different from the person performing the assay, and each interpreted the results within approximately a minute of each other. Each assay result was determined to be either positive (the absence of a colored bar in the test result window) or negative (the presence of a colored bar in the test result window) by the two individuals. Discrepancies between the two analysts were decided by a third individual who was also blind to the origin of the sample.

2.3. Clinical Evaluation and Comparative Study

Clinical specimens, which were positive for amphetamine, benzoylecgonine, morphine, PCP, or THCCOOH, were taken from a frozen sample bank. The specimens were obtained from a commercial laboratory where they had been tested by a drug immunoassay (cutoffs of 1000, 300, 300, 25, and 50 ng/mL for amphetamines, benzoylecgonine, opiates, PCP, and cannabinoids, respectively) and GC/MS confirmed before freezing (cutoffs of 500, 150, 300, 25 and 15 ng/mL for amphetamine, benzoylecgonine, morphine, PCP, and THCCOOH, respectively). Cannabinoid positive specimens were re-confirmed to be greater than or equal to 50 ng/mL by the OnLine assay on the same day they were tested by TesTstik and OnTrak. To conserve the limited volume of sample in the positive specimens, 300 μL was added directly to the sample pad of the TesTstik (approximately the volume of specimen that the sample pad would absorb during a 10-s dip of the TesTstik into a specimen). The frozen sample was first thawed and allowed to reach room temperature. Positive samples were also assayed by OnTrak and OnLine, within one week of testing by TesTstik.

Clinical negative urine specimens were obtained from a testing laboratory, where they had been screened negative by the OnLine assays for the five drugs, and stored at 4°C. Negative specimens were brought to room temperature and tested in the same manner as the positive specimens.

2.4. Specificity

The approximate specificity of the assays for different drugs and metabolites were assessed by comparing the assays' responses with the drugs to that with the target drug. For the purposes of interpreting the assay's response, a color intensity rating system was developed. Each result was visually rated on a scale from 0.0 to 3.0 in 0.5 unit increments. A 0.0 color unit represented no color and a 3.0 color unit represented the strongest color. Photographs of rated results using reference standards served as a reference. Different concentrations of drug containing urine specimens were prepared by serial dilution of a 1 mg/mL stock solution into drug-free urine. Concentrations of drug were based on the

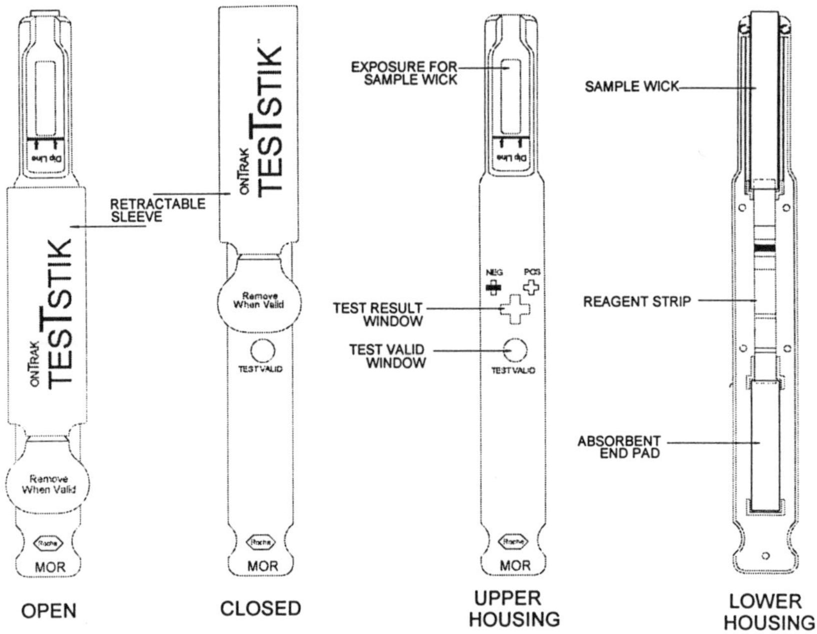

Fig. 2. TesTstik Device Design.

gravitometric addition of drug into the stock solution. No analytical verification of drug concentration was made. Dilutions were tested in the TesTstik by direct addition of 300 μL of the drug containing urine to the sample pad. Dilution and testing of drug compound was continued until a concentration was found that produced an average color rating (five replicates) similar to the average of color ratings produced by the target analyte at its cutoff concentration (typically a 0.0 to 0.5 color rating). Concentrations of drug at ± 25% of this "cutoff-equivalent" concentration were tested to confirm relative crossreactivity. The percent crossreactivity of a particular drug compound was calculated by dividing the cutoff-equivalent concentration of the drug by the cutoff concentration of the target analyte and multiplying by 100.

3. *The TesTstik Device*

The OnTrak TesTstik is a self-contained device that has all the reagents necessary to test a specimen for a particular illicit drug or its metabolites. As shown in Fig. 2, it consists of a plastic housing that encases a sample pad, reagent strip and an end pad. A retractable outer plastic sleeve covered the sample pad in the closed position and exposed the pad in the open position.

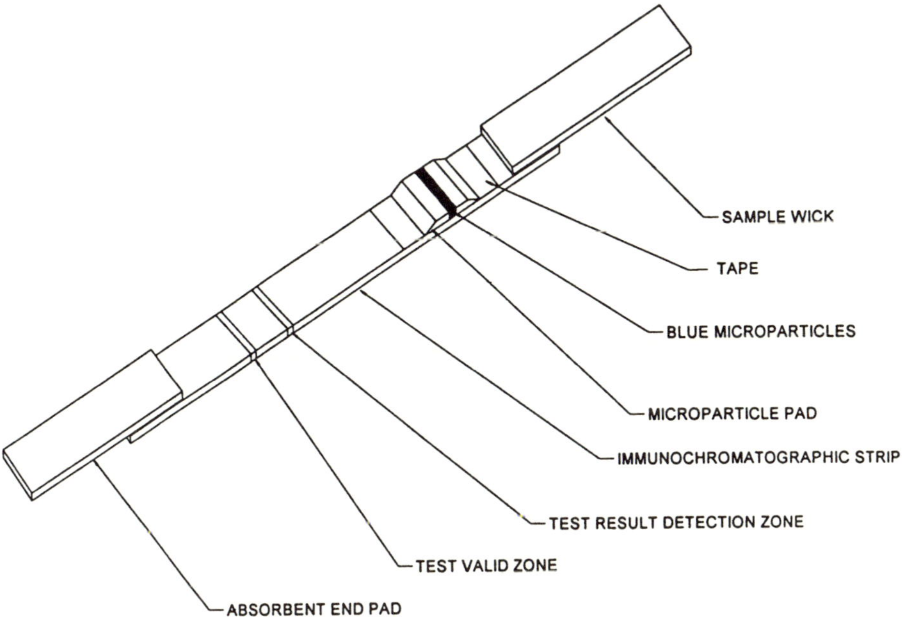

Fig. 3. TesTstik Strip Design.

The reagent strip, as depicted in Fig. 3 is comprised of four segments: a nitrocellulose strip with a nitrocellulose pad containing antibody-coated blue microparticles and a cellulose pad at each of the strip. The sample wick contains dried buffer and chemicals to condition the urine before it enters the nitrocellulose strip. The end pad serves to wick off the excess urine that runs down the test strip. The test result detection zone contains an immobilized drug-protein bound conjugate specific for the particular drug that is being tested. The test valid zone contains an immobilized monoclonal antibody that can interact with a nondrug antigen that is absorbed on the surface of the blue colored microparticles.

4. Principle of Procedure

The OnTrak TesTstik assay is based on the principle of microparticle capture inhibition using a modified immunochromatographic design *(16)*. The test relies on the competition between drug, which may be present in the urine being tested, and drug conjugate immobilized on membrane for binding to antibody-coated colored microparticles.

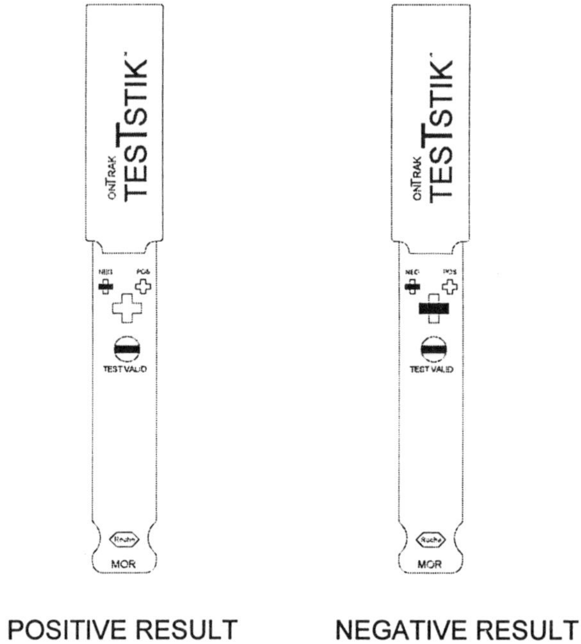

Fig. 4. TesTstik Result Interpretation.

When the TesTstik is immersed in the urine sample, some of the sample is absorbed in the TesTstik sample pad. The absorbed sample travels through a reagent strip contained in the device by capillary action. In the reagent strip, the sample rehydrates and mobilizes antibody-coated blue microparticles on the nitrocellulose pad. The microparticle-urine suspension continues to migrate through the reagent strip and comes in contact with the immobilized drug conjugate. In the absence of drug in the urine, the antibody-coated microparticles bind to the drug conjugate and a blue band is formed at the result window.

When drug is present in the specimen, it binds to the antibody-coated microparticles. If sufficient drug is present, the microparticles are inhibited from binding the drug conjugate and the blue band is not formed at the result window. A positive sample causes the membrane to remain white (Fig. 4).

An additional antibody/antigen reaction occurs at the "TEST VALID" area. The "TEST VALID" blue band forms when antibodies, which are imbedded in the reagent membrane, bind to the antigen on the blue microparticles. The presence of the "TEST VALID" band indicates that the test has completed, the reagents are viable and the results are ready to interpret (Fig. 5).

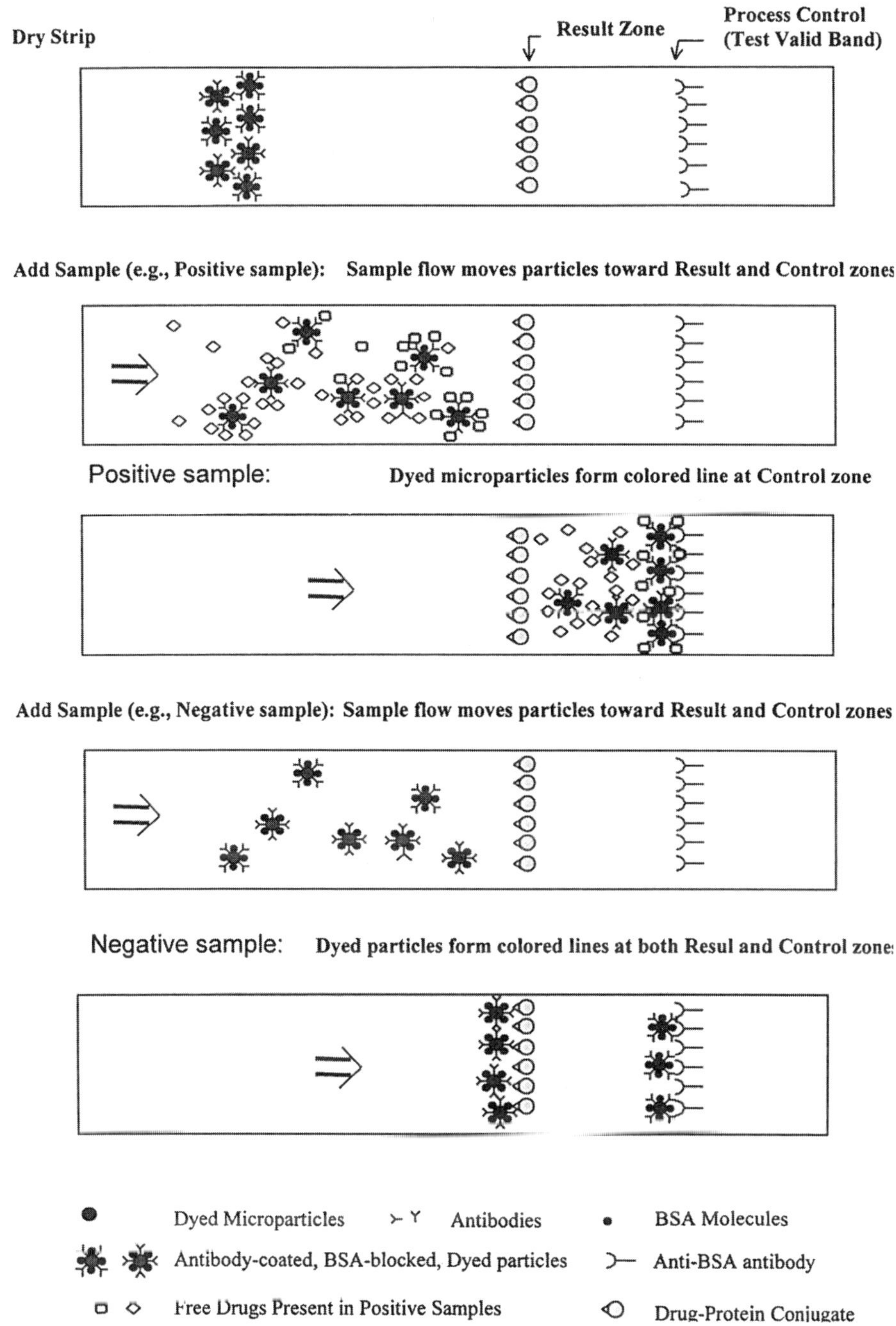

Fig. 5. Illustration of reaction principle.

The improved immunochromatographic design was developed for increased sensitivity. As the urine travels down the main strip it splits in two when it reaches the nitrocellulose pad containing the antibody-coated blue microparticles. The blue microparticles slowly wick out onto the main nitrocellulose strip and travel down to the detection zone. The slow wicking action of the blue microparticles allows for a greater amount of urine to react with the antibody-coated microparticles as compared with traditional immunochromatographic designs which have the antibody-coated particles on the main strip. In addition this modified design allows the drug in the sample more time to interact with the antibody before it reaches the detection zone.

5. Procedure

The TesTstik unit is ready to use when removed from its package. The protective sleeve is retracted and the sample pad end of the TesTstik is dipped into the specimen for approx 10 s. After the TesTstik is removed from the specimen, the sleeve is returned to the starting position. The sleeve helps prevent specimen from splashing and dripping. The sample pad absorbs approx 300 µL of specimen when the TesTstik is dipped into the specimen. The absorbed urine specimen migrates to and through the reagent strip where it interacts with the reagents as described above. Completion of the assay was indicated by the formation of a blue bar in the Test Valid window. Once the blue bar is formed at the Test Valid window, the plastic tab covering the result window is removed from the protective sleeve, and the results are interpreted.

6. Performance

The precision of the TesTstik assay results, using various concentrations of drug standards, is shown in Table 1. All five drug assays produced similar results. All assays demonstrated > 95% positive results using standards with drug concentrations at 1.5 times the cutoff. One hundred percent negative results were produced using standards with drug concentrations at ≤0.25 times the cutoff. At concentrations near the cutoff, the variation was greater. Greater than 90% positive results were obtained for all of the assays at drug concentrations 1.25 times the cutoff. Negative results were obtained 18 to 52 percent of the time for drug concentrations at 0.75 times the cutoff. This demonstrated that the TesTstik assays differentiated negative from positive specimens with a high degree of confidence when the drug concentrations were ≤25% of the cutoff and ≥125% the cutoff respectively.

Table 1
Precision of TesTstik Assay Results

	Standard[a]									
	0		0.25		0.75		1.25		1.5	
Drug	pos[b]	neg[c]	pos	neg	pos	neg	pos	neg	pos	neg
Amphetamine	0	100	0	100	66	34	96	4	98	2
Benzoylecgonine	0	100	0	100	82	18	96	4	97	3
Morphine	0	100	0	100	60	40	97	3	99	1
PCP	0	100	0	100	76	24	92	8	99	1
THC-COOH	0	100	0	100	48	52	98	2	99	1

[a], Standards were 0, 0.25, 0.75, 1.25, and 1.5 times the cutoff concentration for each assay
[b], Number of positive results
[c], Number of negative results

Table 2
Consistency of Result Interpretation
% Agreement Between Analysts[a]

	Standard[b]				
	0	0.25	0.75	1.25	1.5
Drug	% agreement	% agreement	% agreement	% agreement	% agreement
Amphetamine	100	100	75	96	99
Benzoylecgonine	100	100	96	97	96
Morphine	100	100	75	98	98
PCP	100	100	81	93	98
THC-COOH	100	100	94	98	95

[a]Two analysts independently interpreted 100 assays at each standard concentration as positive or negative. The percent agreement was the number interpreted the same by both analysts.
[b]Standards were 0, 0.25, 0.75, 1.25, and 1.5 times the cutoff concentration for each assay.

Because the TesTstik results were visually interpreted by individual analysts, differences in interpretation and scoring the results could have arisen between different individuals. Table 2 shows the percent agreement between the two individuals who interpreted the results of the precision. These results corresponded to the precision results in Table 1. Where there was a high degree of precision there was a corresponding high percentage of agreement between the two analysts and *vice versa*. The drug standard at 0.75 times the cutoff had the highest degree of variability, and, produced the most disagreement between the analysts. Therefore, individual interpretation of the results appeared to be a factor only when the pivotal point between color formation and no color formation was approached. This occurred at drug concentrations near the assay's cutoff concentration. In the evaluation of clinical urine specimens, there was 100% agreement between the two analysts' interpreting the results. Table 3 summarizes the correlation of the TesTstik results with GC-MS results for positive samples, TesTstik versus OnTrak and TesTstik vs OnLine. These results show good correlation between TesTstik and the other testing methods.

In order to assess what drugs and metabolites the TesTstik assay recognized, and how this compared with the OnTrak and OnLine assays, human urine containing related drugs or metabolites was tested. Results, expressed as percent crossreactivity, are summarized in Table 4. Although there were some differences between the TesTstik, OnTrak and OnLine assays in their crossreactivities, generally the crossreactivities were similar (drug crossreactivities for the OnTrak, and OnLine assays were taken from package inserts—data not shown).

In certain circumstances, it may be required that specimens are stored for additional analysis. This may be particularly true for positive specimens if the results were to be used for legal purposes. In these incidences, it would be imperative that the integrity of the stored specimen remain intact. To assess whether the use of TesTstik compromised sample integrity the authors subjected urine standards containing no drug and standards containing drug, to multiple tests with the TesTstik, and determined the drug concentrations before and after testing. Thirty mL of each of two urine standards were subjected to testing by two each of the five TesTstik assays (Ten TesTstiks for each standard). One standard contained no drug and the other contained the five target drugs at approximately cutoff concentration. TesTstiks were dipped into the room-temperature standards for 10 s each. Each TesTstik absorbed approximately 300 µL of specimen, so there was a loss in sample volume of approximately 3 mL. The tested standards and equivalent controls (standards not subjected to TesTstik testing) were shipped, under environmental conditions, by overnight courier to the GC-MS laboratory. At the GC-MS laboratory, the specimens were stored at 4°C until they were tested (within one week of arrival). Results of GC-MS analysis demonstrated that testing by TesTstik did not change the drug concentration in the standards. The drug-free remained negative after testing, and the concentrations of the drugs in the cutoff standard did not chasnge (data not shown).

Table 3
Correlation of TesTstik Results with GC-MS, OnTrak, and OnLine

	Results				
	GC-MS	OnTrak		OnLine	
TesTstik	Positive	Positive	Negative	Positive	Negative
Amphetamine					
positive	50	48	3[a]	50	1[b]
negative	0	1[b]	104	0	105
Benzoylecgonine					
positive	50	50	0	50	0
negative	0	0	106	0	106
THCCOOH					
positive	45	45	0	45	0
negative	0	0	105	0	105
Morphine					
positive	49	50	0	50	0
negative	1[c]	1[c]	105	1[c]	105
PCP					
positive	50	50	0	50	0
negative	0	0	106	0	106

[a]Samples contained 0, 895, and 1282 ng/mL amphetamine, respectively, by GC-MS.
[b]Sample contained 0 ng/mL amphetamine by GC-MS.
[c]Sample contained 394 ng/mL morphine by GC-MS.

Table 4
Drug Crossreactivity in TesTstik

Drug	Approximate Crossreactivity (%)[a] TesTstik
Amphetamine-related compounds	
p-Hydroxyamphetamine	50
Methylenedioxyamphetamine	25
Methamphetamine	<0.2
Phenylpropanolamine	<0.2
Ephedrine	<0.2
Phenethylamine	<0.2
Phentermine	<0.2
Phenylephrine	<0.2
Pseudoephedrine	<0.2
Norpseudoephedrine	<0.2
Tyramine	<0.2

(continued)

Table 4 (cont.)
Drug Crossreactivity in TesTstik

Drug	Approximate Crossreactivity (%)[a] TesTstik
Benzoylecgonine-related compounds	
Cocaine HCl	0.75
Ecgonine HCl	<0.3
Ecgonine Methylester HCl	<0.3
Morphine-related compounds	
Codeine	100
Ethylmorphine HCl	100
Dihydrocodeine Bitartrate	100
Morphine-3-glucuronide	75
Dihydromorphine	75
6-Acetylmorphine	75
Hydrocodone bitartrate	50
Hydromorphone HCl	43
Thebaine	15
N-Norcodeine HCl	1.2
Oxycodone	1.2
Meperidine	0.3
Phencyclidine-related compounds	
1-(1-Phenylcyclohexyl)-pyrrolidine	100
1-[1-(2-Thienyl)cyclohexyl]-piperidine	50
1-(1-Phenylcyclohexyl)-4-hydroxypiperidine	5
4-Phenyl-4-piperidino-cyclohexanol	3
Ketamine	<0.01
Cannabinoid-related compounds	
8-ß-11-Dihydroxy-Δ^9-tetrahydrocannabinol	5
8-±-Hydroxy-Δ^9-tetrahydrocannabinol	5
11-Hydroxy-Δ^9-tetrahydrocannabinol	1.25
11-Hydroxy-cannabinol	0.5
Cannabidiol	<0.05
Cannabinol	<0.05
Δ^9-Tetrahydrocannabinol	<0.05

[a]% Cross-reactivity = the concentration of compound producing a result equivalent to that produced by the cutoff concentration divided by the cutoff concentration times 100 (amphetamine = 1000 ng/mL *d,l*-amphetamine, benzoylecgonine = 300 ng/mL benzoylecgonine, morphine = 300 ng/mL morphine, phencyclidine = 25 ng/mL phencyclidine, cannabinoids = 50 ng/mL THC-COOH).

7. Availability

OnTrak TesTstik may be purchased from Roche Diagnostics Corporation, Indianapolis, IN. Tests are available for amphetamines, barbiturates, benzodiazepines, benzoylecgonine (cocaine metabolite), cannabinoids, opiates and phencyclidine. Tests for methamphetamine, methadone and tricyclic antidepressants are under development. These devices may be stored at room temperature.

8. Acknowledgments

The authors would like to recognize Alex Klimov, Cynthia Kravec, Bernadette Oades, Fauzi Rashid, Lee Anne Talbot, Shiow-Fen Tsai and Barbara Twarowska of Roche Diagnostics Corporation and Steven Bachand, John A. Faux and Stephen K. Schultheis of ANSYS, Corporation for their contribution to the Research and Development of this product. We thank Laboratory Corporation of America, Raritan, New Jersey, for providing urine specimens along with their testing results and ElSohly Laboratories, Oxford, Mississippi, for performing GC-MS analysis.

References

1. Schwartz, R. H., Bogema, S., and Thorne, M. M. (1990) Evaluation of a rapid latex-inhibition screening assay for cocaine in urine. *J. Pediatr.* **117,** 670–672.
2. Cone, E. J., Darwink W. D., and Dickerson, S. L. (1991) Evaluation of the Abuscreen OnTrak assay for cocaine (metabolite). *Clin. Chem. News* **17,** 40.
3. Armbruster, D. A. and Krolak, J. M. (1992) Screening for drugs of abuse with the Roche OnTrak assays. *J. Anal. Toxicol.* **16,** 172–175.
4. Welch, E., Fleming, L. E., Peyser, I., Greenfield, W., Steele, B. W., and Bandstra, E. S. (1993) Rapid cocaine screening of urine in a newborn nursery. *J. Pediatr.* **123,** 468–470.
5. Ferrara, S. D., Tedeschi, L., Frison, G., Brusini, G., Castagna, F., Bernardelli, B., et al. (1994) Drugs-of -abuse testing in urine:statistical approach and experimental comparison of immunochemical and chromatographic techniques. *J. Anal. Toxicol.* **18,** 278–291.
6. Buechler, K. F., Moi, S., Noar, B., McGrath, D., Clancy, M., Shenhav, A., et al. (1992) Simultaneous detection of seven drugs of abuse by the Triage panel for drugs of abuse. *Clin. Chem.* **38,** 1678–1684.
7. Wu, A. H. B., Wong, S. S., Johnson, K. G., Callies, J., Shu, D. X., Dunn, W. E., et al. (1993) Evaluation of the Triage system for emergency drugs-of-abuse testing in urine. *J. Anal. Toxicol.* **17,** 241–245.
8. Koch, T. R., Raglin, R. L., Kirk, S., and Bruni, J. F. (1994) Improved screening for benzodiazepine metabolites in urine using the Triage panel for drugs of abuse. *J. Anal. Toxicol.* **18,** 168–172.

9. Edinboro, L. E. and Poklis, A. (1994) Detection of benzodiazepines and tribenzazolams by Triage: confirmation by solid-phase extraction utilizing SPEC.3ML.MP3 microcolumns and GC-MS. *J. Anal. Toxicol.* **18,** 312–316.
10. Röhrich, J., Schmidt, K., and Bratzke, H. (1994) Application of the novel immunoassay Triage to a rapid detection of antemortem drug abuse. *J. Anal. Toxicol.* **18,** 407–414.
11. Jenkins, A. J., Mills, L. C., Darwin, W. D., Huestis, M. A., Cone, E. J., and Mitchell, J. M. (1993) Validity testing of the EZ-SCREEN cannabinoid test. *J. Anal. Toxicol.* **17,** 292–298.
12. Hwang, S. M., Huang, S. H., Huang, B. C., and Chen, C. S. (1994) Evaluation of five commercial amphetamines and opiates immunoassay test kits in Taiwan. *J. Food Drug Analysis* **2(2),** 89–96.
13. Jenkins, A. J., Darwin, W. D., Huestis, M. A., Cone, E. J., and Mitchell, J. M. (1995) Validity testing of the accuPINCH THC test. *J. Anal. Toxicol.* **19,** 5–12.
14. Towt, J., Tsai, S.-C. J., Henandez, M. R., Klimov, A. D., Kravec, C. V., Rouse, S. L., et al. (1995) OnTrak TesTcup: a novel, on-site, multianalyte screen for the detection of abused drugs. *J. Anal. Toxicol.* **19,** 504–510.
15. Crouch, D. J., Cheever, M. L., Andrenyak, D. M., Kuntz, D. J., and Loughmiller, D. L. (1998) A comparison of OnTrak TesTcup, Abuscreen OnTrak, Abuscreen OnLine, and GC-MS Urinalysis Test Results. *J. Foren. Sci.* **43(1),** 35–40.
16. Klimov, A. D., Tsai, S.-C. J., Towt, J., and Salamone, S. J. (1995) Improved immunochromatographic format for competitive-type assays. *Clin. Chem.* **41(9),** 1360.

Chapter 15

Triage® Device for Drug Analysis

Rafael de la Torre

1. Introduction

The Triage® drugs-of-abuse assay (Biosite Diagnostics) uses an immunological technique known as ASCEND™ MultImmunoassay (AMIA™) (Fig. 1). AMIA is a competitive binding immunoassay that allows the simultaneous detection of multiple analytes in a sample *(1)*. In the first version of Triage, it was used for the detection of seven classes of drugs (*see* Table 1, first row) including the five classes listed by the U.S. Department of Health and Human Services (DHHS) for workplace drug testing.

All reagents required to perform the test are contained in the device. The AMIA technology combines the following features that will be described further: direct assay signal, digital color response at internally calibrated cutoff concentrations, fast assay kinetics, and monoclonal antibody specificity. The test incorporates a solution-phase reaction followed by a solid-phase reaction. The Triage device consists of a reaction cup that contains precisely pre-measured, lyophilized reagent beads for the solution-phase and a solid-phase detection area consisting of a membrane with immobilized monoclonal antibodies in seven discrete drug detection zones for visualization of results (*see* Fig. 2).

The flexibility of Triage has allowed the manufacturer to sell various versions depending on the target market. In the first European version of Triage, phencyclidine was substituted by methadone (Triage plus MTD). In the United States, an eighth drug class, the tricyclic antidepressants, was added (Triage 8) for use in emergency rooms. Another version, the Triage Intervention, marketed for workplace testing, targets the five drug classes specified by DHHS.

Biosite Diagnostics has continued development of the AMIA technology for other analytes of interest in clinical chemistry. A summary of Triage devices is presented in Table 1.

From: *Forensic Science*: *On-Site Drug Testing*
Edited by: A. J. Jenkins and B. A. Goldberger © Humana Press, Inc., Totowa, NJ

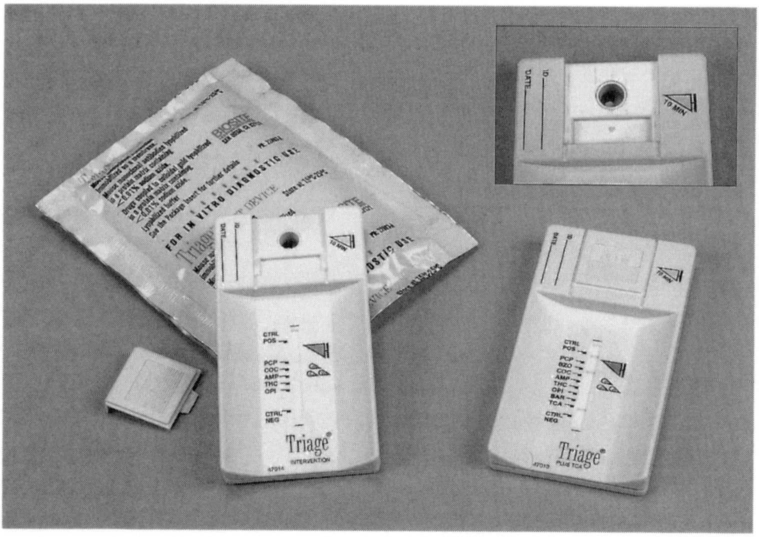

Fig. 1. Triage drugs-of-abuse devices.

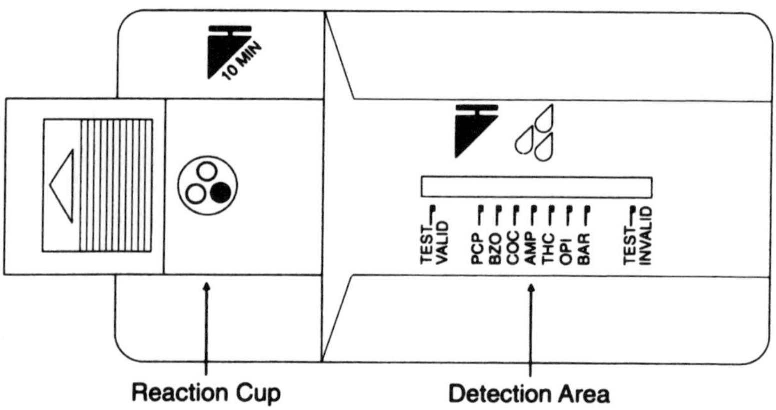

Fig. 2. Design of the Triage analytical device for drugs-of-abuse testing.

2. Test Procedure

The test procedure consists of three steps (*see* Fig. 3). An aliquot of the urine specimen is added to the reaction cup and allowed to react for 10 min (solution-phase reaction). The reaction mixture is transferred to the detection area and the mixture is allowed to soak in completely (solid-phase reaction). Three drops of wash solution are added and the test results are read after the

Table 1
Triage On-Site Test Kits

Product	Purpose	Analytes
Triage	Drugs of Abuse Testing	Phencyclidine Benzodiazepines Cocaine (benzoylecgonine) Amphetamines 11-nor-Δ^9-THC-9-carboxylic acid Opiates (morphine) Barbiturates
Triage Intervention	Drugs of Abuse Testing (Workplace Drug Testing)	Phencyclidine Cocaine (benzoylecgonine) Amphetamines 11-nor-Δ^9-THC-9-carboxylic acid Opiates (morphine)
Triage plus MTD	Drugs of Abuse Testing and Clinical Toxicology (including tricyclic antidepressants and methadone)	Methadone Benzodiazepines Cocaine (benzoylecgonine) Amphetamines 11-nor-Δ^9-THC-9-carboxylic acid Opiates (morphine) Barbiturates Tricyclic antidepressants
Triage plus TCA Triage 8	Drugs of Abuse and Clinical Toxicology (including tricyclic antidepressants)	Phencyclidine Benzodiazepines Cocaine (benzoylecgonine) Amphetamines 11-nor-Δ^9-THC-9-carboxylic acid Opiates (morphine) Barbiturates Tricyclic antidepressants
Triage Micro *C. difficile* Panel	Microbiology	Glutamate dehydrogenase antigen Toxin A
Triage Micro Parasite Panel	Parasitic Testing	*Entamoeba hystolitica/dispar* *Giardia lamblia* *Cryptosporidium parvum*
Triage Cardiac Panel	Cardiac Parameters Testing	CK-MB Myoglobin Troponin I

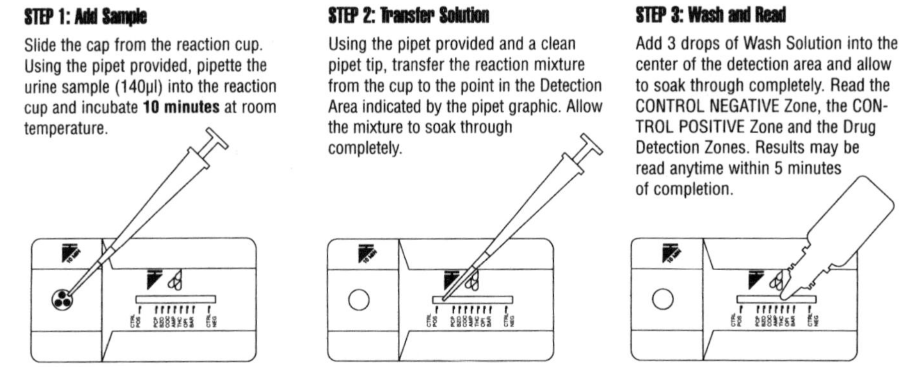

Fig. 3. Summary of the test procedure.

solution has soaked in completely. Positive results are presented by a colored reddish bar in the drug detection zone adjacent to the drug name.

2.1. Solution-Phase Reaction

The solution-phase reagents consist of the following three pre-measured lyophilized beads: one containing monoclonal antibodies, one containing drug conjugates, and a third containing buffer. The antibody bead contains a set of monoclonal antibodies directed against all the targeted drugs in the system. The antibodies have been selected by crossreactivity analysis to eliminate nonspecific drug reactions. The excess amount of monoclonal antibodies present in the AMIA enhances assay kinetics and forces the assay towards equilibrium with an incubation time of 10 min. The drug conjugates consist of conjugates of drug-labeled bovine serum albumin adsorbed to colloidal gold particles. The buffer bead maintains the pH of the reaction mixture between 7.5 and 8.5.

The lyophilized reagent is reconstituted by addition of the urine specimen. A volume of approximately 140 µL of urine is necessary to perform the assay. A pipet with a fixed volume and tips are provided with the device. At the bottom of the reaction well, there is a powdered mixture of citric acid and bicarbonate, separated from the three lyophilized beads by a porous plastic disc. Upon addition of the urine, the powder and the disc create controlled effervescence, which facilitates mixing during the incubation step.

2.2. Solid-Phase Reaction

After 10 min of incubation, the reaction mixture is transferred to the detection area of the device where the solution comes into contact with a membrane containing the discrete drug detection zones of immobilized monoclonal antibodies. The antibodies allow simultaneous reaction and detection of drugs in a single reaction mixture.

Antibodies for the detection of unbound colloidal gold conjugates are immobilized by passive adsorption onto a nylon membrane. The membrane is contained in a plastic device that is designed to maintain contact of the reaction mixture with the entire surface of the membrane before the flow of fluid passes through the membrane. The device design controls the flow, uniformly exposing each drug detection zone on the membrane to the reaction mixture.

If a urine specimen contains one or more drugs at concentrations above the cutoff concentration, the antibodies bind to the conjugate and the free drug, leaving some drug unbound conjugates in the solution phase. Reaction mixtures that do not have free conjugates (negative specimens) flow through the membrane and do not bind to immobilized antibodies. Positive specimens with free conjugates are captured by the immobilized antibodies producing a colored red bar at the zone corresponding to each drug class. Before reading, the detection area is washed with a wash solution consisting of potassium borate, sodium chloride, a detergent, and sodium azide. Refer to Fig. 4 for a summary of the assay.

2.3. Cutoff Definition

One of the most critical features of on-site drug testing devices is how well results above and below the cutoff concentration have been established. At the cutoff concentration, the assay color response should rapidly increase to a maximum visual signal (*see* Fig. 5). Thus, only specimens containing drug at or above the cutoff concentration should generate detectable color responses. Each drug detected by Triage has its own individually selected cutoff concentration and requires no external calibration.

The threshold concentration for each drug is predetermined in terms of the amount of high-affinity monoclonal antibody required to completely bind the drug conjugate and the drug in the sample at concentrations up to the threshold concentration of drug. The assay response is proportional to the concentration of the unbound drug conjugate so that no signal is observed at drug concentrations less than the threshold concentration. At drug concentrations exceeding the threshold concentration, a color response is achieved. The rate of increase of the color response above the threshold concentration is a function of the relative affinities of the antibody for each of the drug metabolites and the drug conjugate and is related to the absolute affinity of the antibody to the drug conjugate. Thus, a response can be achieved at the threshold concentration by using antibodies with the appropriate affinity.

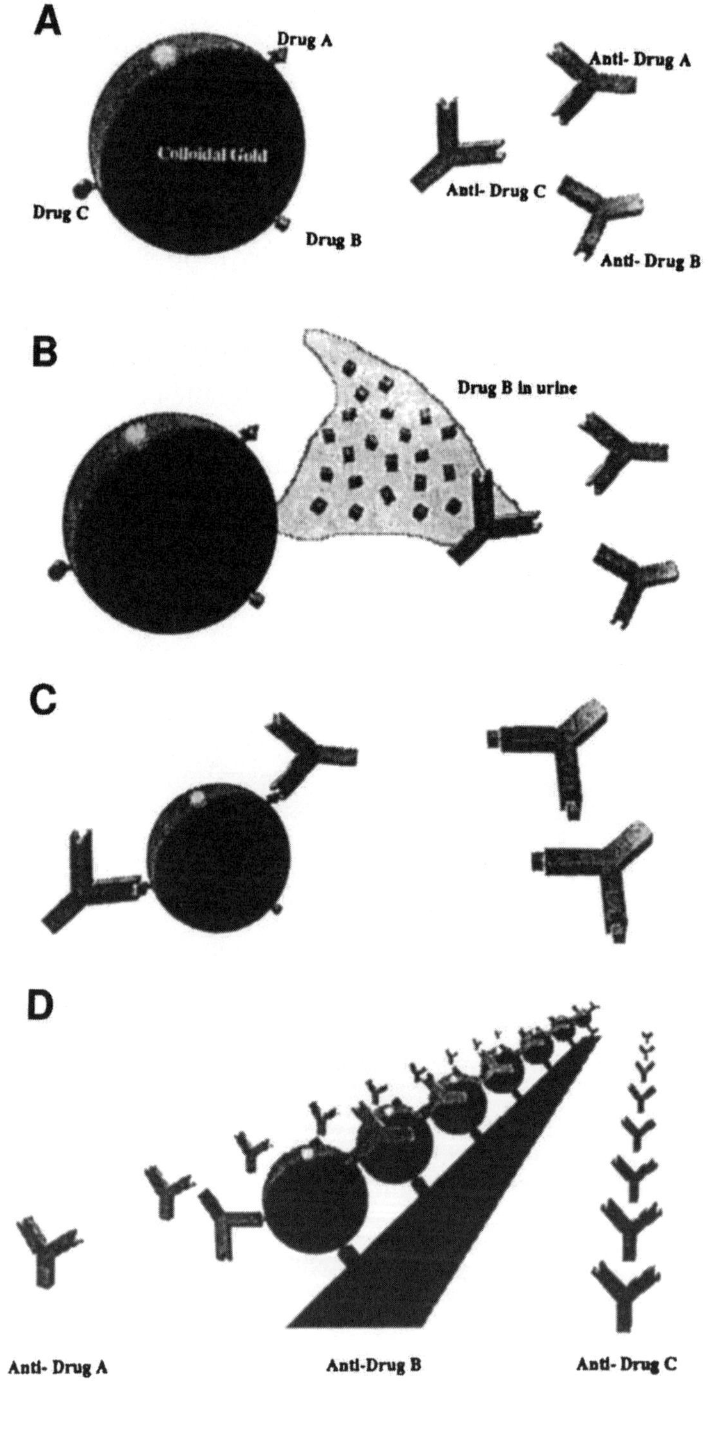
A
Drug A
Anti- Drug A
Colloidal Gold
Anti- Drug C
Drug C
Drug B
Anti- Drug B
B
Drug B in urine
C
D
Anti- Drug A
Anti-Drug B
Anti- Drug C

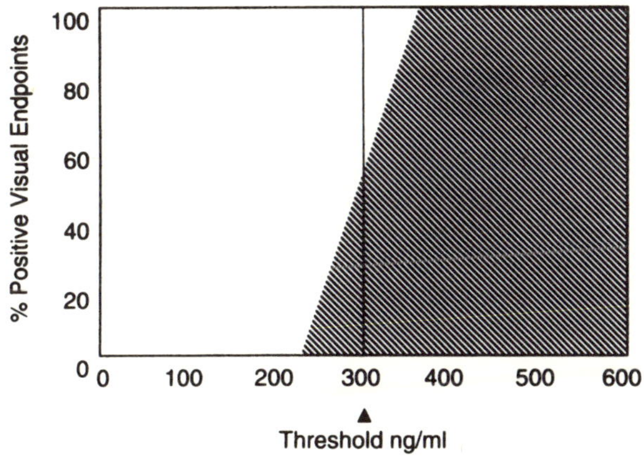

Fig. 5. Theoretical representation of cutoff definition in the Triage analytical device for drugs-of-abuse testing.

The affinity of the monoclonal antibodies and the relative amounts of antibody and drug conjugate in the reaction mixture are selected such that when the concentration of the drug in the sample is below a pre-selected cutoff concentration, no drug conjugate is free to bind to the drug detection zone on the solid-phase. When the concentration of the drug in the sample exceeds the cutoff concentration, drug conjugate is displaced from the appropriate solution-phase antibody and is free to bind to the drug detection zone on the solid phase. A more in depth discussion about the theoretical background on cutoff definition can be found in the literature *(1)*.

Discrepancies between Triage and different immunoassays may occur due to differences in specificity of antibodies, rather than the cutoff specification. Cutoff concentrations are specified by the U.S. Department of Health

---

Fig. 4. (*opposite page*) Schematic representation of the antigen antibody interaction for the AMIA immunoassay used in the Triage analytical device for drugs-of-abuse testing. **(a)** symbols for the colloidal gold particle, drugs, and antisera are defined. **(b)** urine sample containing drug B is added **(c)** antibodies to drug B bind to the free drug; antibodies to drug A and C, in the absence of free drug, bind to the conjugate **(d)** the mixture is apllied to the Traige DOA membrane. Drug B conjugated to the colloidal gold is available for binding to immobilized antibodies located on the Triage DOA membrane surface. Conjugated drugs A and C cannot bind to antibodies on the membrane and no detection is observed.

and Human Services for the five drug classes, and for the four non-regulated classes, previous manufacturer developments have arbitrarily set the limits.

When the Triage device was developed, some novelties were introduced in the design of antibodies. For three drug classes (opiates, cannabinoids and benzodiazepines) emphasis was focused on generating antibodies with good or even better crossreactivity for glucuronide conjugates than for the parent compound (main targeted drugs or their metabolites). The detection of glucuronide conjugates of drugs and/or their metabolites should not change the results in samples well above or below the cutoff concentration but theoretically should expand the time of detection of drugs in urine. In fact, the main discrepancies between Triage and other immunoassays when targeting similar compounds can be found at concentrations close to the cutoff. For amphetamines, the assay developed makes one of the clearest distinction in the market between active (d-) and inactive (l-) enantiomers. The ratio of crossreactivity between enantiomers is 60 and 30 times for amphetamine and methamphetamine respectively. A summary of crossreactivity of related compounds for each drug class is presented in Table 2.

2.4. *Internal Quality Control*

In the solid-phase membrane of the detection area there is the presence of test valid (CTRL POS in the device) and test invalid (CTRL NEG in the device) procedural control zones which ensure that the incubation time has been followed properly and that the reagents are active. For the test valid zone, a ligand-colloidal gold conjugate is provided that binds to that zone upon addition of the reaction mixture to the membrane producing a red bar. The test invalid zone includes both a ligand-colloidal gold conjugate and an antibody specific for that ligand. The amount of antibody provided is just sufficient to bind all the ligand conjugate; therefore, normally no binding of conjugate to the invalid test zone occurs. However, when the reaction mixture is not allowed to come to equilibrium (i.e., if the reaction mixture is added to the membrane after insufficient incubation time) free ligand conjugate will be available to bind to that zone, resulting in the appearance of a red bar, invalidating the assay.

3. *Clinical and Laboratory Evaluations*

The Triage device for drugs-of-abuse testing has been the subject of several evaluations. Table 3 (pp. 210–211) provides a summary of several studies evaluating the performance of the Triage device with established instrumental methods. Overall, the studies demonstrated excellent performance. Regarding its performance with the five drug classes for which testing is regulated by

Table 2(a)

Crossreactivity of Related Drugs for Drug Classes Screened for in the Triage Analytical Device for Drugs-of-Abuse On-Site Testing

Amphetamines	ng/mL	Barbiturates	ng/mL	Benzodiazepines	ng/mL	Cocaine	ng/mL	Methadone	ng/mL
Amphetamine, *d*-	650	Allobarbital	300	Alprazolam	450	Benzoylecgonine	300	Methadone, *dl*-	300
Amphetamine, *l*-	40000	Aminogluthetimide	10000	Alprazolam, α-OH	400	Cocaethylene	100000	Methadone, *l*-	400
MDA	1200	Amobarbital	300	Alprazolam G*, α-OH	400	Cocaine	550	EDDP	>100000
MDEA	2500	Aprobarbital	300	Bromazepam	400	Ecgonine	15000	EMDP	>100000
MDMA	2500	Barbital	500	Clorazepate	5000				
Methamphetamine, *d*-	1000	Butabarbital	300	Chlordiazepoxide	1250				
Methamphetamine, *l*-	30000	Butalbital	300	Clobazam	700				
Phenethylamine	750000	Cyclobarbital	300	Clonazepam	350				
		Cyclopentobarbital	300	Demoxepam	2000				
		Pentobarbital	300	Diazepam	350				
		Phenobarbital	400	Estazolam	300				
		Secobarbital	300	Flunitrazepam	350				
		Talbutal	300	Flurazepam	450				
				Flurazepam-OH-ethyl	350				
				Halazepam	750				
				Lorazepam	550				
				Lorazepam-G	400				
				Nitrazepam	750				
				Nordiazepam	300				
				Nordiazepam-G	300				
				Oxazepam	700				
				Oxazepam-G	800				
				Temazepam	550				
				Temazepam-G	500				
				Triazolam	400				
				Triazolam, α-OH	700				

Cutoff concentrations are as follows: Amphetamines 1000 ng/mL (methamphetamine), barbiturates 300 ng/mL, benzodiazepines 300 ng/mL, cocaine 300 ng/mL (benzoylecgonine), methadone 300 ng/mL.

G*, refers to glucuronide conjugate

Table 2(b)
Crossreactivity of Related Drugs for Drug Classes Screened for in the Triage Analytical Device for Drugs-of-Abuse On-Site Testing

Phencyclidine (PCP)	ng/mL	Opiates	ng/mL	Cannabinoids	ng/mL	Tricyclic Antidepressants	ng/mL
PCE	500	Acetylmorphine,6-	400	11-nor-9-carboxy-Δ^9–THC	50 (100)	Amitriptyline	1000
PCP	25	Codeine	300	11-nor-9-carboxy-Δ^9–THC-G	(125)	Chlorpromazine	50000
PCPy	50	Diacetylmorphine	400	Δ^9-THC	(1500)	Chlorprothixene	12500
TCM	5000	Ethylmorphine	400	Cannabinol	(10000)	Clomipramine	4000
TCP	25	Hydrocodone	500			Cyclobenzaprine	2000
TCPy	125	Hydromorphone	500			Desipramine	1000
		Meperidine	75000			Doxepin	1750
		Morphine	300			Imipramine	1000
		Morphine-3G*	490			Maproptiline	25000
		Nalorphine	2500			Nordoxepin	2000
		Oxycodone	20000			Nortriptyline	1000
		Oxymorphone	40000			Perphenazine	40000
		Thebaine	2000			Phenothiazine	60000
						Promazine	10000
						Protriptyline	2000
						Thiothixene	20000
						Trimipramine	3500

Cutoff concentrations are as follows: PCP 25 ng/mL, opiates 300 ng/mL, THC 50 ng/mL (11-nor-9-carboxy-Δ9-tetrahydrocannabinol) (crossreactivities in parenthesis refer to those calculated for a previous version of Triage with a cutoff concentration of 100 ng/mL), Tricyclic antidepressants 1000 ng/mL.

G*, refers to glucuronide conjugate.

DHHS, Triage performance is similar with the observed for instrumental methods such as the Behring EMIT and Abbott FPIA, especially in those cases where urinary concentrations of drugs are well above the cutoff concentration.

The Triage approach of screening for benzodiazepines in the early 1990s targeting antibodies based on their crossreactivity with glucuronides, was an innovative one and many users now prefer Triage over instrumental methods for the detection of these compounds *(3,5,7)*. The same has been also reported for amphetamine-like compounds *(2)*. Nevertheless, there are reports suggesting that tyramine, a compound produced by decarboxylation of tyrosine and other phenethylamines generated during putrefaction, may be the source of false positive amphetamine test results *(6,9,10)*. However, similar false positive results are commonly observed with other immunoassays for this drug class.

It can be a matter of debate to what extent the lack of objectivity, or if preferred a certain degree of subjectivity, in the reading of results could be a source of errors if personnel lacking laboratory skills performs the analysis with on-site drug testing devices. Independent reports have shown that results between laboratories are comparable *(8)* and that results between highly trained personnel in chemistry laboratories are similar *(3)*. In addition, it has also been demonstrated that results with a minimum training are independent of laboratory skills of personnel performing analysis *(7)*. A report *(11)* emphasizes that Triage has to be operated properly and that the presence of the three reagent beads has to be verified as if the buffer bead is missing false positive results may arise in urine samples with acidic pH *(4–5)*.

Biosite has used the same technology applied to diagnostic areas other than drugs-of-abuse testing to demonstrate that the performance of quantitative/semi-quantitative estimations of analytes is feasible *(12)*. Triage is currently used in many different clinical and forensic settings; several reports have confirmed its usefulness *(9,10,13–15)*.

References

1. Buechler, K. F., Moi, S., Noar, B., McGrath, D., Vilella, L., Clancy, M., et al. (1992) Simultaneous detection of seven drugs of abuse by the TRIAGE™ panel for drugs of abuse. *Clin. Chem.* **38,** 1678 1684.
2. Wu, A. H. B., Wong, S. S., Johnson, K. G., Callies, J., Shu, D. X., Dunn, W. E., et al. (1993) Evaluation of the TRIAGE system for emergency drugs-of-abuse testing in urine. *J. Anal. Toxicol.* **17,** 241–245.
3. Koch, T., Raglin, R. L., Kirk, S., and Bruni, J. F. (1994) Improved screening for benzodiazepine metabolites in urine using TRIAGE™ panel for drugs of abuse. *J. Anal. Toxicol.* **18,** 168–172.
4. Ferrara, S. D., Tedeschi, L., Frison, G., Brusini, G., Castagna, F., Bernardelli, B., et al. (1994) Drugs-of-abuse testing in urine: statistical approach and experimental

Table 3

Summary of Clinical Evaluations of the Triage Device for Drugs-of-Abuse On-Site Testing

Analyte	Reference Method	Samples tested (%positive/ %negative	Sensitivity (%)	Specificity (%)	Observations	Reference
PCP Opiates Δ^9-COOH-THC Amph/Methamph Cocaine Barbiturates	EMIT GC/MS	About 200 for each parameter (50/50)	Essentially similar	Essentially similar except for Amph/Methamph, Triage better than EMIT	Agreement of 93–100% for positive samples and from 95 to 100% for negative samples	Wu et al. 1993 (2)
Benzodiazepines	FPIA EMIT GC/MS	326 (50/50) by EMIT	97.5 Triage better than EMIT and FPIA	94.3 Triage equal than FPIA and better than EMIT	Observations independent of the analyst (experienced)	Koch et al. 1994 (3)
Opiates Δ^9-COOH-THC Amph/Methamph Cocaine Barbiturates	GC/MS	202 (10/90 to 30/70) depending on the parameter	44.4 to 95	89.7 to 99.5	Best positive predictive value among IA with EMIT	Ferrara et al 1994 (4)
Benzodiazepines	EMIT GC/MS	103 (60/40)	Not available	Not available	85% overall agreement Triage better for lorazepam and temazepam	Edinboro et al. 1994 (5)

(continued)

Table 3 (continued)

Opiates Δ^9-COOH-THC Amph/Methamph Cocaine Barbiturates Benzodiazepines	FPIA GC/MS	100 all were positive for at least one parameter	Not available	Not available	Agreement between 81.5% for amphetamines to 100% for opiates and barbiturates	Rörich et al. 1994 (6)
Opiates Δ^9-COOH-THC Cocaine Benzodiazepines	FPIA GC/MS HPLC	125 (emergency room) 138 (methadone maintenance program)	100 97–100 97–100 97–98 (all figures referred to FPIA)	98 97–99 87–92 74–75 (all figures referred to FPIA)	Triage better than FPIA for benzodiazepines	De la Torre et al. 1996 (7)
Amphetamines Benzodiazepines Cocaine Δ^9-COOH-THC Opiates	EMIT GC/MS	65 (20/45) positive samples stratified	Δ^9-COOH-THC 85.7 Cocaine 100	Δ^9-COOH-THC 88.3 Cocaine 100	Higher tendency to report positive results unconfirmed by GC/MS following DHHS regulations	Crouch et al. 1998 (8)

comparison of immunochemical and chromatographic techniques. *J. Anal. Toxicol.* **18,** 278–291.

5. Edinboro, L. E. and Poklis, A. (1994) Detection of benzodiazepines and tribenzolams by TRIAGE™: confirmation by solid-phase extraction utilizing SPEC®.3ML. MP3 microcolumns and GC-MS. *J. Anal. Toxicol.* **18,** 312–316.
6. Rörich, J., Schmidt, K., and Bratzke, H. (1994) Application of the novel immunoassay TRIAGE™ to a rapid detection of antemortem drug abuse. *J. Anal. Toxicol.* **18,** 407–414.
7. De la Torre, R., Domingo-Salvany, A., Badia, R., Gonzalez, G., McFarlane, D., San, L., et al. Clinical evaluation of the Triage analytical device for drugs-of-abuse testing. (1996) *Clin. Chem.* **42,** 1433–1438.
8. Crouch, D. J., Frank, J. F., Farrell, L. J., Karsch, H. M., and Klaunig, J. E. (1998) A multiple-site laboratory evaluation of three on-site urinalysis drug-testing devices. *J. Anal. Toxicol.* **22,** 493–502.
9. Moriya, F. and Hashimoto, F. (1996) Application of the Triage panel for drugs of abuse to forensic blood samples. *Nippon Hoigaku Zasshi.* **50,** 50–56.
10. Moriya, F. and Hashimoto, F. (1997) Evaluation of Triage screening for drugs of abuse in postmortem blood and urine samples. *Nippon Hoigaku Zasshi.* **51,** 214–219.
11. Poklis, A. and O'Neal, C. L. (1996) Potential for false-positive results by the TRIAGE™ panel of drugs-of-abuse immunoassay. *J. Anal. Toxicol.* **20,** 209–210.
12. Apple, F. S., Christenson, R. H., Valdes, R., Andriak, A. J., Berg, A., Duh, S.-H., et al. (1999) Simultaneous rapid measurement of whole blood myoglobin, creatine kinase MB, and cardiac troponin I by the Triage Cardiac Panel for detection of myocardial infarction. *Clin. Chem.* **45,** 199–205.
13. Wiernikowski, A., Soltycka, M., Kosecka-Grybek, E., Groszek, B., and Brodkiewicz, A. (1996) Acute poisonings in the course of drug addiction: chemicotoxicological diagnostics. *Przegl. Leck.* **53,** 334–337.
14. Valentine, J. L. and Komorski, E. M. (1995) Use of a visual panel detection method for drugs of abuse: clinical and laboratory experience with children and adolescents. *J. Pediatr.* **126,** 135–140.
15. Nihira, M., (1998) Urinalysis of body packers in Japan. *J. Anal. Toxicol.* **22,** 61–65.

Chapter 16

Visualine II™ Drugs-of-Abuse Test Kits

Scott A. Kuzdzal and James H. Nichols

1. Introduction

Visualine II™ drug-abuse, test kits are one-step, rapid immunoassay kits developed by Sun Biomedical Laboratories (Cherry Hill, NJ) for the quantitative analysis of drugs-of-abuse in human urine. The test kits are marketed for use by professional laboratories, physician offices, clinics, institutions, law-enforcement agencies, and pre-employment testing laboratories.

2. Principle

The Visualine II drug abuse test kits (Fig. 1) are homogeneous immunochromatographic assays based on the principle of antigen/antibody complexation. The assay is based on the competition for limited antibody sites between the drug or drug metabolite in the specimen and a drug conjugate immobilized on a porous membrane support. An aliquot of a urine specimen is placed into the window in the device that holds the porous membrane. The urine is automatically wicked along the chromatographic membrane to mobilize the microspheres coated with antibody specific to the particular drug. These microspheres then move along the membrane by capillary action to the probe area on the membrane. If the drug is absent, the colored microspheres are attached to the drug conjugate probe, forming a visible line as the antibody complexes with the drug conjugate. Therefore, the formation of a visible red precipitin at the probe line occurs when the urine is negative for the drug. Results are read after a five-minute incubation period.

When the drug is present in the urine specimen, the drug or drug metabolite competes for the limited antibody sites on the microspheres. When an

From: *Forensic Science: On-Site Drug Testing*
Edited by: A. J. Jenkins and B. A. Goldberger © Humana Press, Inc., Totowa, NJ

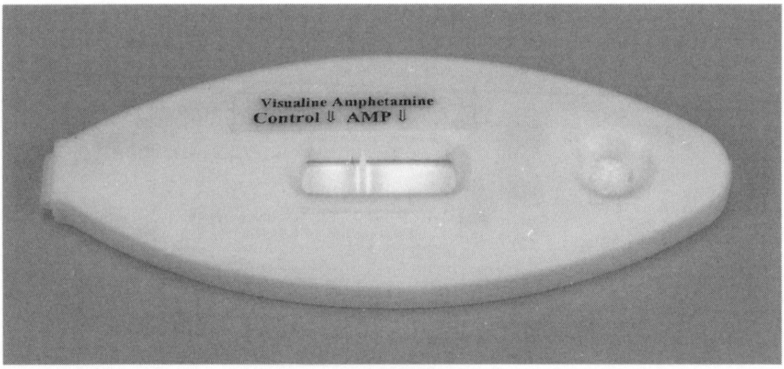

Fig. 1. Visualine II drugs-of-abuse test kit. Device shown is used for the detection of amphetamines.

adequate amount of drug is present, it will fill the limited antibody binding sites. This prevents attachment of the colored microspheres to the probe site on the membrane. Therefore, a positive urine specimen will not form a line at the probe area. The testing procedure is illustrated in Fig. 2.

A reference or control line with a different antigen/antibody reaction is also added to the immunochromatographic membrane strip to indicate that the test result is valid. The control line should always be visible. A negative urine specimen will produce two colored lines, and a positive specimen will produce only one line. The test kits are also available with simultaneous testing for multiple drugs (Fig. 3).

3. Description of Test Kits

Each Visualine II test kit is housed in a single plastic device. The device contains a membrane strip with a defined amount of microspheres coated with an anti-drug monoclonal antibody (mouse) in a pH 7.4 buffer. The kits contain mouse monoclonal antibody directed against benzoylecgonine (cocaine), morphine glucuronide (opiates), 11-nor-Δ-9-tetrahydrocannabinol-9-carboxylic acid (cannabinoids, THC), oxazepam glucuronide (benzodiazepines), amphetamine, and methamphetamine.

A second antibody (goat antimouse IgG) is incorporated to form the aforementioned reference line. Antigenic probe and animal serum are also absorbed onto the membrane. The membrane is treated with stabilizer and preservative and is then dried before assembly and use. All necessary reagents for performing the test are included in the individual test device; no additional reagents are required.

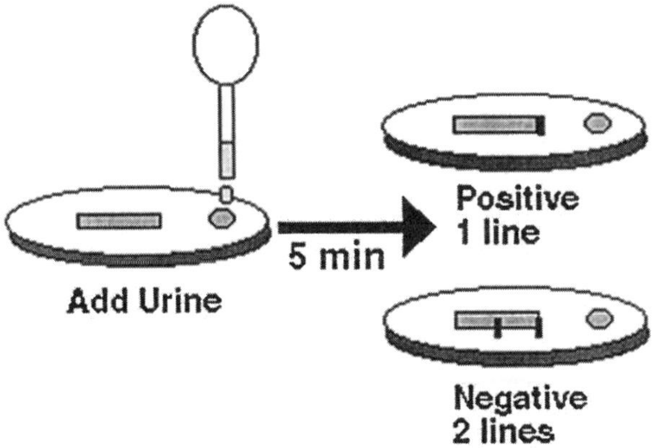

Fig. 2. Testing procedure for Visualine II drugs-of-abuse tests. Three drops of urine are added to the specimen well. After five minutes, the result is read. Presence of one line (control) indicates a positive test result.

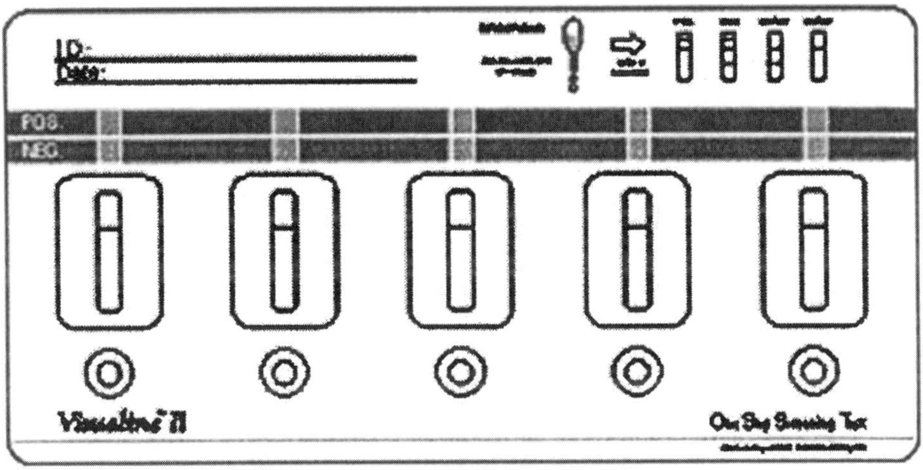

Fig. 3. Visualine II test kits for the simultaneous detection of multiple drugs.

4. Performance Evaluation

The precision, stability, analytical sensitivity, accuracy, and analytical specificity (interferences) of Visualine II test kits for cocaine metabolite (benzoylecgonine), opiates, cannabinoids, benzodiazepines, amphetamine, and methamphetamine were evaluated in the authors' laboratory at the Johns Hopkins Hospital to determine its applicability to a hospital clinical laboratory.

Table 1
Comparison of the Visualine II Drugs-of-Abuse Test Kits with the Abbott FPIA (ADx) and Behring EMIT Assays (Boehringer-Mannheim Hitachi 704)

Analyte and Cutoff Concentration	Sensitivity	Specificity	+PV	–PV	Efficiency	*N*
Cocaine Metabolite – 300 ng/mL	100%	94.7%	95.0%	100%	97.4%	151
Opiates – 300 ng/mL	100%	86.2%	84.0%	100%	92.0%	150
Cannabinoids – 100 ng/mL	100%	86.7%	88.6%	100%	93.5%	153
Benzodiazepines – 300 ng/mL	100%	97.4%	97.4%	100%	98.7%	150
Amphetamine – 500 ng/mL	100%	95.0%	90.7%	100%	96.6%	119
Methamphetamine – 500 ng/mL	100%	96.3%	93.2%	100%	97.5%	123

Abbrev: +PV, positive predictive value; -PV, negative predictive value; N; number of tests performed

The intra-assay (within day) and inter-assay (day-to-day) precision were examined with three lots of Visualine II test kits using control samples from Bio-Rad Laboratories (Lyphocheck Urine Toxicology Control, Hercules, CA). Specimens were analyzed in duplicate, twice daily over five consecutive days by a single researcher. The results were scored as percentage of correct (positive or negative) responses. Visualine II tests demonstrated >99% precision for within run, run-to-run, within day, day-to-day, within lot and lot-to-lot experiments.

Visualine II test kits were quantitatively compared to the Abbott Laboratories ADx (Abbott Park, IL) for cocaine metabolite, opiates and cannabinoids and to the Behring Diagnostics Emit Assay (Palo Alto, CA) for benzodiazepines, amphetamine and methamphetamine. The sensitivity, specificity, positive and negative predictive values, and efficiency for approximately 75 positive and 75 negative urine specimens are summarized in Table 1. According to the manufacturer, sensitivity of the test is 300 ng/mL for cocaine metabolite and benzodiazepines, 100 ng/mL for opiates and cannabinoids, and 500 ng/mL for amphetamine and methamphetamine. False negative and positive results were confirmed by GC/MS when specimen volume allowed. The false positive test results were because of an increased sensitivity of the Visualine II tests when compared with other drugs-of-abuse assays.

The analytical specificity (interference) of these test kits was evaluated by spiking negative urine specimens with up to 100 mg/L of common prescription, over-the-counter, and illicit drugs. Compounds that did not interfere with the Visualine II test kits are listed in Table 2. Interfering substances are listed in Table 3.

Table 2
Compounds That Will Not Interfere With the Visualine II Test Kits

Analyte	Concentration
Acetaminophen	100 mg/L
Acetylsalicylic acid	100 mg/L
Brompheniramine	100 mg/L
Caffeine	100 mg/L
Clonidine	100 mg/L
Creatinine	10 mg/L
Dimenhydrinate	100 mg/L
Diphenhydramine	100 mg/L
Ethanol	0.5% v/v
Fluoxetine	100 mg/L
Haloperidol	100 mg/L
Ibuprofen	100 mg/L
Meclizine	100 mg/L
Pentobarbital	100 mg/L
Protein	1% w/v
Simethicone	100 mg/L
Sodium chloride	60 g/L
Urea	40 g/L

5. Management and Clinical Utility

Visualine II test kits are very easy to use and require minimal training. The devices contain a built-in integrity check that reduces the potential for errors. Additional laboratory instrumentation is not required, which results in reduced laboratory overhead. The test kits contain an expiration date and have a shelf life of up to 18 mo (no refrigeration is required). Despite their ease of use, the tests are considered moderately complex and require strict laboratory documentation.

Visualine II drugs-of-abuse test kits have been used by physicians who routinely test for drugs-of-abuse, institutions interested in rapid drug detection, drug rehabilitation facilities and drug counselors interested in monitoring patients, probation officers testing individuals as a condition of probation, and those who administer drug tests for workplace and sports-related activities. The kits have also found utility in emergency room and OB/GYN screening. They have been used extensively in judicial programs.

Table 3
Compounds That Produce Positive Test Results with the Visualine II Test Kits

Compound	Concentration (ng/mL)	Assay
Benzoylecgonine	300	Cocaine metabolite
Cocaine, HCl	300	Cocaine metabolite
Cocaine, freebase	300	Cocaine metabolite
Morphine	100	Opiates
Codeine	300	Opiates
Hydromorphone	1000	Opiates
Morphine Sulphate	2000	Opiates
Naloxone	1000	Opiates
Methamphetamine	1000	Amphetamine
Amphetamine	1000	Methamphetamine
d-Amphetamine	50,000	Amphetamine and Methamphetamine
Pseudoephedrine	10,000	Amphetamine and Methamphetamine
Ephedrine	100,000	Amphetamine and Methamphetamine
11-nor-Δ^9-Tetrahydro-cannabinol-9-COOH	100	Cannabinoids
11-nor-Δ^8-Tetrahydro-cannabinol-9-COOH	100	Cannabinoids
11-OH-Δ^9-Tetrahydro-cannabinol	200	Cannabinoids

6. Conclusions

Visualine II drugs-of-abuse test kits provide a rapid, one-step point-of-care testing alternative without the need for expensive instrumentation and technical training. The performance of the kits are comparable to marketed immunoassay testing methods. Common over-the-counter and prescription medications do not interfere with the test kit. The stability of the test kit has been demonstrated for up to 12 mo when stored unopened at 2–28°C.

Visualine II test kits are intended as screening only. If required, positive test results should be confirmed by an appropriately sensitive and specific method such as gas chromatography/mass spectrometry.

Chapter 17

Drugs-of-Abuse Test Devices

A Review

Robert E. Willette and Leo J. Kadehjian

1. Introduction

1.1. Background

As part of the Federal government's efforts to assess the reliability and effectiveness of on-site drug testing devices that do not require the use of instruments or extensive operator training, Duo Research was contracted to conduct a study in 1996 for the Administrative Office of the U.S. Courts (AOC), to evaluate the performance and operational characteristics of noninstrumented drug testing (NIDT) devices for use in the federal criminal justice system. Similarly, in 1998, The Department of Health and Human Services' (HHS) Division of Workplace Programs (DWP), as part of its responsibility to oversee drug testing programs and procedures sanctioned under federal regulations, commissioned Duo Research to conduct a similar study in order to expand the knowledge base on the accuracy of these NIDT.

1.2. Study Design

Both studies were designed to test each device with 90 selected clinical specimens and 10 control samples for each of five drugs. The goal of the studies was to challenge the devices with specimens clustered around the cutoff. The specimens were selected from routine specimens submitted by Federal Probation offices to a laboratory under contract with the AOC. Specimens were selected based on initial testing on a Hitachi 717 analyzer using enzyme immunoassay reagents (AOC study, Emit; DWP study, DRI) at the HHS ini-

From: *Forensic Science: On-Site Drug Testing*
Edited by: A. J. Jenkins and B. A. Goldberger © Humana Press, Inc., Totowa, NJ

tial screening test cutoff levels. The absorbance rate data were compared to spiked control values to classify specimens into four categories: Negative, Below cutoff (ranging from about 25% below cutoff to cutoff), Above cutoff (ranging from cutoff to about 25% above the cutoff), High (greater than 25% above the cutoff). To serve as a reference instrument device, a Dade Behring Diagnostic's ETS instrument, using Emit® d.a.u. reagents, was included.

The primary focus of the study, in keeping with the testing requirements of the AOC and the HHS Guidelines, was to test for amphetamines, cocaine, opiates, cannabinoids, and phencyclidine, with the performance assessment made relative to GC/MS confirmation criteria. Two to three technically trained operators were retained to perform the tests.

Specimens were tested on the ETS analyzer and the NIDT devices on the same day in groups of 20–30. The analysts divided the various devices so that on each day each analyst tested all specimens on a group of devices. Each day the analysts rotated devices in an effort that all analysts would have experience with all devices about the same number of times. GC/MS results were obtained for all the samples included in the evaluation results presented below.

1.3. Study Devices

Devices were available in various configurations. Many of the devices are described as "cards" or "cassettes," of which most are plastic holders of various shapes and sizes. The actual test component is an absorbent strip, impregnated with an antibody-dye complex, specific for the drug or drugs to which the test is designated, and one or more zones of immobilized drug. The strips are also available as "dipsticks." There are also devices with the test strips incorporated into the specimen container, so-called "cup" devices. Also, some devices were available as single tests and in multiple-test formats.

The group of devices in the AOC study included five multiple-test cassettes; one cup; and nine different single tests, two of which were dipsticks. The DWP study included four "cup" configurations; seven multi-test devices, of which two were in a multiple dipstick format; and four devices in single drug formats, two of which were dipsticks. The devices, their operation characteristics, manufacturers, and distributors are described in Subheading 2.

Most devices were available for the five drugs included in the studies. The major variable between devices was in the amphetamine assay. In the AOC study, three devices were amphetamine-specific, ten methamphetamine-specific, one both. In the DWP study, six devices contained only methamphetamine-specific strips; five contained only amphetamine-specific strips; one claimed amphetamine and methamphetamine specificity in a single strip; and three devices were available with separate strips for both amphetamine and methamphetamine, with two of them integrated into the same device and one as separate single-test devices.

In addition to the 15 drug devices in the DWP study, one product, AdultaCheck, an adulteration detection device, was also included to evaluate the capability of a dipstick device to correctly detect dilute specimens. AdultaCheck also has test pads for detecting abnormal pH, glutaraldehyde and nitrites. No positive results were observed for these adulterants, which is not unexpected as most specimens from Federal probationers are collected under direct observation.

2. *Results*

2.1. *Introduction*

Operators were instructed to judge all results as positive or negative, but if they were uncertain, those results were recorded as either borderline negative (BN) or borderline positive (BP). The discussion presented herein is based on the more conservative interpretation of the results, that is, all borderline results were scored as negative. This is in keeping with a more traditional approach, and as recommended by most of the package inserts.

The results for each device were ranked based on the concentrations found in the GC/MS analyses. Samples were judged to be positive or negative using the cutoffs established in the AOC contract and by those required under the HHS Guidelines. These are shown in Table 1.

It should be noted that the AOC cutoffs for amphetamines and opiates are one-half those under the HHS Guidelines, which are used for federally-mandated workplace drug testing programs. In addition, there is no amphetamine requirement in order to report methamphetamine as positive (the HHS Guidelines require 200 ng/mL or more), and the opiate assay also included hydromorphone. When the HHS Guidelines cutoffs are applied, most devices gave slightly lower false positive rates but higher false negative rates for these two drug classes.

2.2. *Analysis of Results*

The results of the two studies are summarized in Tables 2–19. There are two tables for amphetamines, opiates and the average of all drug tests for each device to distinguish the different cutoffs used by the AOC and HHS. The tables include the sensitivity (percent of true positive results); specificity (percent of true negative results); positive predictive values (PPV, i.e., of all positive results for a device, how many were confirmed by GC/MS); negative predictive values (NPV, i.e., of all negative results for a device, how many were negative by GC/MS); and accuracy (i.e., of all results for a device, how many were correct).

It is important to understand the distinction between sensitivity and PPV. Sensitivity is the percentage of all confirmed positive specimens that are correctly detected as positive by the screening device. Any of the confirmed positive specimens that are incorrectly determined to be negative are false negatives. In contrast PPV is the percentage of all positive screening results that are correct. Any positive results for specimens that are in fact confirmed negative are false positives. PPV provides a direct indication of false positive results, that simply being 1 – PPV. The same distinction applies to specificity and NPV. Specificity is the percentage of confirmed negative specimens that are correctly detected as negative by the screening device. Any of the confirmed negative specimens that are incorrectly determined to be positive are false positives. In contrast NPV is the percentage of all negative screening results that are correct. Any negative results for specimens that are in fact confirmed positive are false negatives. NPV provides a direct indication of false negative results, that simply being 1 – NPV.

These tables can be used to assist in the selection of devices for one's specific needs. In programs desiring to identify as many drug users as possible, devices with high NPVs might be favored, recognizing that these devices also tend to have lower PPVs and will produce a higher percentage of positive results that will not confirm. For programs testing individuals where there may be immediate actions taken, as in many workplace situations, devices with high PPVs may be favored as they will produce fewer unconfirmed results, with the downside of missing more drug users. Devices located in the middle of the values would represent devices that have better balance between false positive and false negative rates.

2.3. Interpretation of the Results

An observation derived from the data is that there is a trend for devices with a high percentage of true positive results (sensitivity) to have a higher percentage of false positive results as well, with a number of exceptions. That is, a high percentage of the specimens giving positive results for a device were also positive by GC/MS; however, many of the specimens found negative by GC/MS tested incorrectly as positive by the same device. The opposite was also observed; i.e., devices with a high number of true negative results (specificity) also had a higher number of false negative results. In other words, a high percentage of those specimens identified as negative by the device were confirmed as negative by GC/MS, but also a high percentage of specimens positive by GC/MS were identified incorrectly as negative by the same device.

For example, in Table 16 (DWP study, HHS cutoffs) showing the percentages for cannabinoids, the Accutest Single device has the highest true negative rate, 100% (i.e., % of negative specimens identified correctly as negative), but ranks last in true positive rates, 26% (i.e., 74% false negatives). Although other examples similar to this can be found, when the combined scores for all five drugs are ranked by sensitivity and specificity, trends seen with individual drugs are less dramatic. The Accutest device, e.g., now ranks 7th in specificity (66%) and 15th in overall sensitivity.

The biggest deviation from this pattern was seen with the amphetamine assays. For example, in the DWP study, the sample population had 19 confirmed positive specimens, with nine samples containing amphetamine only greater than 500 ng/mL and ten samples containing methamphetamine greater than 500 ng/mL in addition to 200 ng/mL or greater of amphetamine. There were 24 samples with more than 500 ng/mL of methamphetamine (21 with measurable levels of amphetamine) that would have been confirmed positive without applying the 200 ng/mL amphetamine rule. Under the AOC cutoffs, 37 samples were positive for methamphetamine and 10 positive for amphetamine. Many of these specimens gave positive responses in the methamphetamine-specific tests. Obviously, the performance of the devices would have improved significantly if these were deemed positive.

With only a couple of exceptions, in order to obtain maximum performance, separate test areas or strips are provided for amphetamine and methamphetamine. The choice of which to use will depend on the prevalence of these two drugs in the test population. From the data in the DWP study, the methamphetamine-specific devices had a higher range of false negative and false positive results under both cutoff criteria, although false positive rates were lower using the AOC cutoffs because of the inclusion of 28 additional positives.

More revealing is the comparison of the three devices that were available with tests for both drugs. Two of these devices had higher true positive rates and all had lower false positive rates for amphetamine using the HHS cutoffs, but all had higher true positive rates for methamphetamine under the AOC cutoffs. However, when a combination of results is used, i.e., a sample was deemed positive if either drug test was positive, true positive rates increased significantly under either cutoffs (*see* Tables 11 and 12).

Examples can also be seen in the amphetamine results where the use of PPV for device selection can be deceptive. For example, one device in Table 3 had a PPV of 1.00, i.e., all positive results were confirmed, but that was 8 positive samples out of a total of 40 positive results, giving a false negative rate of 80%. Under the HHS cutoffs (Table 2), it had a PPV of 0.88, but a false negative rate of 67%. Clearly, choices of devices must take into account all of the performance measures to achieve the desired testing outcomes.

Of the other drug tests, cocaine appeared to be the "best behaved." There was a fairly wide range of false negative and false positive results, but most devices had fewer false negative results than with other drugs.

The opiates present another complex pattern, similar to amphetamines, as two analytes—morphine and codeine—are included, as well as hydromorphone in the AOC confirmation criteria. In the mix of specimens included in both studies, the higher cutoff used under HHS criteria produced lower specificity values (more false positives) and lower PPVs (*see* Tables 5, 6, 14,15).

The cannabinoid results showed a wide range of false negative and false positive results. This can probably be attributed to differences in antibody specificity, although products included in both studies did show improvement, e.g., one device had 72% false negative results in the AOC study, but only 48% in the DWP study, and the PPVs were also generally higher in the DWP study.

PPV results for phencyclidine were fairly low in both studies, suggesting that metabolites or other substances may be contributing to the lack of confirmation.

Comparing the amphetamine and opiate results using the two different cutoff criteria, HHS and AOC, it is obvious that device performance improves significantly if the confirmation cutoffs are lowered. In non-government regulated programs, this may be a desirable modification in order to minimize potential false positive results.

If one is planning to use a multi-test device, a review of Tables 9, 10, 18, and 19 is helpful. These tables summarize the overall performance of the devices across all tests for which they were available. In the AOC study, two obvious "conservative" devices standout, having low false positive rates and high PPV rates; however, they both have high false negative rates. They are classed as conservative as they will produce fewer unconfirmed positives, but miss many positives as well. The rest of the devices have lower false negative rates, being more able to identify positive specimens. There were fewer distinctions across all devices in the DWP study, with most devices clustered together with their overall results. This can be seen in the narrow range of all performance measures in the tables. These aggregate figures can be deceptive as some devices performed better for some drugs than others, so the overall picture of individual drugs and the combined scores should be taken into account in choosing a device.

The results of these studies may be interpreted in terms of how well the devices establish cutoffs—the primary focus of the studies, as well as differences in antibody specificity. The differences in performance may also be due to manufacturing issues as devices produced by the same manufacturer, but sold under different names, do not perform the same. These data suggest that there are lot-to-lot variations in production, a factor that has not been well studied. A comparison of several devices originating from the same manufacturers in the DWP study is illustrated in Table 20. The last four all had different lot numbers, presumably being manufactured at different times. In all of the above cases, it is not clear if the original manufacturing process contributes to these variations and/or the subsequent handling and final device assembly steps play a role.

Because of the practical trade-off between sensitivity and specificity, or the ability to identify drug users and not falsely identify non-users, the optimal test device will depend on the goals or objectives of the testing program. For example, in criminal justice settings, if the purpose is to identify as many drug users as possible, devices with high sensitivity, i.e., low percentage of false negative results, would be favored. However, these devices also tend to have a higher number of false positive results, thus requiring confirmation prior to any adverse action. Likewise, if the result is going to be used immediately, without confirmation (which could follow at a later time if necessary), those devices with a low percentage of false positive results might be favored.

The AdultaCheck device was evaluated against quantitative concentrations determined by a routine laboratory assay. The results are included in all of the tables for the DWP study. If AdultaCheck indicated a specimen was below 20 mg/dL, which is considered dilute under the federal regulations, but the quantitative result was above that level, the result was scored as a false positive. The opposite was the case for false negatives. Of the 450 specimens included in the study, 57 (12.6%) were judged dilute (less than 20 mg/dL) by the quantitative results. Of these, the AdultaCheck device missed 7 (12.3% false negatives). Of the 393 "normal" specimens, 33 (8.4% false positives) were scored as dilute using the AdultaCheck device. The overall accuracy for the device was 91.1%. It was concluded that the AdultaCheck device could be very useful in identifying dilute specimens in conjunction with on-site testing.

2.4. Operator Variability

One key issue regarding the use and observed performance of NIDT devices is operator subjectivity in reading results. Reading of results by the presence or absence of a colored line or spot (or its intensity relative to a control spot) would be expected to be operator dependent. According to the operator assessments, some devices demonstrated more clearly distinguishable results for positive or negative specimens than others.

It is to be expected that strongly positive or "clean" negative specimens would give more easily distinguishable results. Also, any operator subjectivity and variability in reading results would be expected to be most prevalent when specimens had concentrations at or near the cutoff values. The studies were specifically designed to truly challenge the devices and operators, with the goal of selecting clinical specimens such that approximately two-thirds of them had immunoreactive drug concentrations at or near the screening cutoffs (as judged by initial immunoassay results). Although this borderline specimen-weighted distribution was met using immunoreactive results at screening cutoffs, subsequent specific GC/MS results showed that overall less than half of the specimens were within ±25% of the confirmation cutoffs. It must be remembered that the screening cutoffs are based on immunoreactive concentrations, whereas the confirmation cutoffs are based on specific GC/MS concentrations.

The study protocols did not allow for the independent reading of each result by multiple operators, as the focus of the evaluation was to simulate "field" conditions. To assess whether there was any significant operator variability, an examination was made of the relative number of borderline results reported by each operator, taking into account that all operators did not perform tests on the same number of borderline specimens. Reporting of results as borderline reflects the operator's judgement that the result was not clearly positive or negative. An analysis did not indicate any significant differences.

2.5. Operational Characteristics

The above discussion focused on one of the most important criteria in judging the suitability of a test device for a given testing application, i.e., accuracy. Of secondary, but essential importance, are the operational characteristics, i.e., ease of use, well-defined result indicators, and storage. Several observations are discussed briefly below.

Table 21 on page 238, "Product Descriptions, Operation, and Distributor Information, AOC and DWP Studies," outlines briefly the test procedures for each device, together with a time estimate and distributor information. It is important to note that devices designed to test for multiple drugs will obviously take less time than individual test devices for each drug. For example, one of the multi-assay devices takes about 8 min to test for 5 drugs, but using five single tests would require 8 min per drug. However, these times can overlap, adding urine sequentially to the five different devices, thus requiring as little as 10 to 12 min.

It should also be noted that some devices require careful timing, with a warning such as: "Do not read after 10 min." This is because of fading of the control and/or detection bands, or the development of color across the entire test strip. Clearly, those devices that are less time sensitive will provide simpler testing procedures and minimize the potential for errors in the interpretation of results.

In addition to the time factor, the number of steps or procedural complexities contributes to operator acceptance and reduction of errors. Most devices included in the study required minimal manipulations, e.g., requiring only the use of a pipette provided in the kit to add one or more drops to a well on the test plate or card. The test strips only require the dipping of the strip into the urine sample.

The most convenient devices from an operational perspective are the cups, which require no "handling" of the urine. The four cups in the DWP study (one of which was in the AOC study) are all activated by different means. One, the Roche TesTcup is activated by tipping the closed collection cup to expose the test strip (which is embedded into the side of the cup) to the sample. The Syva Rapid Cup requires the twisting of the cap, which depresses a plunger that allows an aliquot to enter and be trapped in the test chamber. The lid is tamper-evident, not allowing it to be removed. The V-Tech Drug Check Cup requires no activation, the urine starts wicking into the test strips as soon as it enters the cup. The fourth device does not have the test strips integrated into the cup, but the American Bio Medica Rapid Drug Screen requires that the test card be inserted through a slot in the lid to run the test. If the result is positive, the lid and card are removed and replaced with a solid lid. In all cases, the entire cup can then be submitted for confirmation.

As part of the study, each operator maintained a log of comments, recording operational observations. The most frequent complaint was the general lack of clear endpoints to distinguish positive results from negative ones. Also, several devices "failed," in that the control band was invalid or no wicking of the sample occurred. In the DWP study, these were replaced and the samples retested.

Other operator comments included: easy to use; easy to read results; sample failing to evenly "wick" across the test strip or not at all; hard to distinguish between positives and negatives; and takes too long to develop. Comments specific to each device are included in the product descriptions from the DWP study (the comments were not tabulated during the AOC study).

3. Summary

This chapter has summarized the data analysis of results from two controlled studies of 15 different NIDT and one instrument on-site drug test devices. They may also serve as an introduction to the issues and limitations involving the use of on-site test systems or devices, including the accuracy, as compared to standard GC/MS confirmation methods, and some operational considerations. The favorable performance of some of the devices was encouraging considering the simplicity of their design and operational requirements, especially in light of the challenging set of specimens that were clustered around the screening cutoffs. It was hoped that this study could clearly identify one or more devices that showed significant superiority over others, but it appears that no single product is ideally suited for all applications. Other chapters in this text discuss several of these devices in more detail.

Nevertheless, the results described herein indicate that with proper training, controls and other operational requirements, NIDT devices can be sufficiently accurate to serve as useful screening tests in criminal justice and workplace drug testing programs.

Table 1
Drug Cutoffs (ng/mL)

Drug	Screening	GC/MS AOC	GC/MS HHS
Amphetamines	1000	250	500
Cocaine	300	150	150
Opiates	300	150	300
Cannabinoids	50	15	15
Phencyclidine	25	25	25

Table 2
Amphetamine Test Results vs GC/MS – AOC Study, HHS Cutoffs

Device	Sensitivity	Specificity	PPV	NPV	Accuracy
A/Q Rapid Test (Meth)	100%	19%	0.14	1.00	28%
AccuSign DOA 4 (Meth)	70%	87%	0.41	0.96	85%
AccuSign Single (Meth)	60%	85%	0.35	0.94	82%
First Check (Meth)	60%	84%	0.33	0.94	81%
MicroLINE (Meth)	78%	72%	0.25	0.96	72%
One Step Card (Meth)	100%	23%	0.15	1.00	32%
One Step Strip (Meth)	100%	32%	0.17	1.00	40%
PharmScreen (Amp)	80%	73%	0.29	0.96	74%
EZ-SCREEN Profile (Amp)	100%	72%	0.33	1.00	76%
QuickScreen (Meth)	60%	77%	0.26	0.93	75%
Triage (Both)	78%	77%	0.30	0.96	77%
Verdict (N/A)	N/A	N/A	N/A	N/A	N/A
Visualine D (Meth)	50%	60%	0.14	0.90	59%
Visualine II (Meth)	50%	67%	0.17	0.91	65%
Emit (ETS)	100%	69%	0.30	1.00	72%
TesTcup (Amp)	33%	97%	0.88	0.83	83%
Emit (ETS) with TesTcup	95%	62%	0.43	0.98	70%

(continued)

Table 3
Amphetamine Test Results vs GC/MS – AOC Study, AOC Cutoffs

Device	Sensitivity	Specificity	PPV	NPV	Accuracy
A/Q Rapid Test (Meth)	100%	20%	0.23	1.00	35%
AccuSign DOA 4 (Meth)	44%	86%	0.41	0.87	78%
AccuSign Single (Meth)	50%	87%	0.47	0.88	80%
First Check (Meth)	50%	86%	0.44	0.88	79%
MicroLINE (Meth)	73%	75%	0.39	0.93	75%
One Step Card (Meth)	100%	25%	0.24	1.00	39%
One Step Strip (Meth)	100%	35%	0.27	1.00	48%
PharmScreen (Amp)	81%	78%	0.46	0.95	79%
EZ-SCREEN Profile (Amp)	94%	77%	0.50	0.98	80%
QuickScreen (Both)	44%	77%	0.30	0.85	70%
Triage (Both)	53%	76%	0.35	0.87	72%
Verdict (N/A)	N/A	N/A	N/A	N/A	N/A
Visualine D (Meth)	50%	61%	0.23	0.84	59%
Visualine II (Meth)	38%	65%	0.20	0.82	60%
Emit (ETS)	100%	75%	0.48	1.00	80%
TesTcup (Amp)	20%	100%	1.00	0.61	64%
Emit (ETS) with TesTcup	85%	76%	0.74	0.86	80%

Table 4
Cocaine Test Results vs GC/MS – AOC Study, HHS/AOC Cutoffs

Device	Sensitivity	Specificity	PPV	NPV	Accuracy
A/Q Rapid Test	100%	44%	0.62	1.00	71%
AccuSign DOA 4	95%	77%	0.79	0.94	85%
AccuSign Single	90%	84%	0.83	0.90	87%
First Check	97%	56%	0.66	0.96	75%
microLINE	95%	43%	0.59	0.90	67%
One Step Card	100%	21%	0.52	1.00	58%
One Step Strip	97%	38%	0.59	0.94	67%
PharmScreen	100%	47%	0.63	1.00	72%
EZ-SCREEN Profile	90%	52%	0.64	0.85	70%
QuickScreen	97%	44%	0.61	0.95	70%
Triage	51%	100%	1.00	0.69	77%
Verdict	81%	64%	0.67	0.79	72%
Visualine D	92%	44%	0.60	0.86	67%
Visualine II	100%	51%	0.65	1.00	74%
Emit (ETS)	90%	98%	0.97	0.91	94%
TesTcup	66%	97%	0.97	0.67	79%
Emit (ETS) with TesTcup	66%	100%	1.00	0.67	80%

(continued)

Table 5
Opiates Test Results vs GC/MS – AOC Study, HHS Cutoffs

Device	Sensitivity	Specificity	PPV	NPV	Accuracy
A/Q Rapid Test	100%	39%	0.34	1.00	54%
AccuSign DOA 4	100%	55%	0.41	1.00	66%
AccuSign Single	95%	49%	0.35	0.97	59%
First Check	100%	52%	0.38	1.00	63%
microLINE	100%	41%	0.33	1.00	54%
One Step Card	100%	32%	0.31	1.00	48%
One Step Strip	100%	27%	0.29	1.00	44%
PharmScreen	100%	36%	0.33	1.00	51%
EZ-SCREEN Profile	100%	13%	0.26	1.00	33%
QuickScreen	100%	55%	0.42	1.00	66%
Triage	94%	66%	0.44	0.98	72%
Verdict	90%	52%	0.36	0.94	60%
Visualine D	100%	30%	0.30	1.00	47%
Visualine II	100%	29%	0.30	1.00	45%
Emit (ETS)	95%	71%	0.49	0.98	76%
TesTcup	100%	68%	0.57	1.00	78%
Emit (ETS) with TesTcup	92%	73%	0.59	0.96	79%

Table 6
Opiates Test Results vs GC/MS – AOC Study, AOC Cutoffs

Device	Sensitivity	Specificity	PPV	NPV	Accuracy
A/Q Rapid Test	97%	47%	0.54	0.96	66%
AccuSign DOA 4	91%	65%	0.63	0.92	75%
AccuSign Single	91%	58%	0.58	0.91	71%
First Check	97%	65%	0.64	0.97	77%
microLINE	94%	48%	0.53	0.93	66%
One Step Card	100%	41%	0.53	1.00	65%
One Step Strip	100%	35%	0.50	1.00	60%
PharmScreen	100%	47%	0.58	1.00	69%
EZ-SCREEN Profile	97%	14%	0.43	0.88	48%
QuickScreen	100%	65%	0.60	1.00	77%
Triage	91%	80%	0.74	0.93	84%
Verdict	85%	60%	0.58	0.86	70%
Visualine D	94%	35%	0.48	0.90	58%
Visualine II	97%	35%	0.49	0.95	59%
Emit (ETS)	82%	80%	0.73	0.87	81%
TesTcup	88%	90%	0.91	0.86	89%
Emit (ETS) with TesTcup	75%	90%	0.90	0.76	82%

(continued)

Table 7
Cannabinoids Test Results vs GC/MS – AOC Study, HHS/AOC Cutoffs

Device	Sensitivity	Specificity	PPV	NPV	Accuracy
A/Q Rapid Test	98%	49%	0.67	0.95	74%
AccuSign DOA 4	77%	85%	0.85	0.77	81%
AccuSign Single	77%	82%	0.83	0.76	80%
First Check	96%	54%	0.70	0.91	76%
microLINE	83%	50%	0.69	0.70	69%
One Step Card	98%	38%	0.65	0.93	70%
One Step Strip	95%	37%	0.63	0.88	68%
PharmScreen	100%	58%	0.73	1.00	80%
EZ-SCREEN Profile	79%	51%	0.67	0.67	67%
QuickScreen	88%	74%	0.77	0.86	81%
Triage	43%	97%	0.95	0.60	69%
Verdict	33%	100%	1.00	0.60	67%
Visualine D	81%	74%	0.78	0.78	78%
Visualine II	11%	97%	0.83	0.49	51%
Emit (ETS)	84%	87%	0.88	0.83	86%
TesTcup	28%	98%	0.93	0.55	61%
Emit (ETS) with TesTcup	70%	95%	0.94	0.75	82%

Table 8
Phencyclidine Test Results vs GC/MS – AOC Study, HHS/AOC Cutoffs

Device	Sensitivity	Specificity	PPV	NPV	Accuracy
A/Q Rapid Test	100%	29%	0.53	1.00	60%
AccuSign DOA 4	N/A	N/A	N/A	N/A	N/A
AccuSign Single	N/A	N/A	N/A	N/A	N/A
First Check	88%	67%	0.69	0.87	77%
microLINE	90%	41%	0.56	0.83	63%
One Step Card	N/A	N/A	N/A	N/A	N/A
One Step Strip	N/A	N/A	N/A	N/A	N/A
PharmScreen	100%	39%	0.58	1.00	67%
EZ-SCREEN Profile	61%	57%	0.54	0.64	59%
QuickScreen	N/A	N/A	N/A	N/A	N/A
Triage	71%	98%	0.97	0.80	85%
Verdict	93%	60%	0.66	0.91	75%
Visualine D	N/A	N/A	N/A	N/A	N/A
Visualine II	N/A	N/A	N/A	N/A	N/A
Emit (ETS)	100%	67%	0.72	1.00	82%
TesTcup	N/A	N/A	N/A	N/A	N/A
Emit (ETS) with TesTcup	N/A	N/A	N/A	N/A	N/A

(continued)

Table 9
All Drugs Test Results vs GC/MS – AOC Study, HHS Cutoffs

Device	Sensitivity	Specificity	PPV	NPV	Accuracy
A/Q Rapid Test	99%	33%	0.45	0.99	57%
AccuSign DOA 4	87%	75%	0.64	0.92	79%
AccuSign Single	83%	74%	0.61	0.90	77%
First Check	92%	65%	0.59	0.94	74%
microLINE	90%	51%	0.51	0.90	65%
One Step Card	99%	28%	0.41	0.98	52%
One Step Strip	97%	33%	0.42	0.96	55%
PharmScreen	99%	52%	0.54	0.99	69%
EZ-SCREEN Profile	81%	49%	0.48	0.82	61%
QuickScreen	91%	64%	0.56	0.93	73%
Triage	61%	85%	0.70	0.79	76%
Verdict	72%	66%	0.60	0.77	69%
Visualine D	86%	51%	0.47	0.88	62%
Visualine II	61%	58%	0.42	0.74	59%
Emit (ETS)	92%	76%	0.69	0.94	82%
TesTcup	55%	89%	0.78	0.74	75%
Emit (ETS) with TesTcup	76%	79%	0.71	0.83	78%

Table 10
All Drugs Test Results vs GC/MS – AOC Study, AOC Cutoffs

Device	Sensitivity	Specificity	PPV	NPV	Accuracy
A/Q Rapid Test	99%	36%	0.51	0.98	61%
AccuSign DOA 4	82%	78%	0.71	0.87	80%
AccuSign Single	81%	78%	0.70	0.86	79%
First Check	90%	68%	0.66	0.91	77%
microLINE	89%	53%	0.57	0.87	68%
One Step Card	99%	31%	0.48	0.98	58%
One Step Strip	98%	36%	0.50	0.96	61%
PharmScreen	98%	56%	0.61	0.98	73%
EZ-SCREEN Profile	82%	52%	0.55	0.80	65%
QuickScreen	88%	66%	0.61	0.90	74%
Triage	61%	89%	0.80	0.77	78%
Verdict	73%	70%	0.66	0.75	71%
Visualine D	84%	53%	0.54	0.84	65%
Visualine II	62%	60%	0.51	0.71	61%
Emit (ETS)	90%	80%	0.76	0.92	84%
TesTcup	52%	97%	0.94	0.65	73%
Emit (ETS) with TesTcup	73%	89%	0.88	0.75	81%

(continued)

Table 11
Amphetamines Test Results vs GC/MS – HHS Study, HHS Cutoffs

Device	Sensitivity	Specificity	PPV	NPV	Accuracy
Accutest Single (Meth)	26%	85%	0.31	0.81	72%
DiPro 10 Panel (Amp)	26%	94%	056	0.83	80%
DiPro 10 Panel (Meth)	47%	68%	0.28	0.83	63%
DiPro 10 Panel (Combined)	74%	66%	0.37	0.90	68%
Drug Check Cup (Both)	63%	53%	0.27	0.84	55%
DTx 520 (Meth)	47%	78%	0.36	0.85	71%
Syva Rapid Cup (Amp)	79%	92%	0.71	0.94	89%
Syva Rapid Cup (Meth)	42%	68%	0.26	0.81	62%
Syva Rapid Cup (Combined)	90%	66%	0.41	0.96	71%
InstaCheck (Meth)	37%	89%	0.47	0.84	78%
One-Step Single (Amp)	84%	70%	0.43	0.94	73%
One-Step Single (Meth)	68%	32%	0.21	0.79	40%
One-Step Single (Combined)	95%	32%	0.27	0.96	46%
PharmScreen DS Card (Meth)	53%	63%	0.28	0.83	61%
PharmScreen Multi-4 (Meth)	42%	83%	0.40	0.84	74%
QuickScreen (Amp)	95%	75%	0.50	0.98	79%
Rapid Drug Screen Cup (Amp)	58%	96%	0.79	0.90	88%
Status DS-5 (Amp)	53%	85%	0.48	0.87	78%
Syva Rapid Test (Meth)	5%	86%	0.09	0.77	69%
TesTcup 5 (Amp)	63%	86%	0.55	0.90	81%
TesTstik (Amp)	47%	97%	0.82	0.87	87%
Emit (ETS) (Both)	90%	51%	0.33	0.95	59%
AdultaCheck	74%	85%	0.56	0.92	82%

Table 12
Amphetamines Test Results vs GC/MS – HHS Study, AOC Cutoffs

Device	Sensitivity	Specificity	PPV	NPV	Accuracy
Accutest Single (Meth)	30%	95%	0.88	0.55	61%
DiPro 10 Panel (Amp)	17%	98%	0.89	0.52	56%
DiPro 10 Panel (Meth)	64%	95%	0.94	0.71	79%
DiPro 10 Panel (Combined)	75%	93%	0.92	0.77	83%
Drug Check Cup (Both)	62%	62%	0.64	0.59	62%
DTx 520 (Meth)	47%	93%	0.88	0.62	69%
Syva Rapid Cup (Amp)	40%	95%	0.90	0.59	67%
Syva Rapid Cup (Meth)	57%	93%	0.90	0.67	74%
Syva Rapid Cup (Combined)	77%	91%	0.90	0.78	83%
InstaCheck (Meth)	32%	100%	1.00	0.57	64%
One-Step Single (Amp)	62%	81%	0.78	0.66	71%

(continued)

Table 12 (continud)
Amphetamines Test Results vs GC/MS – HHS Study, AOC Cutoffs

Device	Sensitivity	Specificity	PPV	NPV	Accuracy
One-Step Single (Meth)	87%	54%	0.67	0.79	71%
One-Step Single (Combined)	98%	54%	0.70	0.96	77%
PharmScreen DS Card (Meth)	72%	95%	0.94	0.76	83%
PharmScreen Multi-4 (Meth)	40%	98%	0.95	0.60	68%
QuickScreen (Amp)	68%	91%	0.89	0.72	79%
Rapid Drug Screen Cup (Amp)	28%	98%	0.93	0.55	61%
Status DS-5 (Amp)	40%	95%	0.90	0.59	67%
Syva Rapid Test (Meth)	9%	84%	0.36	0.46	44%
TesTcup 5 (Amp)	45%	98%	0.95	0.62	70%
TesTstik (Amp)	23%	100%	1.00	0.54	60%
Emit (ETS) (Both)	89%	77%	0.81	0.87	83%
AdultaCheck	74%	85%	0.56	0.92	82%

Table 13
Cocaine Test Results vs GC/MS – HHS Study, HHS/AOC Cutoffs

Device	Sensitivity	Specificity	PPV	NPV	Accuracy
Accutest Single	88%	85%	0.93	0.73	87%
DiPro 10 Panel	97%	69%	0.89	0.90	89%
Drug Check Cup	95%	46%	0.81	0.80	81%
DTx 520	86%	85%	0.93	0.71	86%
Syva Rapid Cup	91%	73%	0.89	0.76	86%
InstaCheck	91%	77%	0.91	0.77	88%
One-Step Single	80%	100%	1.00	0.67	86%
PharmScreen DS Card	64%	92%	0.95	0.51	72%
PharmScreen Multi-4	89%	92%	0.97	0.77	90%
QuickScreen	81%	92%	0.96	0.67	84%
Rapid Drug Screen Cup	66%	89%	0.93	0.51	72%
Status DS-5	72%	100%	1.00	0.59	80%
Syva Rapid Test	64%	92%	0.95	0.51	72%
TesTcup 5	97%	81%	0.93	0.91	92%
TesTstik	86%	85%	0.93	0.71	86%
Emit (ETS)	70%	100%	1.00	0.58	79%
AdultaCheck	100%	95%	0.71	1.00	96%

Table 14
Opiates Test Results vs GC/MS – HHS Study, HHS Cutoffs

Device	Sensitivity	Specificity	PPV	NPV	Accuracy
Accutest Single	93%	57%	0.30	0.98	63%
DiPro 10 Panel	100%	39%	0.25	1.00	49%
Drug Check Cup	87%	39%	0.22	0.94	47%
DTx 520	100%	24%	0.21	1.00	37%
Syva Rapid Cup	100%	32%	0.23	1.00	43%

(continued)

Table 14 (continued)

Opiates Test Results vs GC/MS – HHS Study, HHS Cutoffs

Device	Sensitivity	Specificity	PPV	NPV	Accuracy
InstaCheck	100%	29%	0.22	1.00	41%
One-Step Single	100%	35%	0.23	1.00	0.46%
PharmScreen DS Card	87%	64%	0.33	0.96	68%
PharmScreen Multi-4	100%	33%	0.23	1.00	44%
QuickScreen	93%	59%	0.31	0.98	64%
Rapid Drug Screen Cup	80%	64%	0.31	0.94	67%
Status DS-5	93%	53%	0.29	0.98	60%
Syva Rapid Test	100%	57%	0.32	1.00	64%
TesTcup 5	93%	64%	0.34	0.98	69%
TesTstik	87%	80%	0.46	0.97	81%
Emit (ETS)	87%	81%	0.48	0.97	82%
AdultaCheck	90%	90%	0.53	0.99	90%

Table 15

Opiates Test Results vs GC/MS – HHS Study, AOC Cutoffs

Device	Sensitivity	Specificity	PPV	NPV	Accuracy
Accutest Single	75%	65%	0.59	0.80	69%
DiPro 10 Panel	97%	52%	0.57	0.97	70%
Drug Check Cup	86%	48%	0.53	0.84	63%
DTx 520	97%	32%	0.49	0.94	58%
Syva Rapid Cup	97%	43%	0.53	0.96	64%
InstaCheck	100%	41%	0.53	1.00	64%
One-Step Single	100%	48%	0.56	1.00	69%
PharmScreen DS Card	67%	70%	0.60	0.76	69%
PharmScreen Multi-4	94%	43%	0.52	0.92	63%
QuickScreen	86%	74%	0.69	0.89	79%
Rapid Drug Screen Cup	67%	72%	0.62	0.76	70%
Status DS-5	78%	61%	0.57	0.80	68%
Syva Rapid Test	86%	70%	0.66	0.88	77%
TesTcup 5	78%	76%	0.68	0.84	77%
TesTstik	56%	85%	0.71	0.74	73%
Emit (ETS)	39%	75%	0.52	0.65	61%
AdultaCheck	90%	90%	0.53	099	90%

Table 16

Cannabinoids Test Results vs GC/MS – HHS Study, HHS/AOC Cutoffs

Device	Sensitivity	Specificity	PPV	NPV	Accuracy
Accutest Single	26%	100%	1.00	0.47	56%
DiPro 10 Panel	98%	36%	0.70	0.93	73%
Drug Check Cup	85%	36%	0.67	0.62	66%
DTx 520	98%	36%	0.70	0.93	73%
Syva Rapid Cup	63%	78%	0.81	0.58	69%

(continued)

Table 16 (continued)

Cannabinoids Test Results vs GC/MS – HHS Study, HHS/AOC Cutoffs

Device	Sensitivity	Specificity	PPV	NPV	Accuracy
InstaCheck	74%	69%	0.78	0.64	72%
One-Step Single	96%	36%	0.69	0.87	72%
PharmScreen DS Card	52%	75%	0.76	0.51	61%
PharmScreen Multi-4	56%	83%	0.83	0.56	67%
QuickScreen	50%	56%	0.63	0.43	52%
Rapid Drug Screen Cup	91%	47%	0.72	0.77	73%
Status DS-5	54%	94%	0.94	0.58	70%
Syva Rapid Test	57%	64%	0.71	0.50	60%
TesTcup 5	52%	86%	0.85	0.54	66%
TesTstik	76%	67%	0.77	0.65	72%
Emit (ETS)	52%	94%	0.93	0.57	69%
AdultaCheck	94%	89%	0.68	0.99	90%

Table 17

Phencyclidine Test Results vs GC/MS – HHS Study, HHS/AOC Cutoffs

Device	Sensitivity	Specificity	PPV	NPV	Accuracy
Accutest Single	97%	27%	0.41	0.94	51%
DiPro 10 Panel	97%	31%	0.42	0.95	53%
Drug Check Cup	77%	46%	0.43	0.79	57%
DTx 520	90%	36%	0.42	0.88	54%
Syva Rapid Cup	100%	27%	0.42	1.00	52%
InstaCheck	61%	73%	0.54	0.78	69%
One-Step Single	90%	53%	0.50	0.91	66%
PharmScreen DS Card	100%	25%	0.41	1.00	51%
PharmScreen Multi-4	N/A	N/A	N/A	N/A	N/A
QuickScreen	94%	49%	0.49	0.94	64%
Rapid Drug Screen Cup	71%	76%	0.61	0.83	74%
Status DS-5	90%	54%	0.51	0.91	67%
Syva Rapid Test	100%	32%	0.44	1.00	56%
TesTcup 5	94%	42%	0.46	0.93	60%
TesTstik	61%	64%	0.48	0.76	63 %
Emit (ETS)	87%	92%	0.84	0.93	90%
AdultaCheck	100%	98%	0.00	1.00	98%

Table 18

All Drugs Test Results vs GC/MS – HHS Study, HHS Cutoffs

Device	Sensitivity	Specificity	PPV	NPV	Accuracy
Accutest Single	65%	66%	0.57	0.73	66%
DiPro 10 Panel*	86%	57%	0.55	0.87	68%
Drug Check Cup	85%	44%	0.51	0.81	61%
DTx 520	87%	48%	0.54	0.85	64%
Syva Rapid Cup*	80%	59%	0.54	0.83	67%
InstaCheck	76%	65%	0.60	0.80	69%

*Includes combined results for amphetamine and methamphetamine.

(continued)

Table 18 (continued)

All Drugs Test Results vs GC/MS – HHS Study, HHS Cutoffs

Device	Sensitivity	Specificity	PPV	NPV	Accuracy
One-Step Single*	87%	50%	0.51	0.86	64%
PharmScreen DS Card	67%	60%	0.53	0.73	63%
PharmScreen Multi-4	72%	66%	0.61	0.77	69%
QuickScreen	77%	64%	0.59	0.80	69%
Rapid Drug Screen Cup	74%	75%	0.67	0.81	75%
Status DS-5	69%	72%	0.63	0.77	71%
Syva Rapid Test	65%	64%	0.55	0.73	64%
TesTcup 5	79%	70%	0.64	0.83	74%
TesTstik	75%	80%	0.72	0.82	78%
Emit (ETS)	71%	79%	0.70	0.80	76%
AdultaCheck	88%	92%	0.60	0.98	91%

Table 19

All Drugs Test Results vs GC/MS – HHS Study, AOC Cutoffs

Device	Sensitivity	Specificity	PPV	NPV	Accuracy
Accutest Single	61%	69%	0.68	0.62	65%
DiPro 10 Panel*	78%	61%	0.68	0.72	70%
Drug Check Cup	82%	48%	0.63	0.72	66%
DTx 520	83%	52%	0.65	0.74	68%
Syva Rapid Cup*	73%	64%	0.69	0.69	69%
InstaCheck	72%	70%	0.72	0.71	71%
One-Step Single*	85%	59%	0.69	0.79	72%
PharmScreen DS Card	68%	67%	0.68	0.66	67%
PharmScreen Multi-4	70%	75%	0.78	0.66	72%
QuickScreen	74%	70%	0.72	0.71	72%
Rapid Drug Screen Cup	65%	76%	0.74	0.67	70%
Status DS-5	65%	76%	0.74	0.67	70%
Syva Rapid Test	60%	64%	0.64	0.60	62%
TesTcup 5	72%	73%	0.74	0.71	73%
TesTstik	63%	79%	0.76	0.67	71%
Emit (ETS)	67%	86%	0.84	0.71	76%
AdultaCheck	88%	92%	0.60	0.98	91%

*Includes combined results for amphetamine and methamphetamine.

Table 20

Variation in Test Results for Products Manufactured by the Same Company (from HHS Study, HHS Cutoffs)

Manufacturer	Device	False positive	False negative
Princeton BioMeditech	Status DS-5	28.1%	30.6%
	Syva Rapid Test	36.3%	35.0%
Roche Diagnostics	TesTcup	30.5%	20.8%
	TesTstik	20.2%	25.1%
Forefront Diagnostics	InstaCheck	35.2%	24.0%
	DTx 520	51.7%	12.6%

Table 21
Product Descriptions, Operation, and Distributor Information, AOC and DWP Studies

Test devices	Description/Operation	Distributor
AOC Study Multiple Test Devices		
AccuSign	Each device is packaged in a sealed pouch with an attached pipet. Storage does not require refrigeration, but 40° to 86°F is recommended. Expiration dates are stamped on the pouches. The devices are well labeled, with clear result designations. The device includes a "control" or validity check. The test requires the addition of three (3) drops of urine to a well at one end of the device. Results can be read within 3 to 5 minutes, but should be read within 10 minutes. The endpoint for a positive result is the absence of a line at the test band.	Drug Test Resources International 1489 West Palmetto Park Road, Suite 465 Boca Raton, Florida 33486 Phone: 800-498-8583 There are several local distributors
First Check	Each device is packaged in a sealed pouch with an attached pipet. Storage does not require refrigeration, but 40° to 86°F is recommended. Expiration dates are stamped on the pouches. The devices are well labeled, with clear result designations. The device includes a "control" or validity check. The test requires the addition of three (3) drops of urine to a well at one end of the device. Results can be read within 3 to 5 minutes, but should be read within 10 minutes. The endpoint for a positive result is the absence of a line at the test band.	Worldwide Medical Corporation 199 Technology Drive, Suite 150 Irvine, California 92718 Phone: 800-788-5716 Fax: 714-727-0602
microLINE	Each device is packaged in a sealed pouch. Sample dispensers (pipets) are provided. Storage requires refrigeration, 35° to 40°, but the device must be brought to room temperature prior to use (ca. 1 hour). Expiration dates are stamped on the	Drug Screening Systems, Inc. P.O. Box 579 Blackwood, New Jersey 08012 Phone: 800-247-3784 Fax: 609-228-8571

	pouches. The devices are well labeled, with clear result designations and areas for donor ID and date. The device includes a "control" or validity check. The test requires the addition of three (4) drops of urine to a separate well for each drug included. Results are to be read at 10 minutes, but no longer than 10 minutes. The endpoint for a positive result is the absence of a line at the test band.	
EZ-SCREEN Profile	Each device is packaged in a sealed pouch. Additional supplies include reagents, buffer, wipes and pipets. Storage requires refrigeration, 36° to 46°F is recommended. Expiration dates are stamped on the pouches. The devices are well labeled, with clear result designations. The device includes a "control" or validity check. The testing procedure is extensive, requiring the addition of one (1) drop of urine to each of six wells spaced along the device. In succession, a drop of reagent A is added to each well, then buffer B, excess liquid wiped off, then one drop of substrate is added to each well. Results are to be read in 3 min. The endpoint for a positive result is the appearance of a colored spot at the test band that is equal to or lighter than that of the control spot.	MedTox Laboratories, Inc. 354 West County Road D Saint Paul, Minnesota 55112 Phone: 800-832-3244 Fax: 651-628-6150 (Fomerly EDITEK, Inc.)
QuickScreen	Each device is packaged in a sealed pouch with an attached pipet. Package insert does not state if refrigerated storage is required, but implied as the device is to be brought to room temperature prior to use. Expiration dates are stamped on the pouches. The devices are not clearly labeled, with number designations for each test band, three on a side (the device has two parallel wicking channels). The device includes a "control" or validity check on each channel. The test requires the addition of six (6) drops of urine to a well at one end of the	Syntron Bioresearch, Inc. 2774 Loker Avenue West Carlsbad, California 92008 Phone: 619-930-2200 Fax: 619-930-2212

(continued)

Table 21 (continued)
Product Descriptions, Operation, and Distributor Information AOC and DWP Studies

Test devices	Description/Operation	Distributor
	device. Results are to be read in 10 min. The endpoint for a positive result is the absence of a line at the test band.	
TesTcup	Each device is packaged in a sealed bag. Storage does not require refrigeration, but 65° to 85°F is recommended. Expiration dates are stamped on the bags. The devices are well labeled, with clear result designations. The device includes a "control" or validity check. The device is a self-contained collection and storage cup, that has the drug test strips imbedded in its side. The cup is closed with a screw-cap lid after specimen collection. At the time of testing, the lid is turned to its "test" position, the cup tilted until the urine covers _ to _ of the lid (do not invert fully). It is held in this position for 10 seconds, then returned to its upright position. Results can be read as soon as the "TEST VALID" window develops a blue color, usually within 5 min. The endpoint for a positive result is the absence of a line at the test band. Timing is said not to be important. An adhesive covering strip is removed from the test display windows and placed on a small "breather" hole on the back of the cup. The lid should then be returned to the sealed position if the specimen is to be stored or sent for confirmation.	Roche Diagnostic Corporation 9115 Hague Road Indianapolis, Indiana 46256 Phone: 800-428-5074 Fax: 317-521-4240 There are local representatives
Triage	Each device is packaged in a sealed pouch and is provided with a vial of wash solution, a pipet and disposable pipet tips. Storage does not require refrigeration, but 59° to 77°F is recommended. Expiration dates are stamped on the kit box. The devices are well labeled, with symbolic instructions and clear	Biosite Diagnostics 11030 Roselle Street, Suite D San Diego, California 92121-9437 Phone: 800-745-8026 Fax: 619-623-1392

	result designations. The device includes positive and negative "control" or validity checks. The test requires the addition of a measured volume (140 μL) of urine, using the pipet, to a well at one end of the device. This is allowed to incubate for 10 min. The pipet is then used to transfer the urine reaction mixture from the well to the Detection Area. After all the liquid is absorbed, the Wash Solution is added to the test band. Results are to be read within 5 min. Upon standing, the band will all turn a dark color. The endpoint for a positive result is the appearance of a line at the test band.	
Single Test Devices		
A/Q Rapid Test	Each device is packaged in a sealed pouch with an attached pipet. Storage does not require refrigeration, but can be if desired. Expiration dates are stamped on the pouches. The devices are not well labeled. The device includes a "control" or validity check. The test requires the addition of five (5) drops of urine to a well at one end of the device. Results can be read within 3 min, but must be read within 8 min. The endpoint for a positive result is the absence of a line at the test band.	Bionike Laboratories 1015 Grandview Drive S. San Francisco, California 94080-4910 Phone: 415-737-7937 Fax: 415-737-5902
AccuSign	Each device is packaged in a sealed pouch with an attached pipet. Storage does not require refrigeration, but 40° to 86°F is recommended. Expiration dates are stamped on the pouches. The devices are well labeled, with clear result designations. The device includes a "control" or validity check. The test requires the addition of three (3) drops of urine to a well at one end of the device. Results can be read within 3 to 5 min, but should be read within 10 min.	Drug Test Resources International 1489 West Palmetto park Road, Suite 465 Boca Raton, Florida 33486 Phone: 800-498-8583 There are several local distributors

(continued)

Table 21 (continued)

Product Descriptions, Operation, and Distributor Information AOC and DWP Studies

Test devices	Description/Operation	Distributor
First Check	Each device is packaged in a sealed pouch with an attached pipet. Storage does not require refrigeration, but 40° to 86°F is recommended. Expiration dates are stamped on the pouches. The devices are well labeled, with clear result designations. The device includes a "control" or validity check. The test requires the addition of three (3) drops of urine to a well at one end of the device. Results can be read within 3 to 5 min, but should be read within 10 min.	Worldwide Medical Corporation 199 Technology Drive, Suite 150 Irvine, California 92718 Phone: 800-788-5716 Fax: 714-727-0602
One Step Card	Each device is packaged in a sealed pouch with an attached pipet. Storage does not require refrigeration, but 40° to 86°F is recommended. Expiration dates are stamped on the pouches. The devices are not well labeled. The device includes a "control" or validity check. The test requires the addition of three (3) to five (5) drops of urine to a well at one end of the device. Results can be read within 3 to 5 min, but should be read within 10 min. The endpoint for a positive result is the absence of a line at the test band.	International Immuno-Diagnostics 1155 Chess Drive, Suite 121 Foster City, California 94404 Phone: 415-345-9518 Fax: 415-578-1810
One Step Strip	Each device is packaged in a sealed pouch with an attached pipet. Storage does not require refrigeration, but 40° to 86°F is recommended. Expiration dates are stamped on the pouches. The devices are not well labeled. The device includes a "control" or validity check. The test requires the dipping of the device into a urine sample up to a mark on the device. Results can be read within 3 to 5 min, but should be	International Immuno-Diagnostics 1155 Chess Drive, Suite 121 Foster City, California 94404 Phone: 415-345-9518 Fax: 415-578-1810

	read within 10 min. The endpoint for a positive result is the absence of a line at the test band.	
PharmScreen	Each device is packaged in a sealed pouch, which also contains a pipet. Storage does not require refrigeration, but 36° to 86°F is recommended. Expiration dates are stamped on the pouches, are for at least one year. The devices are fairly well labeled, with result designations. The device includes a "control" or validity check. The test requires the addition of a measured amount (0.2 mL as marked on the pipet) of urine to a well at one end of the device. Results can be read within 3, but must be read within 8 min.	PharmChem, Inc. 4600 North Beach Haltom City, Texas 67137 Phone: 800-446-5177 Fax: 817-605-6417
Verdict	Each device is packaged in a sealed pouch with an attached pipet. Storage does not require refrigeration, but 40° to 77°F is recommended. If stored under refrigeration, the shelf life is extended to the expiration dates stamped on the pouch. The devices are well labeled, with space for the donor's ID.	MedTox Laboratories, Inc. 354 West County Road D Saint Paul, Minnesota 55112 Phone: 800-832-3244 Fax: 651-628-6150 (Formerly EDITEK, Inc.)
Visualine D	The device includes a "control" or validity check. The test requires the addition of five (5) drops of urine to a well at one end of the device. Results can be read within 5 min, but should be read within 10 min. The endpoint for a positive result is the absence of a line at the test band. Each device is packaged in a sealed pouch with an attached pipet. Storage does not require refrigeration, but 36° to 86°F is recommended. Expiration dates are stamped on the pouches. The devices are not well labeled. The device includes a "control" or validity check. The test requires the dipping of the device into a urine sample up to a mark on the	Sun Biomedical Laboratories, Inc. 2040 Fairfax Avenue Cherry Hill, New Jersey 08003 Phone: 609-751-4668 Fax: 609-751-0681

(continued)

Table 21 (continued)

Product Descriptions, Operation, and Distributor Information AOC and DWP Studies

Test devices	Description/Operation	Distributor
	device. Results can be read within 5 min, but should not be read after 5 min. The endpoint for a positive result is the absence of a line at the test band.	
Visualine II	Each device is packaged in a sealed pouch with an attached pipet. Storage does not require refrigeration, but 36° to 86°F is recommended. Expiration dates are stamped on the pouches. The devices are not well labeled. The device includes a "control" or validity check. The test requires the addition of three (3) drops of urine to a well at one end of the device. Results can be read within 5 min, but should not be read after 5 min. The endpoint for a positive result is the absence of a line at the test band.	Sun Biomedical Laboratories, Inc. 2040 Fairfax Avenue Cherry Hill, New Jersey 08003 Phone: 609-751-4668 Fax: 609-751-0681
DWP Study Multiple Test Devices		
Dipro 10 Panel	Each device is packaged in a sealed pouch. The device consists of a flat plastic card that has five dipsticks extending from one edge. Two of these are connected back-to-back providing for ten separate test strips. The strips are covered with a protective cap. Storage does not require refrigeration, but 36° to 86° is recommended. Expiration dates are stamped on the pouches. The devices are well labeled, with clear result designations and areas for donor ID and date. The device includes a "control" or validity check. The test requires the	Dipro Diagnostics Products, Inc. 3415 Hycliffe Avenue Louisville, Kentucky 40207 Phone: 502-899-3108

	removal of the cap, insertion of the dipsticks into the specimen for about 10 seconds. The cap can be replaced. The endpoint for a positive result is the absence of a line at the test band windows. Manufactured by Applied Biotech Inc. Operators comments: Device was easy to use and results easy to read. Messy to handle. Difficult package to open.	
Drug Check Cup	Each device is packaged in a sealed bag. Expiration dates are stamped on the bags. The devices are well labeled, with clear result designations. The device includes a "control" or validity check. The device is a self-contained collection and storage cup, that has the drug test strips imbedded in its side. The cup is closed with a screw-cap lid after specimen collection. The test begins as soon as the urine is added to the cup. There is no other activation step required. Results can be read within 5 to 9 min. The endpoint for a positive result is the absence of a line at the test band. The test strips are manufactured by V-Tech. Operators comments: Device took up to 10 min to show results, slow compared to other devices. Results unclear, hard to tell the difference between positive and negative results. Difficult to determine if test is valid due to time required. Some strips tend to streak.	Job Services Inc. 32107 West Lindero Canyon Road Westlake Village, California 91361 Phone: 818-599-2512
DTx 520	Each cassette-style device is packaged in a sealed pouch with an attached pipet. Storage does not require refrigeration, but 36° to 86°F is recommended. Expiration dates are stamped on the pouches. The devices are well labeled, with clear result designations. The device includes a "control" or validity check. The test requires the addition of 4 to 5 drops of urine	Universal Drug Testing Company 467 Route 51 Large, Pennsylvania 15025 Phone: 888-822-7120

(continued)

Table 21 (continued)
Product Descriptions, Operation, and Distributor Information AOC Sand DWP Studies

Test devices	Description/Operation	Distributor
	to a well at one end of the device. Results can be read within 3 to 8 min, but should be read within 8 min. The endpoint for a positive result is the absence of a line at the test band. Manufactured by Forefront Diagnostics, Inc. Operators comments: Device was easy to use and results easy to read. Plastic well over strips unneccesary.	
Syva Rapid Cup	Each device is packaged in a sealed bag. Expiration dates are stamped on the bags. The devices are well labeled, with clear result designations. The device includes a "control" or validity check. The device is a self-contained collection and storage cup, that has the drug test strips imbedded in its side. The cup is closed with a screw-cap lid after specimen collection. At the time of testing, the lid is turned to its fully closed position. This depresses a plunger to trap a portion of the specimen in the test chamber. Results can be read as soon as a line appears in the "test valid" area. The endpoint for a positive result is the absence of a line at the test band. Timing is said not to be important. The test strips were manufactured by Applied Biotech Inc. Operators comments: Device was easy to use and results easy to read. Results were quite distinct. (Product first marketed by Point of Care Technologies under the name "Genie Cup.")	Dade Behring Inc. Glasgow Business Community Newark, Delaware 19702 Phone: 800-242-3233 (Formerly Chimera Research and Chemicals, Inc.)

InstaCheck	Each cassette-style device is packaged in a sealed pouch with an attached pipet. Storage does not require refrigeration, but 36° to 86°F is recommended. Expiration dates are stamped on the pouches. The devices are well labeled, with clear result designations. The device includes a "control" or validity check. The test requires the addition of 4 to 5 drops of urine to a well at one end of the device. Results can be read within 3 to 8 min, but should be read within 8 min. The endpoint for a positive result is the absence of a line at the test band. Manufactured by Forefront Diagnostics, Inc. Operators comments: Device was easy to use and results easy to read.	Forefront Diagnostics, Inc. 23561 Ridge Route Drive, Suite D Laguna Hills, California 92653 Phone: 949-595-0673 Fax: 949-595-0152
PharmScreen Drug Screen Card	Each device is packaged in a sealed pouch. The device consists of a flat plastic card that has five dipsticks extending from one edge. The strips are covered with a protective cap. Storage does not require refrigeration, but 36° to 86° is recommended. Expiration dates are stamped on the pouches. The devices are well labeled, with clear result designations and areas for donor ID and date. The device includes a "control" or validity check. The test requires the removal of the cap, insertion of the dipsticks into the specimen for about 10 seconds. The cap can be replaced. The endpoint for a positive result is the absence of a line at the test band windows. Manufactured by Applied Biotech Inc. Operators comments: Device was easy to use, although can be messy. Results easy to read.	PharmChem Laboratories, Inc.. 4600 North Beach Hatton City, Texas 76137 Phone: 800-446-5177 Fax: 817-605-6417

(continued)

Table 21 (continued)

Product Descriptions, Operation, and Distributor Information AOC and DWP Studies

Test devices	Description/Operation	Distributor
PharmScreen Drug Screen Multi-4	Each cassette-style device is packaged in a sealed pouch. Storage does not require refrigeration, but 36° to 86° is recommended. Expiration dates are stamped on the pouches. The devices are well labeled, with clear result designations and areas for donor ID and date. The device includes a "control" or validity check. The test requires the addition of 4 to 5 drops of urine to a well at one end of the device. Results can be read within 3 to 8 min, but should be read within 8 min. The endpoint for a positive result is the absence of a line at the test band windows. Manufactured by Applied Biotech Inc. Operators comments: Device was easy to use and results easy to read.	PharmChem Laboratories, Inc.. 4600 North Beach Hatton City, Texas 76137 Phone: 800-446-5177 Fax: 817-605-6417
Rapid Drug Screen	The device is a cup and a separate card containing the individual test strips. It is packaged in a sealed pouch. Expiration dates are stamped on the pouches. The devices are well labeled, with clear result designations and areas for donor ID and date. The device includes a "control" or validity check. The test requires the insertion of the test card through a slit in the lid and into the specimen. Results can be read within 3 min, but should be read within 8 min. The endpoint for a positive result is the absence of a line at the test band windows. Manufactured by American Bio Medica Corporation Operators comments: Results easy to read. Problems with cards wicking inspite of dipping up to line. Messy to use.	American Bio Medica Corporation 300 Fairview Avenue Hudson, New York 12534 Phone: 800-227-1243

Status DS-5	Each cassette-style device is packaged in a sealed pouch with an attached pipet. Storage does not require refrigeration, but 35° to 86°F is recommended. Expiration dates are stamped on the pouches. The devices are well labeled, with clear result designations. The device includes a "control" or validity check. The test requires the addition of 3 drops of urine to a well at one end of the device. Results can be read within 3 to 5 min, but should be read within 10 min. The endpoint for a positive result is the absence of a line at the test band. Manufactured by Princeton BioMeditech. Operators comments: Device was easy to use and results easy to read.	Orion Diagnostica Inc. 71 Veronica Avenue Somerset, NJ 08873 Phone: 800-526-2125
Syva Rapid Test	Each cassette-style device is packaged in a sealed pouch with an attached pipet. Storage does not require refrigeration, but 35° to 86°F is recommended. Expiration dates are stamped on the pouches. The devices are well labeled, with clear result designations. The device includes a "control" or validity check. The test requires the addition of 3 drops of urine to a well at one end of the device. Results can be read within 3 to 5 min, but should be read within 10 min. The endpoint for a positive result is the absence of a line at the test band. Manufactured by Princeton BioMeditech. Operators comments: Device was easy to use and results easy to read.	Dade Behring Inc. Glasgow Business Community Newark, Delaware 19702 Phone: 800-242-3233 (Formerly Chimera Research and Chemicals, Inc.)
TesTcup 5	Each device is packaged in a sealed bag. Storage does not require refrigeration, but 65° to 85°F is recommended. Expiration dates are stamped on the bags. The devices are well labeled, with clear result designations. The device includes a "control" or validity check. The device is a self-contained	Roche Diagnostic Corporation 9115 Hague Road Indianapolis, Indiana 46256 Phone: 800-428-5074 Fax: 317-521-4240 There are local representatives

(continued)

Table 21 (continued)

Product Descriptions, Operation, and Distributor Information AOC and DWP Studies

Test devices	Description/Operation	Distributor
	collection and storage cup, that has the drug test strips imbedded in its side. The cup is closed with a screw-cap lid after specimen collection. At the time of testing, the lid is turned to its "test" position, the cup tilted until the urine covers _ to _ of the lid (do not invert fully). It is held in this position for 10 seconds, then returned to its upright position. Results can be read as soon as the "test valid" window develops a blue color, usually within 5 min. The endpoint for a positive result is the absence of a line at the test band. Timing is said not to be important. An adhesive covering strip is removed from the test display windows and placed on a small "breather" hole on the back of the cup. The lid should then be returned to the sealed position if the specimen is to be stored or sent for confirmation. Manufactured by Roche Diagnostic System. Operators comments: Deviced was easy to use and results easy to read.	
Single Test Devices		
Accutest	Each cassette-style device is packaged in a sealed pouch with an attached pipet. Storage does not require refrigeration, but 36° to 86°F is recommended. Expiration dates are stamped on the pouches. The devices are well labeled, with clear result designations. The device includes a "control" or validity check. The test requires the addition of urine from a pipet marked for about 0.2 mL to a well at one end of the device.	Jant Pharmacal Corporation 16255 Ventura Boulevard, Suite 505 Encino, California 91436 Phone: 818-986-8530

	Results can be read within 3 to 8 min, but should be read within 8 min. Manufactured by Jant Pharmacal Corporation Operators comments: Device was easy to use and results easy to read.	
One Step	Each device is packaged in a sealed pouch with an attached pipet. Storage does not require refrigeration, but can be if desired, or at room temperature, 65° to 85°F. Expiration dates are stamped on the pouches. The devices are well labeled. The device includes a "control" or validity check. The test is in the form of a dipstick, requiring the dipping of the strip into the urine, preferably a samll aliquot in a test tube. Results can be read within 3 min, but must be read within 5 min. The endpoint for a positive result is the absence of a line at the test band. Manufactured by Technical Chemicals & Products, Inc. Operators comments: Device was easy to use and results easy to read. Needs small container for sample, which is not included in the kit.	Technical Chemicals & Products, Inc. P.O. Box 9748 Ft. Lauderdale, Florida 33310 Phone: 954-979-0400
QuickScreen	Each cassette-style device is packaged in a sealed pouch with an attached pipet. Storage does not require refrigeration, but 40° to 86°F is recommended. Expiration dates are stamped on the pouches. The devices are well labeled. The device includes a "control" or validity check. The test requires the slow addition of 4 drops of urine to a well at one end of the device. Results can be read within 10 min. The endpoint for a positive result is the absence of a line at the test band. Manufactured by PhamaTech. Operators comments: Device takes too long to use. Slow addition of drops too cumbersome.	PhamaTech 9265 Activities Road San Diego, California 92126 Phone: 619-635-5840

(continued)

Table 21 (continued)

Product Descriptions, Operation, and Distributor Information AOC Sand DWP Studies

Test devices	Description/Operation	Distributor
TesTstik	Each device is packaged in a sealed pouch with an attached pipet. Storage does not require refrigeration, but 36° to 86°F is recommended. Expiration dates are stamped on the pouches. The devices are well labeled. The device includes a "control" or validity check. The test requires the dipping of the device into a urine sample up to a mark on the device for 5 to 7 seconds. Results can be read within 5 min, but should not be read after 30 min. The endpoint for a positive result is the absence of a line at the test band. Manufactured by Roche Diagnostic System, Inc. Operators comments: Device was easy to use and results easy to read.	Roche Diagnostic Corporation 9115 Hague Road Indianapolis, Indiana 46256 Phone: 800-428-5074 Fax: 317-521-4240 There are local representatives
Non-Drug Device		
AdultaCheck 4	The devices are packaged in a capped bottle. Storage does not require refrigeration, but 59° to 86°F is recommended. Expiration dates are stamped on the label. The dipstick contains four test pads, for pH, creatinine, glutaraldehyde, and nitrite. The test requires the dipping of the device into a urine sample over the top pad and removing it immediately. The strip is to be held in a horizontal position with the pads upward. The pads are visually compared to the color chart on the bottle label. Only the creatinine pad was evaluated in this study. Manufactured by Chimera Research and Chemical, Inc. Operators comments: Device was easy to use, results must be read immediately, only one test can be conducted at a time.	Dade Behring Inc. Glasgow Business Community Newark, Delaware 19702 Phone: 800-242-3233 (Formerly Chimera Research and Chemicals, Inc.)

Chapter 18

Sample Adulteration and On-Site Drug Tests

John T. Cody

1. Introduction

This chapter addresses the adulteration of urine samples and its effect on drugs-of-abuse testing using on-site testing devices. The technical aspects of on-site testing methodologies are described in detail elsewhere in this book and will not be described in this chapter. Current literature regarding adulteration of urine samples and its impact on on-site tests is nearly non-existent. As a result, this chapter describes some adulterants and focuses on their effects on the analyte of interest along with some relevant discussion of effects of the adulterants on laboratory immunoassay and GC-MS testing. Those adulterants that directly effect the drug (or metabolite) will impact results regardless of which methodology is used, including on-site tests. In addition, tests available for the detection of adulterants that can be used at the collection-site are also described in this chapter.

Adulteration of urine samples to prevent detection of illicit drug use has a history nearly as long as drug testing itself. Adulteration was often accomplished using a wide variety of different products including: alcohol, ammonia, ascorbic acid, aspirin, bicarbonate, bleach, blood, detergent, Drano®, ethylene glycol, golden seal root, lemon juice, Lime-A-Way®, peroxide, potassium hydroxide, salt, soap, sodium phosphate, vanish, vinegar and Visine®. These adulterants, their effects and detection have previously been reviewed in depth in several publications *(1–14)*.

From: *Forensic Science: On-Site Drug Testing*
Edited by: A. J. Jenkins and B. A. Goldberger © Humana Press, Inc., Totowa, NJ

In these cases, the adulteration was accomplished with readily available products that could be easily and inexpensively obtained. They were used to adulterate urine samples to avoid detection of drug use which was not the intended purpose of the product. While several of these adulterants were very effective in preventing a sample from being properly identified as containing drugs, the adulterant often left a telltale sign of its presence (i.e. smell, color, precipitate, etc.).

More recently, a cottage industry has grown up around the drug testing program. Now, products are being marketed whose sole purpose is to cause a sample to not test positive despite drug abuse by the user. These items are readily available through magazine advertisements and the internet. They are designed to be consumed by the individual prior to testing, or to be placed into the urine sample in the privacy of the collection process.

Many of the adulterants interfere with the screening assay causing it to produce negative or invalid results. Such adulterants do not themselves chemically alter the drugs or metabolites but do not allow the laboratory to produce forensically defensible positive test results. Others do effect the drug (or drug metabolite) directly impacting testing results regardless of the methodology used.

Identification of adulterants has become an important part of a viable drug testing program. The very nature and utility of a drug testing program is the production of accurate and reliable results. Any deterrent effect of a drug testing program is negated if the abuser is confident that they are indeed free to use drugs since they have the ability to foil the drug test to prevent proper detection of their illicit use. Recently, as a response to this in the federally regulated programs, the U.S. Department of Health and Human Services (HHS) Substance Abuse and Mental Health Services Administration (SAMHSA) published guidelines for the testing and reporting of adulteration and dilution of urine samples. These measures are an important step in helping the program maintain its useful deterrent effect.

To that end, several analytical tests have been developed to identify adulteration, substitution or dilution of a urine sample. These tests include simple procedures such as measurement of specific gravity, creatinine and pH. Although simple analyses, these procedures can detect many different types of adulteration, dilution and substitution. In addition, more sophisticated analytical procedures have been put into place to address several other adulterants.

The current literature is nearly devoid of information regarding the utility of on-site tests that can be used to detect the presence of an adulterant. The initial requirements for measuring the temperature of a sample to ensure it was consistent with having recently been voided from a person, is a viable test to identify dilution or substitution of most samples. However, the attentiveness of the collection-site staff is also important, being attentive to unusual smells and appearance can be important in the detection of adulteration of samples.

Methods used to defeat the proper testing of samples have become more sophisticated in recent years. Although methods for preparing samples so they are within the acceptable temperature range have been tried in the past (i.e., holding a small amount of liquid against the body in the arm pit or groin area *[15]*), a small battery operated device is now available whose intended purpose is to allow for heating a liquid, to be used to dilute or substitute for the donor's own urine, to the proper temperature. This device coupled with commercially available liquid or freeze-dried urine that is guaranteed to be drug free is impossible to detect by any tests and is dependent on the collection-site staff and observers to detect.

The remainder of this chapter is divided into several sections. The first section discusses dilution of samples and methods used for detection of dilution or substitution. The next section describes commercially available adulterants. Those discussed are designed and marketed specifically to be used as adulterants. A list of available adulterants is shown in Table 1. Other common adulterants, such as bleach, etc., are not described because their use and detection have been described in detail in previous publications. In addition, since detection methods have been developed, these are far less commonly used. The final section of this chapter discusses devices designed to detect adulteration on-site.

2. Dilution

A number of different solutions are available for the in vivo adulteration (dilution) of samples. In this case, the user is directed to drink the liquid and to then consume additional amounts of water. These products state they purify the urine of any toxins, but there is no evidence they have any ability to mask drug use other than that associated with dilution of the urine. Two such products are Quick Flush® and Eliminator®. Coleman and Baselt *(16)* studied these two products and compared them to no treatment (control) and the consumption of 1.2 L of water. The use of both products resulted in the decrease in concentration of amphetamine, THC-COOH, benzoylecgonine and codeine as measured by GC-MS. In this study, little effect was noted in the immunoassay results (RIA). The simple consumption of water gave results comparable to those seen with the use of these two commercial products. None of the treatments caused the pH, specific gravity or creatinine to be outside the normally acceptable physiological range. Skopp et al. *(17)* evaluated the effect of 'The Ultimate Blend', a carbohydrate drink touted as causing elimination of drug testing positives. Eight regular marijuana users (one or more marijuana

Table 1
List of Adulterants

Adulterant	Active ingredient
Amber-13	Strong acid
THC-Free	Strong acid
UrinAid	Glutaraldehyde
Clear Choice	Glutaraldehyde
LL418	Pyridinium chlorochromate
Urine Luck	Pyridinium chlorochromate
Urine Luck	Chromate
Urine Luck	Iodic acid/Hydrofluoric acid
Klear	Nitrite
Whizzies	Nitrite
Randy's Klear	Nitrite
Stealth	Peroxidase

cigarettes per day) were given this drink following the directions for use on the package. A urine sample was collected from each subject prior to administration of the drink and another sample was collected 2.5–3 h following administration. The samples provided after use of the drink showed some dilution, as expected, based on the volume of fluid intake. The authors reported significant decrease in creatinine levels in all but one subject whose initial creatinine was 4 mg/dL and following use increased to 15 mg/dL. Four of the eight subjects had creatinine levels <20 mg/dL (one of the two criteria required to report a sample as diluted following SAMHSA guidelines). Unfortunately, specific gravity was not reported, therefore it is not possible to determine if the samples would have met the criteria for being reported as diluted under those guidelines.

Several on-site tests were used as part of this study (Triage, Toxi Quick test strips, and Quick Screen 6). All of these tests were positive for the presence of marijuana metabolite in all samples following administration of the drink. Several of the samples had less than 50 ng/mL of THC-COOH as measured by GC-MS and were presumably positive due to crossreactivity with other metabolites. Three of the samples taken after the drink was administered were negative by the EMIT assay, one of which also tested negative by the ABUSCREEN OnLine and CEDIA immunoassays. All eight samples showed

THC-COOH concentrations of > 15 ng/mL by GC-MS. There were significant decreases in concentration for all samples ranging from 45–83% of the initial value. Given these data, it is clear that dilution of this sort could cause decreases that would result in negative (below the cutoff level) drug test results depending on initial concentrations. Dilution of drug concentration was also described by Cone et al. who demonstrated that consumption of large volumes of liquid could cause samples to test negative for marijuana and cocaine metabolites *(18)*.

Evaluation of specific gravity and creatinine and their potential utility in assessing dilution and substitution has been described by a number of different investigators *(18–25)*. Based on the available scientific data, SAMHSA set acceptable ranges for these parameters. For a sample to be reported as diluted, it must have a creatinine of less than 20 mg/dL and a specific gravity of less than 1.003. Substitution is reported when the creatinine is less than or equal to 5 mg/dL and a specific gravity of less than or equal to 1.001 or greater than or equal to 1.020. Guidelines for the collection of samples in the HHS program eliminate ready access to water thus preventing easy dilution of the sample with water at the collection-site. A recent proposal for revision of validity testing criteria has been announced (Fed. Reg., 66(162) 43876-82). Recommended revisions include a proposed change from less than or equal to 1.001 to less than 1.002 for specific gravity. In practice, this does not alter the criteria since refractometers read to the third decimal point, thus a reading of 1.000 or 1.001 would be outside the range in either case. These recommendations change the wording to a mathematically simpler form consistent with other cutoffs used in the program. A change for the acceptable pH range from less than or equal to 3 to less than 3 does change the criteria slightly as does the change from less than or equal to 5 mg/dL to less than 5 mg/dL for creatinine. These changes are designed to eliminate the potential problems caused by truncation of numbers in determination of acceptance limits. Final implementation of these recommended changes will follow policy guidelines for changes to existing criteria and readers are referred to the latest guidelines for final rules.

3. Adulterants

3.1. Acid

Strong acid has a significant impact on some drugs and testing methodologies. Several adulterants are merely strong acids which are added to the urine sample to interfere with the testing process. These include Amber-13 and THC-Free which both contain hydrochloric acid. While these strong acids are effective as an adulterant, they leave the pH of the sample outside the acceptable range (pH less than or equal to 3 or greater than or equal to 11)

(26). Before reporting a sample as adulterated based on its pH, the pH must be measured by two different techniques using two different aliquots. Urine dipsticks widely used in clinical laboratories typically measure urine pH and can easily be used on-site. In addition, the AdultaCheck 4 test strip, which is specifically designed for the detection of adulteration, has pH as one of the four tests.

3.2. Chromate

Chromate is another compound that has been used as an adulterant to invalidate urine drug tests. The process involves the use of chromate, in one of several forms, to interfere with the test. Initially, Urine Luck contained pyridinium chlorochromate. A GC-MS test was developed for the detection of this product based on the analysis of pyridinium *(27)*. The product LL418 also contains chromate. Since the actual active ingredient in this adulterant is the strong oxidant chromate, using chromate in a different form yields the same interference with the drug test, but would not be detected by this assay.

A simple spot test method for detection of chromate anions was described by Wu et al. *(27)* which employed the use of two drops of 10 g/L 1,5-diphenylcarbazide added to one mL of urine resulting in the production of a reddish-purple color. While not as convenient as a test strip, this procedure could easily be carried out on-site if there was a suspicion of adulteration. It is also likely that a test strip could be developed for the detection of this adulterant. Currently, there is no data available on the effect of chromate on on-site testing devices.

3.3. Glutaraldehyde

Glutaraldehyde is a chemical fixative commonly used in the histological preparation of tissues for microscopic examination. It has been packaged and marketed as an adulterant in the form of UrinAid and Clear Choice. The use of glutaraldehyde decreases the pH of the sample, however, in many cases the pH would remain within acceptable range for all but a few samples that started out at the low end of the acceptable range (pH less than or equal to 3 or greater than or equal to 11). There is also an odor associated with glutaraldehyde which is characteristic and can assist in identification. It was demonstrated, however, that concentrations as low as 2% glutaraldehyde gave rise to false negative results when using the EMIT assay. At that concentration, there was no noticeable change to the color or odor of the urine samples *(28)*. Another study has reported the effects of glutaraldehyde on immunoassays (EMIT, FPIA, KIMS and RIA) *(29)*. Unfortunately, there is currently no data available on the effect of glutaraldehyde on on-site drug testing devices.

The AdultaCheck 4 test strip tests for the presence of glutaraldehyde as one of its four parameters. King *(30)* evaluated the ability of this on-site test and found it was effective in detection of samples adulterated with glutaraldehyde. Since glutaraldehyde is not a urine constituent normally evaluated clinically, unlike nitrite, pH etc., clinical urine dipsticks are not designed to detect this compound.

3.4. Nitrite

Nitrite, in several forms, has been used to adulterate urine samples with the intention of making urine drug testing results invalid. Nitrite is the active ingredient in a number of different adulterating agents including Klear, Whizzies, and Randy's Klear.

Unlike many of the other adulterants, nitrite can be found in urine without addition of the substance for purposes of adulteration. Although not a normal constituent of urine, nitrite is found in some pathological conditions. The amount of nitrite found in samples for various clinical reasons has been evaluated by several investigators *(31,32)*. Accounting for the potential natural presence of nitrite in samples, SAMHSA has published guidelines for the testing and reporting of adulteration of samples with nitrite. If the measured concentration of nitrite in a sample is greater than or equal to 500 micrograms/mL, the sample is to be reported as adulterated. Nitrite adulteration testing must be accomplished using two different methods, one of which must be quantitative, with both tests accomplished on a separate aliquot before reporting the sample as adulterated *(26,33)*.

Detection of nitrite has been described by Singh et al. using high performance ion chromatography *(31)*. While this is a very accurate method, it requires some sophisticated laboratory equipment and is not amenable to on-site testing. However, most commercially available urine dipsticks detect nitrite. Pathologically, the presence of nitrite is an indicator of bacteriuria resulting from bacteria that convert nitrate to nitrite, a common indicator of a urinary tract infection. The AdultaCheck 4 test strip also includes a test for nitrite.

An evaluation of the on-site drug testing device, ONTRAK TESTCUP-5 (Roche Diagnostics), showed no effects on the results for amphetamine, THC COOH, benzoylecgonine, morphine and PCP, even at concentrations as high as 1.0 *M* sodium or potassium nitrite. In this study, the analyses were conducted 48 h following adulteration of the sample. Given that the on-site devices properly identified samples that contained drug 48 h after the nitrite was added, it is reasonable to assume they would have performed the same if used on-site shortly after addition of the adulterant (a more likely scenario for on-site testing). The Roche OnLine instrument based immunoassay became more sensitive to the presence of amphetamine and far less sensitive to the presence of THC-COOH when testing nitrite adulterated urine. GC-MS confirmation was also seriously effected by this adulterant. Recovery of deuterium labeled internal standard was negatively effected with the presence of as little as 0.03 *M* nitrite *(34)*. The amount of deuterated THC-COOH recovered was shown to be time dependent. Nitrite caused a rapid effect on recovery, but the effect was not complete. The effect of nitrite on the THC-COOH metabolite in the urine would be expected to mirror what is seen with the internal standard and, in fact, the effect on recovery of the internal standard was the initial sign that lead investigators to identify this adulterant. Once identified, methods were developed to eliminate the interference using bisulfite *(35)* or sulfamic acid *(36)*. Both bisulfite and sulfamic acid react with the nitrite remaining in the urine, thus eliminating its presence and therefore its effect on the extraction of drug and internal standard. Using either of these methods, the effect on the confirmation assay can be eliminated. It must be remembered, however, that any chemical change to the THC-COOH in the sample can not be reversed.

The magnitude of effect of nitrite on THC-COOH proved to be pH dependent. Samples containing 50 ng/mL of THC-COOH and stored at pH 7.0 showed recovery of the THC acid metabolite of 47.3 ng/mL after two days and 43.4 ng/mL at two weeks. Subsequent evaluation of samples after storage at pH 5 or 6 showed no recovery of the THC-COOH even with bisulfite treatment. At pH 8.0, > 90% of the THC-COOH could be recovered after three weeks. The amount of recovery was shown to be little effected by amount of nitrite (0.294–11.765 m*M*) when compared to the effect of sample pH *(34)*. Since the pH of the sample is not controlled, the extent of the degradation of THC-COOH is not consistent from sample to sample.

The effects of pH and time were also confirmed by Tarnai et al. *(37)* who saw the effect of sodium nitrite in Whizzies as well as samples spiked with sodium nitrite on immunoassay (Roche OnLine and Diagnostic Reagents reagents) results for the THC metabolite as well as GC-MS analysis. Their results also confirmed the effect of pH on the degradation of the metabolite and the utility of bisulfite treatment to stop the destructive effect of the adulterant on the THC-COOH and internal standard.

3.5. Other Adulterants

As the ability of laboratories to detect adulterants improves, those that prepare and market adulterants develop new ones to meet the demand. One adulterant that is not detected by any of the current adulteration tests is Stealth. Stealth is provided as two vials, one containing a solid and the other a liquid

(38,39). The solid was determined to contain peroxidase and the liquid is peroxide. The reaction of peroxide with peroxidase results in a strong reduction-oxidation reaction in the urine sample. Reaction of peroxide to produce the desired effect by chemically changing the THC acid metabolite can happen quite rapidly.

On-site analysis of urine adulterated by Stealth would be expected to be significantly effected by this product. Only minutes were required to show a dramatic drop in the concentration of THC metabolite following the addition of this adulterant. The effect of the adulterant is directly on the drug metabolite itself. As a result, any and all tests that are designed to identify the THC acid metabolite would be effected. Many immunoassays are targeted to the THC acid metabolite but have crossreactivity with other metabolites as well. As a result, the degree of crossreactivity of these immunoassays would be dependent on the specificity of the reagent. Those that are very specific for the acid metabolite would be most effected. Additionally, since GC-MS analysis is very specific, it would ultimately be unable to detect the acid metabolite since it would have been chemically altered and no longer present in the urine. For an on-site test, the effect of this adulterant would depend on the rate at which the chemical conversion takes place which has not yet been clearly defined. On-site analysis with a Boehringer Mannheim ChemStrip 10 indicated a positive nitrite, glucose greater than 1000 mg/dL and hemoglobin greater than 250 erythrocytes per microliter. Stealth also affected analyses of opiates and LSD *(40,41)*. The effect on opiates was shown to be concentration dependent with concentrations near the cutoff giving negative results. Samples containing LSD were also negative following adulteration with Stealth. In the case of LSD, there was no indication of concentration dependency.

Other adulterants available that, at the time of this writing, have not yet been characterized will surely be identified soon and will just as surely be replaced by others. Often these new adulterants are given new names; however, in some cases, such as Urine Luck (*see* Table 1), the name has remained the same but the ingredients have changed.

4. ON-SITE ADULTERATION TESTS

Evaluation of the suitability of a sample for testing can be assessed by on-site tests for such parameters as pH and specific gravity. These are commonly found as part of the tests available on test strips available from a variety of manufacturers routinely used in clinical laboratories.

One product specifically designed to detect adulteration of a sample is AdultaCheck 4 (Chimera Research and Chemical). AdultaCheck 4 is a test strip designed, as the name implies, to test four different parameters including pH, creatinine and for the presence of glutaraldehyde and nitrite to assess possible adulteration of a sample. This product has been evaluated by King *(30)* and found to be effective in detection of samples that are adulterated or exceed acceptable limits.

5. Conclusion

As can readily be seen by the discussion in this chapter, the adulteration of urine samples to defeat the drug testing program is a problem which continues to this day. The actual extent of the problem is not clear since adulteration testing is currently not mandated, therefore, the actual number of samples that are adulterated is not known. Even if the testing was conducted on all samples, several adulterants mentioned above do not as yet have analytical procedures available for their detection and confirmation. Even for those adulterants that are known and have readily available tests, the effect of these adulterants on on-site tests has, with rare exception, not been evaluated. On-site detection of adulteration would be a valuable tool in a drug testing program, since the program allows for observed collection when the suspicion exists that a sample is adulterated. Discovery of adulteration in the laboratory, although still valuable, does not allow for the immediate collection of another sample to assess whether or not drug use was present at the time of initial collection.

References

1. Linder, M. W. and Valdes, R., Jr (1994) Mechanism and elimination of asprin-induced interference in Emit II d. a. u. assays. *Clin. Chem.* **40,** 1512–1515.
2. Wagener, R. E., Linder, M. W., and Valdes, R., Jr (1994) Decreased signal in Emit assays of drugs of abuse in urine after ingestion of asprin: potential for false-negative results. *Clin. Chem.* **40,** 608–612.
3. Baiker, C., Serrano, L., and Lindner, B. (1994) Hypochlorite adulteration of urine causing decreased concentration of delta-9–THC-COOH by GC/MS. *J. Anal. Toxicol.* **18,** 101–103.
4. Bronner, W., Nyman, P., and von Minden, D. (1990) Detectability of phencyclidine and 11-nor-delta-9-tetrahydrocannabinol-9-carboxylic acid in adulterated urine by radiommunoassay and fluorescence polarization immunoassay. *J. Anal. Toxicol.* **14,** 368–371.
5. Cassells, N. P. and Craston, D. H. (1998) The effects of commonly used adulterants on the detection of spiked LSD by an enzyme immunoassay. *Sci. Just.* **38,** 109–117.
6. Cody, J. T. (1990) Specimen adulteration in drug urinalysis. *Forensic Sci Rev.* **2,** 63–75.
7. Cody, J. T. (1995) Adulteration of urine specimens, in Handbook of workplace drug testing. (Liu, R. H. and Goldberger, B. A., eds.) AACC Press, Washington, DC, pp. 181–208.

8. Cody, J. T. and Schwarzhoff, R. H. (1989) Impact of adulterants on RIA analysis of urine for drugs of abuse. *J. Anal. Toxicol.* **13,** 277–284.
9. Mikkelsen, S. L. and Ash, K. O. (1988) Adulterants causing false negatives in illicit drug testing. *Clin. Chem.* **34,** 2333–2336.
10. Pearson, S. D., Ash, K. O., and Urry, F. M. (1989) Mechanism of false-negative urine cannabinoid immunoassay screens by Visine eyedrops. *Clin. Chem.* **35,** 636–638.
11. Schwarzhoff, R. and Cody, J. T. (1993) The effects of adulterating agents on FPIA analysis of urine for drugs of abuse. *J. Anal. Toxicol.* **17,** 14–17.
12. Kapur, B. M. (1993) Drug-testing methods and clinical interpretations of test results. *Bull. Narc.* **45,** 115–154.
13. Liu, R. H. (1994) Comparison of common immunoassay kits for effective application in workplace drug urinalysis. *Foren. Sci. Rev.* **6,** 19–57.
14. O'Conner, E., Ostheimer, D., and Wu, A. H. B. (1993) Limitations of forensic urine drug testing in methodology and by adulteration. *AACC TDM/Tox* **14,** 277–288.
15. Person, N. B. and Ehrenkranz, J. R. L. (1988) Fake urine samples for drug analysis: hot but not hot enough. *JAMA* **259,** 841.
16. Coleman, D. E. and Baselt, R. C. (1997) Efficacy of two commercial products for altering urine drug test results. *Clin. Toxicol.* **35,** 637–642.
17. Skopp, G., Potsch, L., Rohrich, J., Becker, J., and Mattern, R. (1999) Effect of the detoxifying carbohydrate drink The Ultimate Blend on urine screening for cannabinoids, in Proceedings of the 1998 joint SOFT/TIAFT international meeting. (Spiehler, V., ed.) SOFT/TIAFT, Newport Beach CA, pp. 66–73.
18. Cone, E. J., Lange, R., and Darwin, W. D. (1998) In vivo adulteration: excess fluid ingestion causes false-negative marijuana and cocaine urine test results. *J. Anal. Toxicol.* **22,** 460–473.
19. Edwards, C., Fyfe, M. J., Liu, R. H., and Walia, A. S. (1993) Evaluation of common urine specimen adulteration indicators. *J. Anal. Toxicol.* **17,** 251,252.
20. George, S. and Braithwaite, R. A. (1995) An investigation into the extent of possible dilution of specimens received for urinary drugs of abuse screening. *Addiction* **90,** 967–970.
21. Lafolie, P., Beck, O., Blennow, G., Boreus, L., Borg, S., Elwin, C. E., et al. (1991) Importance of creatinine analyses of urine when screening for abused drugs. *Clin. Chem.* **37,** 1927–1931.
22. Needleman, S. B., Porvaznik, M., and Ander, D. (1992) Creatinine analysis in single collection urine specimens. *J. Foren. Sci.* **37,** 1125–1133.
23. Homer, G. M. and Born, B. (1993) A discussion of creatinine analysis in single urine specimens. *J. Foren. Sci.* **38,** 501.
24. Ottinger, W. O. (1993) A discussion of creatinine analysis in single collection urine specimens. *J. Foren. Sci.* **38,** 502,503.
25. Simpson, D., Jarvie, D. R., and Moore, F. M. L. (1993) Measurement of creatinine in urine screening for drugs of abuse. *Clin. Chem.* **39,** 698,699.
26. Stephenson, R. L., II (1998) Guidance for reporting specimen validity test results (PD 035). Division of applied research, NIDA, 28 September, Rockville MD.
27. Wu, A. H. B., Bristol, B., Sexton, K., Cassella-McLane, G., Holtman, V., and Hill, D. W. (1999) Adulteration of urine by "Urine Luck". *Clin. Chem.* **45,** 1051–1057.

28. George, S. and Braithwaite, R. A. (1996) The effect of Glutaraldehyde adulteration of urine specimens on Syva EMIT II drugs-of-abuse assays. *J. Anal. Toxicol.* **20,** 195,196.
29. Goldberger, B. A. and Caplan, Y. H. (1994) Effect of glutaraldehyde (UrinAid) on detection of abused drugs in urine by immunoassay. *Clin. Chem.* **40,** 1605,1606.
30. King, E. J. (1999) Performance of AdultaCheck 4 test strips for the detection of adulteration at the point of collection of urine specimens used for drugs-of-abuse testing. *J. Anal. Toxicol.* **23,** 72.
31. Singh, J., Elberling, J. A., Hemphill, D. G., and Holmstrom, J. (1999) The measurement of nitrite in adulterated urine samples by high-performance ion chromatography. *J. Anal. Toxicol.* **23,** 137–140.
32. Urry, F. M., Komaromy-Hiller, G., Staley, B., Crockett, D. K., Kushnir, M., Nelson, G., et al. (1998) Nitrite adulteration of workplace urine drug-testing specimens. I. Sources and associated concentrations of nitrite in urine and distinction between natural sources and adulteration. *J. Anal. Toxicol.* **22,** 89–95.
33. Stephenson, R. L., II (1999) Specimen validity testing (PD 37). Division of applied research, NIDA, 28 Jul, Rockville MD.
34. Tsai, S. C., ElSohly, M. A., Dubrovsky, T., Twarowska, B., Towt, J., and Salamone, S. J. (1998) Determination of five abused drugs in nitrite-adulterated urine by immunoassays and gas chromatography-mass spectrometry. *J. Anal. Toxicol.* **22,** 474–480.
35. ElSohly, M. A., Feng, S., Kopycki, W. J., Murphy, T. P., Jones, A. B., Davis, A., Carr, D. (1997) A procedure to overcome interferences caused by the adulterant "Klear" in the GC-MS analysis of 11-nor-delta-9-THC-9-COOH. *J. Anal. Toxicol.* **21,** 240–242.
36. Frederick, D. L. (1998) Improved procedure for overcoming nitrite interferences in GC-MS procedures for cannabinoids. *J. Anal. Toxicol.* **22,** 255,256.
37. Tarnai, L. D., Knachel, K. L., and Crooks, C. R. (1999) Whizzies - a urine drug screen adulterant, in Proceedings of the 1998 joint SOFT/TIAFT international meeting. (Spiehler, V., ed.) SOFT/TIAFT, Newport Beach CA, pp. 93–102.
38. Davis, K. (1999) Adulterants update, Presented at the NLCP lab director/inspector workshop, Society of Forensic Toxicologist annual meeting, San Juan, PR.
39. Davis, K. (2000) Aulterlants. Presented at NLCP lab director/inspector workshop, Society of Forensic Toxicologist annual meeting, Milwaukee, WI.
40. Cody, J. T. and Valtier, S. (2001) Effects of Stealth adulterant on immunoassay testing for drugs of abuse. *J. Anal. Toxicol.* **25,** 471–475.
41. Cody, J. T., Valtier, S., and Kuhlman, J. Analysis of morphine and codeine in samples adulterated with Stealth™, *J. Anal. Toxicol.*, **25,** 572–575.

Index

From: *Forensic Science: On-Site Drug Testing*
Edited by A. J. Jenkins and B. A. Goldberger © Humana Press, Inc., Totowa, NJ